—The—
Lost Ravioli Recipes
of Hoboken

ALSO BY LAURA SCHENONE

*A Thousand Years Over a Hot Stove: A History of American
Women Told Through Food, Recipes, and Remembrances*

HOBOKEN FERRY, HOBOKEN, N. J.

—THE—

LOST RAVIOLI RECIPES

OF HOBOKEN

*A Search for Food
and Family*

LAURA SCHENONE

W. W. NORTON & COMPANY
New York | London

A note: The spellings used in this book are generally Italian-American versions. For example, Adalgisa in Italy, Adalgiza in New Jersey. In addition, some conversations and very small successions of events have been combined for ease of reading.

For information about permission to reproduce
selections from this book, write to Permissions,
W. W. Norton & Company, Inc.,
500 Fifth Avenue, New York, NY 10110

For information about special discounts for bulk purchases,
please contact W. W. Norton Special Sales at
specialsales@wwnorton.com or 800-233-4830

Manufacturing by The Courier Companies, Inc.
Book design by Judith Stagnitto Abbate/Abbate Design
All food photography by Dan Epstein
Production manager: Andrew Marasia

Library of Congress Cataloging-in-Publication Data

Schenone, Laura.
The lost ravioli recipes of Hoboken : a search for
food and family /
Laura Schenone.—1st ed.
p. cm.
Includes bibliographical references.
ISBN 978-0-393-06146-8 (hardcover)
1. Cookery (Pasta) 2. Stuffed foods (Cookery) 3. Cookery—
New Jersey—Hoboken. I. Title.
TX809.M17S243 2007
641.8'22—dc22

2007028262

W. W. Norton & Company, Inc.
500 Fifth Avenue, New York, N.Y. 10110
www.wwnorton.com

W. W. Norton & Company Ltd.
Castle House, 75/76 Wells Street, London W1T 3QT

1 2 3 4 5 6 7 8 9 0

For my sons, Gabriel and Simon, with love forever.

Still here I carry my old delicious burdens;
I carry them, men and women—I carry them with me
        wherever I go;
I swear it is impossible for me to get rid of them;
I am fill'd with them, and I will fill them in return.

WALT WHITMAN
"Song of the Open Road"

You know, honey, us colored folks is branches without roots and
that makes things come round in queer ways. You in particular.

ZORA NEALE HURSTON
Their Eyes Were Watching God

Cooking is a troublesome sprite. Often it may drive you to
despair. Yet it is also very rewarding, for when you do succeed,
or overcome a difficulty in doing so, you feel the satisfaction of
a great triumph.

PELLEGRINO ARTUSI
Science in the Kitchen and the Art of Eating Well,
translated from the Italian by Murtha
Baca and Stephen Sartare

CONTENTS

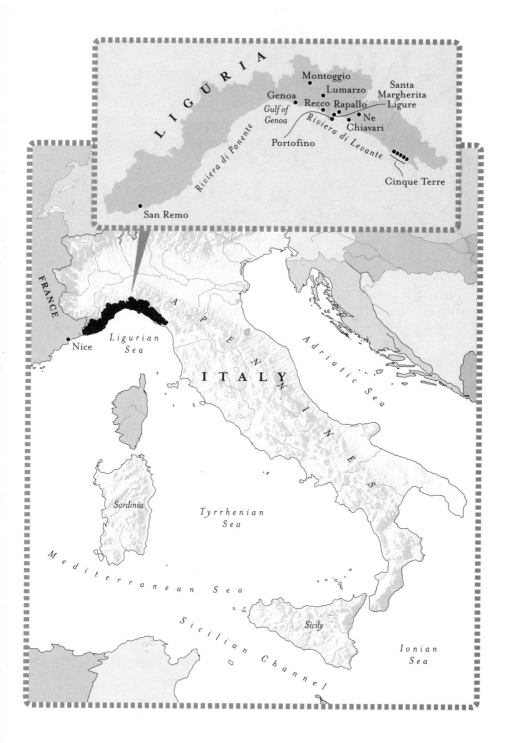

—The—
Lost Ravioli Recipes
of Hoboken

MEMORY WAS HER GIFT. She never told a story the exact same way—never dreamed of dishonoring a story that way. She added twists and turns, her own rhythms and trills depending upon what each telling required, what the people needed to hear—whether it was a time of coming together or falling apart. She never forgot the events she witnessed or the tales she inherited, but her art also had much to do with drawing attention to just the right details—and suspense, of course, that ultimate question of questions: What will happen? Where does the story lead? How will it all turn out?

I wanted to know the stories, so I turned to her. One night, she told this one that comes from the old era, when magic was still in the stories—not just words words words. She told me when we were cooking side by side in the kitchen (the place where she often whispers to me). Or perhaps she told it to me before I was born, or when I was still a baby, and all the world's sounds were still flowing together in a sea that holds past and present lives. It was the story that explained how we came to be, the story that I needed most.

There was a strong young man from the hills, a poor but able man who did not work with the land but with the hard truth of the land—which is to say he was a mason who labored in stone. He was as handsome as he was poor, raised on the steep green hills of rock and chestnut woods, born in a small stone home, raised with six brothers and sisters on the taste of smoked chestnuts, gathered greens, polenta mush, cabbage soups, and when possible, foraged snails and mushrooms that sprang up from the forest floor.

This all takes place long ago, during the days when hunger was real—the years when children ran without shoes in summer, and when the people came out of the mountains looking thin if the chestnuts had been poor that season, and plump if they had been good. The chestnut and the people were practically one. And the mountain people not only ate the chestnuts but built walls and tables and floors from chestnut wood. They lived with chestnuts hanging over the fire to smoke in the fall.

Each day, he left the hills and went down to the water—down to the city where women wore pretty blouses and men had nice jackets and hard top hats, and the boats were always coming and going—and he found work for himself. On hands and knees, he put in the stone-tiled floors of rich families.

It was there, on the road down to the village one spring, that he first saw her. She stood outside the front door of a fine, small stone house, working in her garden plot of vegetables and flowers—it was there on that road that he first stared at her and she turned away, afraid. Day after day the scene repeated, as he stared and she looked away, until one morning when he descended from the hills on his long walk to work she turned her head and looked him straight in the eyes. Her face was not beautiful, but lovely in the boldness and directness of her gaze, which said, *Now I am ready to see you.*

That night, on his way home, it was raining lightly, but he saw a flower, left with apparent deliberateness across a large stone in the front of her house. And he imagined her running out in the mist to place it there just moments before.

Later, traveling back up the road, flower in hand, the day fading behind him, he made his way into the cool and quiet air of the hills. Out of habit, a forager's habit, his eye caught some mushrooms that had sprung up off the edge of the road, a few feet into the forest. From his pocket he took out a handkerchief and stepped into the woods, then reached in among the old leaves of last fall, the moss and bark scrapings, to pluck a nice handful of damp mushrooms by their stems. He filled the center of his handkerchief and tied the whole thing up loosely, put the parcel in his pocket, and continued his walk home, barely aware of what he had done.

Ten minutes passed when a most astonishing thing occurred. He believed he felt the mushrooms moving in his pocket. Incredulous, he pulled out the sack and untied the whole thing, at which moment he did indeed discover the largest and most beautiful of the mushrooms squirming about on the cloth, as though pleading for its life. Holding it up to examine the thing closely, not only did he see the mushroom move before his eyes, he believed that, in the quiet of the hills, he could hear it speak.

He laughed at himself. Impossible. But just the same, he put his ear toward it, and this time, he was certain that the mushroom was imploring him to be set free, promising in exchange a reward of three wishes.

Ridiculous. Ridiculous! But what could he lose? He whispered this: "To have her. To go on one of those ships. To leave behind this hunger."

Fine—but there was one condition. He had to agree never to look back. He would have riches and luxuries. Plenty to eat. A beautiful home. A lovely wife and many children. But he would have to never see these mountains again. He'd have to give up his songs. He'd have to abandon everything and everyone else he loved in exchange for his ambition. He tossed all the mushrooms back into the woods and headed up to the hills.

And so he agreed. And so it came true.

CHAPTER I

Maiden Voyage

A LITTLE SQUARE OF RAVIOLI is like a secret. You look at the out-side and see the neatly crimped dough, puffed up in the center with a lovely pillow of something mysterious inside. It is an envelope with a message. Before you bite into it, all is unknown. And much is still possible.

You're not supposed to make Christmas ravioli alone, really. It's too hard. It takes hours of work. Far better you should have people at your side, probably the women of your family—daughters, mothers, and sisters helping you, nagging you, and bumping into you in the kitchen. The men too—the husbands or fathers who periodically come in to peer over your shoulder and give (tolerated) supervision, or better yet, an extra hand to help press (gently, gently) the dough packets shut, or lift them to the place where they will dry. All this, plus perhaps some gossip, will help the job go faster.

But this cold and damp Christmas Day, I am making ravioli by myself. While I mingle the old-world ingredients of Mediterranean Italy, a gray fog settles about the brown empty tree limbs of my suburban backyard frozen with the onset of a Northeast winter. Outside, all is lethargic and quiet beneath the cold slate-colored sky. Even our street, busy as a race-track on most days, is quiet and still.

Four cups of flour on the wooden board, measured into a small hill. I hollow out the center so it looks like a volcano. The initial touch of my fingers to this soft white powder brings a frisson through my body. My vision sharpens and I see with great focus the grain of the wooden board, the particles of flour, the delicate white of eggshells. Into the volcano I crack my eggs, one by one. Then, with a fork, I burst each yolk and scramble them, drawing in flour, bit by bit, catching runaway egg and pulling it back into the whole. Something awakens—there can be no denying it. Is it in my body or my mind? A door opens. And through that opening, I see a bright place, the hope, once again in my life, for perfection and beauty—this time, a taste that can change everything. I want to go to this place, wherever it is.

On this day of my maiden voyage, I have not yet been in the vast mountains of Liguria. I have not yet heard the love story of my great-grandfather Salvatore coming down at night from the hills on his mission of love to find Adalgiza. I have not yet gone hunting for his mandolin serenatas, nor for the shreds of documents that might give me enough—just barely enough—to make a history for myself. All I've got at this early point in my journey is a broken ravioli tool that once hung on the kitchen wall, a recipe card that makes no sense to me, and these ravioli I intend to make for the first time as taught me by Maria Carla, a kind woman in Genoa, a generous woman—not even a relative. True, I found joy the day she showed me. But does her recipe for ravioli have anything to do with me?

I am not yet sure, but I go forward just the same.

First, the dough is too wet and sticky. Then too dry and stiff. One hunk after the next goes into the garbage. Another white hill of flour, another volcano. More eggs cracked, and soon the kitchen is covered in flour crunching beneath my feet. Perhaps it is my imagination—far too active—but I believe there is an intrusion. Is it sound? Strings, voices, the sound of water moving in and out slapping a rhythm against a boat, against a dock, against the shore? As suddenly as it comes, all is silent again.

IN THE LIVING ROOM, my two sons—all wrapped up in plush robes and slippers that Santa brought—play with their toys. They are seven and two years old, still perfect, in the age of lost worlds where we cannot go, a clattering of pretend where laser beams shoot through space, where animals fly, where spies in dark cloaks save the planet. My husband is in his lost world as well, reading by the fire beneath yellow lamplight. He's holding a book I gave him for Christmas, a book about love and passion.

For the first time in our seventeen years, we are staying home together for Christmas Day. We will not rush off to relatives for Christmas dinner, we will not present our children to their grandparents. We will not, above all, participate in the rituals of gifts. Yes, of course, we'll bring presents for the children of the family. But that is all. We requested in advance to be excluded. It's not that we're stingy. It's not that we don't like to give. It's just that the giving and receiving have grown to take up the better part of the day. I do not doubt my family's good intentions. But finally we are simply saying that we'd rather not.

And so I knead.

And so finally, a dough comes, and I think I like the way it feels, though it's hard to tell.

"It's like giving a massage," Maria Carla had told me when I stood in her kitchen in Genoa six months earlier. I was the awkward apprentice while she, with utmost confidence, showed the way. "One, two, three," with the heels of the hand, fold the dough on itself, and turn the lump a quarter turn. Do it again. "One, two, three, fold, turn, . . ."

The rhythm was never imprinted at an early age in my body, so I must go about it all like an idiot—using the words to get the rhythm and send it down to my hands. It is a translation project. I have no choice but to use the language of cookbooks, and I have read them all. I am to knead the dough until it is "satiny," "smooth," "elastic," "like a baby's bottom." But what do those words actually mean? My hands cannot remember how the dough felt six months ago in Maria Carla's kitchen. A last resort: I turn to the kitchen clock. Twelve minutes of kneading. The books say ten minutes so, gosh, I must be done. In this ridiculous manner, I figure out what my ancestors knew and passed down for hundreds of years.

Later, after my dough is rested, I'll press it out into sheets and wrap it around dollops of *ripieno*—the Italian word for "filling"—in this case, meat that has been cooked under a long slow flame and ground with many flavors and ideas early this morning.

It was not my intention to be making ravioli on Christmas Day. I had planned to have it all completed ahead of time and in the freezer days ago. (Yes, the freezer, even though my great-grandmother would have made them fresh, up early and kneading on Christmas morning.) But I stumbled—my lack of experience with the magic and science of gluten, my troubles with equipment—such as the previous night when my meat grinder mysteriously was missing its blade—and then, of course, my uncertainty as a novice, my second-guessing, which brings countless mistakes.

There was no choice: the big, messy, ravioli-making event carried over to Christmas morning, and now, while the others are playing and relaxing, I am in the kitchen alone with the doors shut so the rest of the family is not forced to listen to the repetitive drone of my new electric-powered pasta machine, its automated rollers going over the dough again and again—*mmmmwaaah, mmmmwaaah, mmmmwaaah*—compressing one strip of dough after the next, thinner and thinner with each pass. (No, the old ladies didn't use machines either.)

As hour moves into hour, the first gust of inspiration fades. My neck and shoulders hurt from looking down, and the weariness of repetition grinds on . . . strip after strip of dough through the pasta machine, row after row of little olive-sized dots of meat, again and again, dough folded over, then fingertips to seal shut each and every raviolo (no air bubbles, no imprints from fingernails), and finally, with my fluted wheel, running over what must add up to miles of ruffled edges around the borders of so many little packets of pasta. No, you're not supposed to do such a thing alone, for sure.

"Is it ready yet, Honey?"

My husband comes into the kitchen and sees the operation and shakes his head. I know the thought that goes through his mind: *Why must she make things so hard?* But thanks to our peaceful and quiet day, he is feeling generous.

"If it makes you happy . . ."

His voice is a little strained. He'd rather have me sitting in the living room with him, just being together. And his voice suggests the question,

Wouldn't you rather be here with me than there in the kitchen? However, he has never eaten homemade ravioli, and let's face it, he's curious.

My oldest son comes through the door too, and I show him how to run some dough through the pasta machine. "Cool!" he says as the lump of dough grows thinner and longer with each pass until it is nearly as translucent as parchment paper. He steps up to my tableau and drops little bits of *ripieno* in a line, then folds over the top piece. But after about ten ravioli, he gets bored.

"Want to do another row?" I ask.

"No thank you." He expertly pads his rejection with politeness, then slips out the door back to his toys and imagination.

THERE WAS a time when producing great holiday food was an emblem of a mother's skill, her love and generosity. What great labors women once put forth so that everyone could enjoy a feast and the mundane austerity of ordinary life would be broken by jubilation. Christ is born. Perhaps in some previous life, I made the sign of the cross in my dough. But now, there can be little doubt that I am a stubborn and selfish woman for holing up like this on Christmas Day with my back to my family as I throw myself into this self-indulgent foray into the wilderness of handmade pasta and its forgotten language. After all, there are plenty of frozen ravioli in the freezer section of my grocery store, just waiting to be tossed into boiling water.

But it comes out all right.

Many hours later, the ravioli are done. I am dressed up and lipsticked, as I bring my crooked little dumplings to the table where my husband and two boys await with rapt curiosity. I begin the usual excuses pertaining to the endless pursuit of perfection. "They're too thick," I say. "Too filled." "Some broke." But when forks are finally raised to lips, my husband and sons fall into a kind of trance, swooning over the softness of the handmade pasta, the many flavors of braised meats cooked with onion, carrot, mushroom, herbs, wine, pignoli, and the faint medieval scent of nutmeg. They slide down their throats—one after the next after the next, two days of effort disappearing in minutes—vanishing inside their bodies. These are my first ravioli, and an undeniable mood of happiness rises from the table, along with some amazement that I have actually achieved these little gems. My littlest boy—not yet three—does not speak, but just keeps putting his bowl forth, barely lifting up his tomato lips and baby cheeks, intent on getting more.

OUR PEACEFUL SOLITUDE does not last. Later that evening, we move from the safety of our inner circle to the wider dimensions of my family. No, we were not going to participate. But in the end, I agreed that we would come at least for some coffee and cake at my sister Andrea's house. The journey up the highway is a mere ten miles, yet the terrain becomes rugged and difficult as soon as we step across the threshold of my sister's front door. Our entrance brings a hush. We find them all—my parents, sisters, and children—at the spent end of the day, dessert table loaded with cakes already cut, presents unwrapped. We missed the presents and the big confusion of holiday food, all according to plan.

Long ago, when I was a child, my parents used to throw an enormous Christmas party, filling our house with family, friends, and wonderful food. We played instruments and sang songs. We ate and drank and stayed up late with aunts, uncles, cousins, and grandparents. But this all ended. My father lost his large family in a bitter feud over the family contracting business where he had worked his entire adult life—a business his father had left behind and one that had sustained several generations of our family. In a parallel series of events, my mother lost her sister in a feud as well. How could such a thing be true on both sides of the family? How could we lose so much family at once? Our parents never fully explained the meaning of these family ruptures to us, their three daughters. They never seemed to be able to explain it to themselves. Over the years, any discussions on the topic ended in utterances of bitterness. The end result was that where there was once a huge extended family, now there was none. My parents lived on their own island with no bridges to the past—only their present and future, which was us and whatever progeny we'd bring forth.

For whatever reason, our holiday cooking was never quite right, never quite the same, again. My mother was still in charge, and she always prepared way too much food, as though she just couldn't get rid of her old habits of setting the table for a hundred people, as though perhaps they might appear at the door any moment.

This excess was the scourge. As any cook knows, if you prepare too many dishes you considerably raise the risk of failure. In this way, my sisters, my mother, and I would make dozens of trips back and forth from the kitchen to the table—ferrying out assorted antipasti of cold meats, vinegary artichokes, roasted peppers, and cheeses. After this, two bowls of store-bought ravioli (some cheese and some meat), a pan of roast chicken, a bloody rare roast beef, overcooked string beans with onion, salad, and additional side dishes (meatballs for the children or a basket of warm rolls, a gravy boat of red sauce)—all of it turning cold in transit—plus the grand finale of cookies, cake, and ice cream. We could never eat this much. What to do with it all?

And yet my mother wanted it this way. She wanted abundance, and since she is a woman who has always asked for little herself, we could not say no.

By the end of the day, I would be as exhausted as if I'd worked a full restaurant shift. My children, feral from all the stimulation, would run from room to room, wondering if more presents would magically appear. Their faces held continued anticipation, eyes wide open, as if to say "Is there more for me?"

THE PREVIOUS YEAR, Andrea, my youngest sister and an evangelical Christian who believes deeply in the holiday and its meanings, suggested that since I was obviously so miserable, perhaps I should take my family elsewhere on Christmas. This was not all that was said, and a three-month silence ensued.

But in the end, she was right. For this reason, we arrive quietly this year, bearing only presents for the nephews—two young boys—and three plastic bags of frozen ravioli, which I put in my sister's freezer.

"Genoese ravioli," I say casually and with little to-do. "One bag for each family. Like our great-grandmother Adalgiza's. At least I think they're like hers."

I hesitate to add that these are *the* ravioli I learned to make when I was in Italy the previous summer. I don't want to draw more attention to the lengths I go through—to that part of me that thinks our Christmas isn't good enough and has to go and get pretentious authentic recipes directly from Italy, from the *real* Italians, rather than our inferior and diluted Italian-Americanized stuff.

My sisters nod at this announcement and smile genially, then turn their attention elsewhere. But my father goes to the freezer and takes hold of a bag and holds it up to the light, examining the ravioli through the plastic, running his fingers over the little ruffled squares. After all, these ravioli have come by way of his Italian name and bloodlines.

"Not bad," he says, low-key as always. But I can tell that he's impressed. "Hey, you did a good job."

"The pasta is too thick," I begin to fret.

"Yes, ours was very thin. But they look pretty good to me. You can't get it perfect the first time."

Then with all the chaos of children and present-opening (apparently we didn't miss it all) and dessert and dishes to clean up—and despite my reminders—everyone forgets to take their ravioli home. And I never hear another word about them—whether my sisters ate them or not, whether they were good or horrible, whether or not my father thought they tasted anything like his memories.

Maybe this sort of thing runs in all families. Months later, when my sister Andrea and I have an even bigger fight and I flee her house with my kids in a whirlwind of fury and tears, as I am speeding down the highway in my car—stunned children in the backseat—I suddenly remember those Christmas ravioli. I wonder if they are still in her freezer, uneaten.

CHAPTER 2

What Can a Recipe Do?

I DON'T KNOW EXACTLY when it began, this search for ravioli—this quest for an authentic family dish. Maybe the desire was with me always.

Surely there came a specific moment in my life when I was especially weary of food fads, fast meals, and the sense of my own disposability. I wanted something enduring—a recipe of my own that did not come from a cookbook or a culinary expert on a television show, a recipe that did not come from the newspaper or my mother's Betty Crocker Golden Treasury collection. I did not need any more recipes to improve me. So many recipes in America tell you what you should eat for better nutrition, what you should serve to impress your guests, what exotic thing you should experiment on to stretch the boundaries of your palate (and perhaps your image)—and most of all, how to cook "quick and easy." I wanted none of this.

I had just written my first book, a sprawling history of American women told through the theme of food. I'd spent years studying ancient cookbooks and anthropologic documents. I'd cooked with older women who worked from memory, and I'd written down their ways. I was a detective on a hunt to uncover meanings of the past. From all this, I'd created a panoramic story to answer many of the questions I'd had about food and women.

When this project was done, it was natural to turn to my own kitchen and seek my own culinary roots.

But to say that I actually set forth on my ravioli quest, my ravioli obsession, my ravioli love because of these reasons . . . well, that would not be entirely true either.

Rather, my ravioli adventure began as a search for something that was not necessarily even a dish or a food.

It began, as many journeys do, in a small way, with an inchoate yearning, a desire for something I only partly understood—perhaps just desire itself, hitting me amidst the sound of cars whooshing by my house on a busy suburban street. Desire rising up against my two sons asking for foods they could suck out of plastic tubes, for aqua blue cereals, for iridescent red strips of corn syrup—things that I am not certain can reasonably be termed "food" but nonetheless are sold as such. Desire for an inner life where advertising could not reach. Desire for religion. Time was running out. Everything going by so fast. I regularly took my lunch standing at the kitchen counter choking down a sandwich and running up to my computer to stare at the screen, tapping with my fingertips. I had left where I came from and climbed the American ladder to a new place. Here, my past did not exist, and it was bothering me. I had a husband and two children I loved intensely. And it was nothing against them, but I was missing something that had to do with home.

When I was a young woman set upon rebellion against my parents, against convention from that limiting life of domestica, I would never have foreseen, never would have dreamed, that I would seek my joy in the kitchen—never. But over the years, I had come to see the importance in food, its brightness in human history. Now I was a mother and home all the time. Children had to eat, and I was constantly in the kitchen. Suddenly I wanted to be able to make something wonderful— wonderful not just because it tasted good but because it could span generations and tell a story—a story I was part of, somehow, a story to which I would add. I decided to find an old recipe, a recipe that preceded the big machine of technological food, before test-tube flavors and before megaindustrial products. A recipe I could trace from my family, back into history, further and further back, into an ancient past. Even more importantly—a recipe that could take me to a landscape more beautiful than postindustrial New Jersey with its traffic and pollution and the house on a racetrack—a landscape somehow more real. I wanted nothing more and nothing less than an authentic old family recipe.

BUT AN AUTHENTIC *WHAT*? My mother was a devoted and eclectic cook who believed in the power of the table, the party, the evening meal. Her repertoire spanned mid- to late-century American—that is to say, heavy on the home economics roasts, iceberg salads, and gelatin molds culled from women's magazines. Not that there's anything wrong with that— she'd fed us well. Her cooking was internationalized with quiche lorraine, humanized by recipes from friends and charitable cookbooks, and immortalized by Italian-American spaghetti-and-meatball Sunday dinners to please her husband. She was good in the kitchen and got respect for it in her circle of family and friends. Her cooking was perfectly authentic suburban America, taken up a couple of notches.

I wanted a deeper food lineage, and this was a problem. My ancestors came from several disparate European places—Ireland, Germany, Italy, and Croatia—with all roads leading to Hoboken, a gritty port perched on the edge of the Hudson River only a mile or so across the water from New York City—so unnaturally close that the astounding line of silver skyscrapers seemed more animation than real.

All our creation myths, all our stories of origin came from this place, a mere two or three generations back, always with the story of a boat trip from far away leading to a rebirth. There was no family tree with clear generations expanding outward over time, no roots digging deeper into the earth. Rather, when looking back to see where I come from, I find a cluster of faces huddled at my shoulder, just a step behind me—faces of parents and grandparents, aunts and uncles. Beyond them, nothing— only the vast expanse of air and stars and the everything that awaits. Fine enough. But before I shut the door again, I would be satisfied with just one old recipe from any of them.

It was out of the question that I'd turn to the Irish and German sides of my family for this recipe. My Irish great-grandmother was an alcoholic and died in an institution. The German one lived in poverty, enduring a husband who beat her, working multiple jobs to help the family survive. Cooking was the least of her concerns.

But who was I kidding? Of course I wanted a recipe from my Mediterranean side. I'd been to southern France and Greece. I'd loved the food and the languages, the ancient histories, the dry hot climate, the beautiful vistas of mountain and sea. Traveling up my maternal line of cooks, from mother to grandmother, I arrived in the Mediterranean kitchens of Croatia along the Dalmatian Coast, one of the most beautiful regions on earth. Here the story of olives, wine, and wheat goes back to the Illyrian and Roman ancients.

I visited Croatia one spring not long ago, in search of those recipes, those stories, those places. I tasted the extraordinary fish and mollusks of the Adriatic and drank fire spirits seeped in green herbs. I fell in love with the undeveloped coasts along the Adriatic and the green gem islands that cluster off Split and Dubrovnik, from where my relatives had once come. I wandered amid the Roman ruins, the Venetian-styled squares, and the big-box architecture of the Communists.

Here, the Mediterranean was not quite part of the Western world, not quite developed, or polluted. I was gripped by the bare intensity of the place, the dizzying mountains along the water, the vineyards by the sea. I listened for the whisperings of my Balkan ancestors. But no culinary ghosts spoke. There were no threads left for me. The reason for this was simple: within ten years of arriving in America, my Croatian great-grandmother severed her ties with the future when she abandoned her three young children and ran off with her lover.

"Bigamist." The first time I ever heard the word was in connection to my Croatian great-grandmother. "Technically, she was a bigamist," explained my mother. "She never divorced her husband. She just got married again." So the chorus went.

The new husband was a cousin of her old husband fresh from Croatia. He'd arrived at the front door in Hoboken, first seeking a place to sleep—and then, later, so much more. Evidently the temptation was too great.

"My mother was a selfish and beautiful woman," my Croatian grandmother often told me, describing the day her mother walked out of her life. "She wore a cape, a Cleopatra haircut, and long earrings. She had suitcases in her hand, and she just kissed us and said good-bye."

When the lovers ran off, my resourceful grandmother (still a child) turned to the kitchen to begin from scratch, with no mother or grand-mother to guide her—and few taste memories to form her vocabulary of food. Just the same, she figured out how to cook, and she did it with rel-ish. She asked neighbors, she used instinct, she read cookbooks, and somehow she developed a near-magical ability to make something from nothing, whether a life from scraps, a pot roast on Sunday, or cake from a box of flour.

Faced with these sad stories of betrayal and a Croatian language that sounded like a wall of impenetrable consonants, I knew there was noth-ing left of this culinary heritage for me to find. All had been wiped away by a colossal failure of love.

And yet, I still wanted an authentic family recipe, and so my challenge remained.

MY FATHER'S Italian family offered the answer. Big and expansive, with many American members, the Schenones had carried forth the recipes of their native Genoa. All I knew was that it was a port city in the north of Italy and that my grandfather had come to America as a baby, and his older sister, Aunt Tessie, was something of a ravioli legend. My mother still recalled with awe the day she witnessed Tessie in action, rolling and flipping dough.

"You ate those ravioli, you know," my mother says. "I'm sure you did."

But I couldn't remember. All I knew was that an old ravioli press—a handmade grid of small squares—had hung on the kitchen wall above us for decades. It was a decoration, an unused relic, and it hung there while we children ate our sweetened breakfast cereals each morning and our roast beef at night. Mine was the generation that would never see its use. I understood only vaguely that a great-grandmother and her daughters had come here from Italy, bringing the craft of pasta. I knew so little; I was lucky to know even her name: Adalgiza. Her husband was Salvatore.

As it turned out, Adalgiza's ravioli was the real deal. A little bit of research quickly revealed, to my delight, that in Genoa ravioli is a crucial and beloved dish, the essential food of Christmas, birthdays, and village *festas*—in short, the food known for celebration and the things that are good in life. Many a writer and artist have paid homage to Genoese ravioli: "the queen of all the first courses," wrote one culinary authority in 1863. "Delicious, appetizing, healthful, substantial" rhapsodized the Genoese poet Martin Piaggio. Even the famous violinist and composer Niccolò Paganini (1782–1840) took an interest in the fine details of this ravioli from his native Genoa. In the last year of his life, he recorded his personal recipe, leaving behind—in addition to his brilliant musical canon—careful documentation for frying butter and onions finely chopped, proper filling, consistent sauce, and "stretched leaves of dough."

Finally, the piece of happy family history I was looking for. This was the sacred dish I wanted—this ravioli and no other. And not just any old version of it, but the holiday recipe carried here by my great-grandmother Adalgiza from Genoa lifetimes ago, her hopes bundled up with her children, on a boat to find her husband who'd sailed before her. Yes, ravioli would be my search, my grail, and I suppose in my private way, a form of protest too, against all that was wrong with my busy modern life.

There were complications, however.

While I had rights to this recipe through my father, we'd been estranged from his family for many years. I feared that the actual lineage of the dish might be a difficult topic. After all, this was the ravioli he'd had in childhood, seated around the table with all of them. I would need his help. Would he be willing to dig up these roots?

Furthermore, my father is a famously reserved man, not prone to sharing many memories about the Italian father he lost, not prone to sharing much of himself in any regard. He draws a wide ring of privacy around himself. I have always sensed a threat of danger if I tread into this forbidden territory by asking too many questions—a continual risk for me, professional question asker, and for him who prefers so much left unsaid.

But to my relief and great surprise, he likes this topic very much, explaining that when he was a boy, Aunt Tessie appeared at various junctures in his life, bringing forth her lovely little handmade squares, distributing them by the hundreds. Aunt Tessie was my Adalgiza's firstborn child and a ravioli hero by anyone's standards. She came to this country as a young girl, but old enough to remember the shape of mountains over the sea and the long cold boat ride to America. And though I'm told she was a practical woman, not one for reminiscing, Tessie kept the ravioli culture going all her life—from the time she was a girl and learned it in Italy until she was in her seventies, too frail to stand up any more at the pasta board without help.

Not that my father ever volunteered any of this, mind you. I learn these stories only when I ask, but he is cooperative and willing, helping me work on a family tree. Mother to daughter, mother to daughter—this is the usual path of recipes, along with talk in the kitchen, where family stories circulate in the onion-scented air. Among more than two hundred or so descendants of Adalgiza and Salvatore, there are still four living granddaughters. And so luckily—because Genoese ravioli is such old history for us—I can skip over the entire troubled story of my father and his siblings and go to other, more distant parts of the family tree—my father's cousins, all older women who have genial feelings about us.

"Don't wait too long to call them—they're getting on in years," my father instructs, giving me their phone numbers. "And make sure you call my cousin Adele. She's Tessie's daughter." And then he adds in a gentler tone, "She's a soft person." When my father uses the word "soft," he doesn't mean weak or lacking, but to the contrary, kind and good. It is a great compliment.

My dad even volunteers that he would like to make the ravioli too. We talk about getting a long rolling pin and board, perhaps repairing the old press.

As instructed, the first person I reach out to is Adele. From the first breath, I find her to be sweet and gentle, as my father promised. Just the same, she is a bit befuddled at what in the world I could be looking for.

Adele has been on the West Coast some forty years. She and my father have long been out of touch, and she's never even met me.

"I didn't cook many Genoese dishes. Italian cooking takes a *long* time, you know," she confesses. "We were in America, so we wanted to be American."

"What about the ravioli?"

"Oh, my daughter and I just made three hundred of them last month for Christmas!" she exclaims, then sighs with fatigue simply remembering the project.

"Do you think you could send me the recipe?" I ask. "Is it written down anywhere?"

"Oh sure," she promises. "I can send it."

But will it ever arrive? Adele is in her early eighties, and though she is perfectly lucid when I talk to her, there is frailness in her voice, a sense that her life is fading. My out-of-the blue request would be easy to forget.

To my surprise, several weeks later an envelope arrives in the mail postmarked from Washington State. It contains three strawberry-bordered recipe cards. "From the kitchen of," they say on top, and someone has written in "Adele Bacigalupi."

Inside the envelope, I find a handwritten note. "Dear Laura, My mother told me you're looking for the ravioli recipe. She's been pretty forgetful lately. If you have any questions, feel free to contact me. We've been out of touch with family so long. It's nice to hear from you. Linda."

I pick up the recipe cards. One for spinach frittata, another for stuffed zucchini, a third for ravioli. Here it is! Adalgiza's ravioli. Tessie's ravioli. My heart jumps. Here it is!

Quickly I scan the list of ingredients: "veal, beef, spinach, eggs, parmigiano cheese . . ." Yes, yes . . . all expected . . . but I stumble on an ingredient that confuses me. I read and reread it again. There must be a mistake.

I email my distant cousin, Linda. "You meant ricotta cheese, right?" She writes back. "No, I mean cream cheese. Cream cheese is correct."

Cream cheese? As in the Philadelphia kind? In Genoese ravioli? I am searching for an authentic family recipe and I get the unctuously rich cream cheese in the silver foil? Cream cheese à la Kraft Foods, megaindustrial producer of Cheez Whiz and Rice Krispies—icon of the convenience-food culture of America?

This cannot be right. No, this cannot be right at all. Surely this is an Americanized substitution. But a substitution for what?

And so the journey begins.

Recipe for: Ravioli   Serves:
From the kitchen of: Adele Barigalupi
5 cups flour
3 tsp salt
2 eggs
1½ cup water (approximate)
Mix together & knead until soft & pliable. Let rest 15 min.

Filling. 1 4oz cream cheese
2 packages spinach (well chopped)
The Fruit of the Spirit is Love

1 lb veal & 1 lb. pork ground fine
3 eggs
½ cup grated cheese
Salt, pepper
Cream all ingredients together
Roll dough very thin. Spread
Filling over half. Fold & press
with Ravioli press. Cut & freeze.

CHAPTER 3

Salvatore and Adalgiza

I DID NOT EXPECT a love story.

I would have assumed their marriage was arranged. After all, such tales litter the immigrant histories here in New Jersey—tales of grand-mothers or great-aunts matched to men their fathers chose for them. Sometimes, the match was lucky enough—a good father, a good provider, a decent guy. Other times not so lucky—there were belligerent men, men who ran with other women, men who stayed out at night, and men who beat their wives.

None of this for Adalgiza. No arranged marriages for her.

Oh, they tried to decide for her. She was engaged to a soldier, you know, the man her parents wanted. She came from a decent family—not rich, but . . . comfortable . . . you know . . . decent. But Salvatore (laughter), well he was another story. He was poor as a peasant—from up in the mountains (a wave of the hand to show boon-docks—way out in the hills, really poor). Of course they didn't want her to marry HIM—not him.

How did they even meet?

Who knows? (Hands in the air. A shrug.) But oh lord, once she saw him, everything changed. Everything.

And then?

She dropped that soldier. She chose Salvatore. But oh boy, was her father mad. She told me he chased her all around the table.

Chased her around the table?

IT'S A STRANGE THING to call distant relatives out of the blue and start asking them questions—relatives I haven't seen in years and some I've never known. They pick up the phone and hear a voice say "Hi, I'm your cousin Peter's daughter. I'm looking for your grandmother's recipes." It is awkward. I feel shy. But I push on just the same, knowing that time is running out, if it hasn't already. A total of eight of my father's cousins and their children receive my strange phone call or letters. Each of them gives a new voice to my chorus. But memory is the most untrustworthy, the most variable of all our songs, and it's not surprising that the memories I dig up do not always agree.

There's this one:

Salvatore left Italy alone. He went to America ahead of Adalgiza to find work. He'd send the money for her later. But the money wasn't coming and the years were going by, and the stories got back to Italy that he had another woman. As soon as she heard about it, that Adalgiza went and packed up her kids and got herself on a boat to America.

And this one:

Oh, Honey, they never talked about Italy. Never expressed a desire to go back. He was a tile man and worked hard here—he did well for himself. He bought a house. They had nothing back there in Italy. Oh no. Nothing.

And this one too:

Adalgiza never should have left Genoa. She'd had it much better there. But you

know how men are. Salvatore had to go on with his big dreams. Oh, what a mis-
take America was.

Catherine is eighty-two years old, and she is the one I want to speak with most of all. When I arrive at her door, she greets me with a big smile and open arms. I haven't seen her since my wedding fifteen years ear-lier, but she is the kind of person who would talk to you day or night and invite you in for coffee. She is looking marvelous too, in a lightweight green pantsuit decorated with dragonflies, wearing feminine sandals with a small heel. The salt-and-pepper hair I remember has turned completely white, but otherwise she is little changed. At eighty-two, she moves with grace and could easily pass for seventy, and you can tell by looking in her eyes and watching her move that she is still sharp, still herself, still fully in the game of life.

"My gosh, you look fabulous," I say, after we hug. "I hope I have some of your genes."

"You do have my genes," she laughs. "You're my cousin!"

Cousin Catherine—Kay as we used to call her—is the closest living link to Adalgiza, the one who knew her best.

"My grandmother raised me," she explains.

Every mother has sadness—and for Adalgiza, it was her daughter Mamie, the child in trouble, the one who suffered lifelong illness. Per-haps nature devises women to be strong later in life so that they can help with grandchildren and ensure the survival of the family. Adalgiza, in her fifties and sixties, gray hair in a bun, her skirt long toward the floor, took young Catherine under her wing, and in her Genoese dialect, taught the girl the survival skills of womanhood: how to cook, how to clean, how to roll out pasta, how to do the dishes properly, and not least of all, to be careful when all those Italian men came over with their man-dolins and homemade wine.

"Never. *Never* sit on anyone's lap," Adalgiza whispered in Catherine's ear. And especially not Salvatore's brother, the artist playboy with the mustache and the big belly who sold his watercolors on the streets of Greenwich Village.

"Please tell me more about this love story," I beg.

"Well . . . ," her voice adjusts once again to a lower tone. "My grandfather was so handsome, you know. *Very* handsome." With this, Catherine says, "Come look," and she guides me to see a hallway wall dedicated to family photos. She points to my great-grandfather Salvatore.

It's true about his looks. No woman would disagree. This is a gorgeous creature—dark hair, dreamy deep eyes, and broad shoulders. There is something about the way he stands with pride, put together in a fine suit and tie. *He is the man you leave home for.* In my mind, I hear these words come from out of nowhere, a line from a poem written by a friend when we were young.

Nearby is a complete family shot, formally posed in a photographer's studio. Salvatore stands beside Adalgiza, his hand on her shoulder. Adalgiza is in her early thirties, dark hair, deep-set eyes, a slightly broad nose. She is pretty, for sure, but not so beautiful as he. In her face, I see her love and worries all bound up, as she sits straight-backed and strong in her chair, Victorian blouse up to chin, long skirt to ankles, hair swept back in a bun. Planted in her lap like a golden flower is a beautiful baby boy, my grandfather, the fair-haired little one, in his christening outfit, which is all white and glorious. Three young daughters—Tessie, Lena, and Mamie—stand tall and immaculate in their stiff little-girl Victorian dresses with big satin bows. As was the habit back then, they do not smile for the camera but look out stoically to the uncertain future that we have become.

"My grandmother used to tell me that he came down from the hills, down to her house in town, at night. He came under her window with a mandolin, and he sang love songs to her in the dark."

I see a silhouette, feet on a rocky road, a shape in the dark. The image disappears. I look at Catherine.

"Are you serious? Sang under her window?"

Catherine smiles, pleased with herself. She continues, "That was the end of the soldier her parents wanted. That was how Salvatore won her."

After a while, the doorbell rings.

"That must be your mom and dad." Catherine walks to the intercom to buzz them up.

Salvatore and Adalgiza's wedding photo, 1895.

When I had located Catherine after all these years, I discovered that she was living on the same block as my parents, a street of apartment towers, popular with many people whose children are grown. How strange. They were neighbors but didn't know it. Catherine invited them over with me. Now everyone hugs and we all sit down.

During this time, I'm carefully observing my father. I never know what to expect of him when it comes to people—whether he'll be warm or aloof—and it has become hard for me to imagine my father actually having any relatives anymore, being anyone's son or brother. But here he is, chatting with Catherine in a wonderfully familiar way, smiling as they go on about their shared clan of cousins and cousins' children.

Salvatore and Adalgiza with their children: from left to right,
Tessie, my grandfather Louis, Mamie, and Lena, about 1906.

To my relief, the conversation finally winds its way on to food.

"Oh, our grandmother was a wonderful cook," says Catherine, emphasizing the word "wonderful" as though I cannot possibly imagine. She rattles off a repertoire of Adalgiza's dishes: pesto pounded in a marble bowl, focaccia with onions, stuffed vegetables, minestrone, anchovies, *torta*, stockfish, the sweet holiday bread called *pandoçe* in Genoese (*pandolce* in Italian)—and of course ravioli, the sacred ravioli for Christmas, Easter, birthday parties, and happy times.

"The one with the spinach and meat and cream cheese?"

"Yes, that one," says Catherine. "That's the only one she ever made."

And of course now is my chance to delve a little deeper into the issue of the famous white cheese in question.

"Was it, uh, really, *cream cheese*?" I ask. "You mean, like, the Philadelphia kind?"

"Oh, yes," Catherine replies confidently. "My grandmother used a lot of cream cheese. She put it in her pesto and her *torta* and in her stuffed vegetables too."

(In my mind, I try to make some adjustment. Okay, cream cheese, I tell myself. What's wrong with that? Why am I so prejudiced against cream cheese?)

My father joins in, remembering all the strange Genoese foods his father used to like: *berodi*—a sausage made of pigs' blood and pignoli—eel and tripe.

I have never heard mention of any of these foods in my family until this moment.

Catherine goes on about Adalgiza. "Oh, she made me clean on Saturdays. My grandmother was a *veerry* clean lady. Work work work. She had a coal stove and set up a board between two chairs where her bread would rise. She soaked her stockfish in the basement so as to keep away the putrid smell—seven days of soaking! And you know what she put in her gravy?" Catherine asks—"gravy," meaning tomato sauce to Italian-Americans in New Jersey.

We shake our heads. No, we don't know. We haven't the foggiest idea.

"It was *very* unusual. She put a pot roast in her gravy."

"A pot roast?"

"Yes, a pot roast."

We fall silent before this mystery, unsure what to say to such a strange concept. Gingerly, I resume the interrogation.

"Did she roll out her pasta with a pin?"

"Oh, of course," says Catherine, almost offended I might suggest it could be any other way. "She rolled it out on a big board. All those Italians did back then. And then she put it on the bed to dry. Once my husband put his coat there and got flour all over it," she laughs. "I made ravioli too, you know. But I gave it up," she shakes her head. "Too much work." She pauses. "You know, there is one cousin left of us who makes it. You've got to call my cousin Millie. Yes, call Millie. She and her daughter do it every Christmas. You want her phone number?"

Catherine's recollection proves excellent on many things. She is the only one who can tell me Adalgiza's maiden name—Amianto—and she knows the address of their first house in Hoboken—120 Willow Avenue.

BEFORE WE LEAVE, Catherine leans toward me and says she has one more story to tell. She is smiling a little mischievously, as though about to reveal something she shouldn't.

This story goes back to the 1960s, Union City, just up the road from Hoboken. In those days, Catherine and her first husband ran a tavern there.

"Your dad had just started going with your mother. And one day he brought her into our tavern. She was so beautiful—such a nice girl."

She smiles and looks at my mother, then continues.

"He brought his guitar too. And when your father played and sang—oh, he was so handsome—she stared at him like a lovesick cow. Oh *my god* was she in love with him."

My mother, with a body that is failing her much too soon at age sixty-two, smiles at the memory. And so does my father.

Catherine is an emissary from another world of family gossip and stories that had long ago faded from us. We are happy for the camaraderie, my parents and I, and delighted to find her doing so well, and to be reminded that happiness is always possible—especially in old age.

Catherine's amazing condition is hardly the result of an easy life—what with that childhood of hers, then all those decades working six days a week night and day, running a tavern with her husband, taking care of two kids and then, finally, nursing her husband through years of fatal cancer. . . . It looks to me like somehow, Catherine held on to her grace so that when another chance came along she was still able to leap. At age seventy-five she remarried and now still seems to hardly believe her happiness. Her husband taught her to play golf, and they spend winters in Florida.

"I don't know how long it will go on for, but it's a good life," she ventures.

True, her husband is Irish and refuses to eat certain dishes like calamari or gnocchi with pesto. But a woman couldn't wish for a more appreciative man at the table. When I finally meet her husband, Joe, he tells me he's a writer too.

"I'm writing a book about Catherine's cooking," he pronounces, going on to describe how he keeps a diary of every dinner she cooks, carefully logging with detail the menu each night. "It's going to solve every woman's cooking problems." He winks, and Catherine giggles, rolling her eyes.

"It's just simple food," she insists. "I made a spinach *torta* last week. I just cook plain food."

At the end of our time together, Catherine offers to take me to the cemetery where all the Schenones are buried.

"They're all lying there in a row," she declares. "We'll go some day and see them. And then we'll have lunch."

CHAPTER 4

May I Borrow Your Mother?

Mix flour and eggs and water.
Knead until pliable.
Roll until very thin.

When I'd first received the Schenone ravioli recipe card, I stared at it over and over again, as though it were an oracle, or at the very least a treasure map to decode.

This got me nowhere. The recipe was not a recipe but a list of ingredients and actions to jog the memory of the cook who already knew what to do. I had not yet made a single ravioli, and so all I had were questions.

How to mix flour and eggs?

What did this word "pliable" mean?

How did one roll?

Then there was that nagging problem of the cream cheese. What was it before America? What was the recipe Adalgiza brought with her, the original one?

It was soon clear that I'd have to go to Italy to answer these questions. I'd have to go to the place where the recipe and Adalgiza came from.

However, there were many problems in this decision, the biggest being that I didn't know where to go.

This was long before I'd called Catherine. I did not yet know the story

of the hills and the seaside and serenatas of life. I did not yet know Adalgiza's name was Amianto. These bits of information might have helped.

"Genoa," said my father. "Genoa is all I know."

This could have meant the actual city of Genoa or one of the dozens
of dramatically different villages in the Genoa province of the Liguria
region. It could have meant just a few steps west of the French Riviera or
up in the rural hills of *contadini* in northern Italy. To say "Genoa" could
have meant rich or poor. There are many worlds in Genoa.

There were plenty more problems too. Even if I knew where my
ancestors were from a hundred years earlier, with whom could I speak
once I arrived? I couldn't exactly go to peoples' houses and knock on
their doors asking for ravioli recipes, could I?

And yet, these minor details did not deter me much. I was convinced
that in the long history of Italian food, a hundred years was not terribly
much, and Adalgiza's recipe—or something like it—still existed. Italy is
a nation where people take memory and food seriously, and I was quite
sure there would be answers for me.

My husband agreed that I could go for a week. I was amazed. No, no,
it wasn't that I had to ask permission—not exactly. But with two young
children, logistics were tough. My oldest was only seven, a quiet young
boy who still anchored himself to the rock of mother and home and
needed me to help him navigate the world. Our youngest was just two
and a half, a little blond boy who burst forth with open arms and smiles
when I entered the room, singing forth "Mommy!" if we had been
parted for only an hour. How could I leave such a vulnerable little babe?

Then there was the money. Oh, our money problems. Perhaps some
food magazines would want a story on ravioli. Could I sell this little bit
of diluted Italian heritage? I wrote to all the editors I knew, and then
some. But it turned out that no one was buying. "Our inventories are
full of Italy and France," they replied. (Better if I were Vietnamese or
from the Kerala Coast of India on a hunt for ancestral dishes made of
coconut, ginger, and curry. These are the new culinary frontiers calling
elite gastronomes in search of the exotic, the primitive, the authentic—
where life is lived "as it once was.") Italy, quite simply put, had already
been done to death.

With no magazine assignment, no one inviting me, and only financial disincentives for me to go, I began to lose my nerve for the prospect of cluelessly walking Genoa's streets in search of a ravioli recipe.

And yet my husband encouraged me. "You should have freedom to live your life," he said, knowing full well that this was part true but also part wish.

It wasn't easy. There would be babysitters. There would be lengthy notes and extensive arrangements. My husband would have to come home early from work, pack lunches by himself, manage the endless minutiae of domesticity. He would be stressed, for sure. Problems would arise. But I was going to have one free week. One quick week. And I would owe him big time.

"You mean you're going to Italy to make pasta with mamas?" a food-writer friend asked incredulously, as though I had won the lottery, because everyone in America knew that Italy was some kind of paradise and old Italian mamas held culinary magic in their stalwart hands. They had what we'd lost. They turned the raw simple materials of the earth into gold, while we Americans—well, the large part of us anyway—had given up all that for our embarrassing frozen foods, our strange microwavable creations.

"Oh, lucky you!" this friend told me, and so did everyone else. Among Americans, the mere concept of Italy evoked rhapsodies of the romantic, the beautiful, and above all a primitive simplicity in the delicious. When I said I was going to Italy, people inevitably fell into lyrical tribute and memory about the unforgettable meal of handmade pasta with lemon sauce once enjoyed on a terrace above the Adriatic, the lasagne béchamel that formed an epiphany in Naples, or the sublimely perfect tomato salad in a trattoria of Tuscany. "So simple!" they all said, shaking their heads at the magic. "So simple, and yet so exquisite!"

I was always suspicious of such displays, such culinary tourism and its reveries of paradise. Yes, Italy is a beautiful country. Yes, the food is great. But it bothered me that Americans glorified it so. Something in this romance seemed false. What?

Maybe it brings up my own mixed feelings about ethnicity. When I grew up in New Jersey in the 1970s, we lived in a place full of immigrants

and their children. My closest friends were Italian, Ecuadorian, Alban-
ian, Polish, Cuban, Jewish, and Irish kids who did step dancing at the
school shows. Here, being merely American seemed not only boring but
deprived. Far better to have some deeper part of yourself that went back
to a beautiful place of memory, even if it was a memory that didn't
belong to you personally but to your parents or grandparents.

When I was young, many people assumed I was Italian. I sported a big
head of long dark curly hair, a New Jersey accent, and an Italian last
name. I had a father who wore gold chains and pinky rings. Relatives and
friends came and went day and night. These were all the markings of
being Italian, and I often allowed that assumption. After all, we were
somewhat Italian, right?

My parents' friends, on the other hand, were truly Italian. Their
families came from Sicily, the Piedmont, Naples. They were the ones
whose families spoke Italian dialects at home, whose fathers made wine,
whose grandmothers lived in the house and rolled out pasta dough on
those legendary boards. I was envious. I think my parents were too.

"Mom, did you raise us Italian?" I recently asked.

"No," she paused. "We just raised you with an Italian bent."

An Italian bent? Was that an actual cultural heritage?

Despite the assumptions, I always knew the truth—I was not Italian.
My father was Italian, but not me. There was simply not enough left by
the time my generation came around. Because of intermarriage and the
passing of time, I was born in the twilight of ethnicity, the barely tail end
of it.

As the years went on, Italians evolved into Italian-Americans, and a
new generation emerged. With few connections left to the actual place
of Italy, they carried out memories heavily faded by time and filtered
through stereotypes from movies and television. Anthropologists might
say that these Americanizations are creolized cultures in the United
States—not inauthentic replicas but new cultures unto themselves. Yes,
they deserve respect. But just the same, these latter-day New Jersey Italians troubled me and sometimes grated on my nerves.

Most irritating to me of all were the macho Italian-American men
with their roles and privileges, to threaten, to raise voices, to have affairs

outside of marriage, and to go out at night with friends while their wives stayed home and cooked and cleaned. By age sixteen, I was wise to these brute injustices and believed them all to be laid at the feet of the Italian patriarchs of New Jersey.

As an adult, I shared some of these feelings with my brother-in-law, who is from Rome.

"You know," he replied, "the Italian men in New Jersey mostly came from the south. The people who came here were very uneducated and very poor."

Was this the old prejudice against the south? Blame it on Naples. Blame it on Palermo. Blame it on the mafia. Even if I'd heard this excuse when I was a miserable teenager at constant odds with authority—my strict father and his tyrannical rules—I doubt it would have helped.

I suffered. I rebelled. And then I finally found a position of strength: I studied French. I became a bookish girl.

What else was there to do? Education trumps machismo—I sensed it then as a sixteen-year-old girl in the Jersey landscape, the unrelenting gray of strip malls, doughnut shops, and motels along Route 46, the bleak swamplands where mafia sins were said to be buried.

A weeklong visit to Italy at age twenty-one satisfied any interest I had in the real Italy with a whirlwind Eurorail tour of Rome, Florence, and Venice, rushing to see Michelangelo's David, the Sistine chapel, and the romantic canals. I was also baffled to discover that these glorious north-ern cities bore little likeness to the Italy I knew in New Jersey, which was mostly descended from peasants in the south. The fair-haired, blue-eyed Tuscans I glimpsed in Florence looked nothing like *our* Italians at home. In fact, as a child, I'd grown up assuming that the darker your skin was, the purer Italian you were—not unlike the blacks with darker skins who were closer to pure African.

I didn't feel a need to return to Italy anytime soon. Whenever I had the chance to travel, I chose my beloved France and the language I'd worked years to learn—the language of Flaubert, Proust, and Camus. What a contrast to our New Jersey dialect, our bare, boiled-down-to-the-bones way of putting things, our tough rhythms that lay beneath the surface of words. This was the exotic refinement, the escape hatch I needed to leave behind my childhood vistas of oil tanks and gargantuan industry along that science-fiction corridor we call the New Jersey Turnpike.

After college, when I went to work in editorial jobs in New York City, I was a curiosity to my colleagues. An Italian intellectual with big hair and red lips. How strange! How novel! A working-class Jersey girl in publishing—and one who knows French!

No. All my logic and education couldn't erase my ambivalence about Italians—the stereotypes, the envy, the confusion over what was real. And so I had chosen France instead, for my dream of elsewhere.

Now, two decades later, here I was turning toward Italy again.

THE DAY OF my departure was a strange one. My husband and I woke up at the same moment. Lying side by side in bed in the half-wake, half-sleep moment of morning, he told me he'd dreamed he was in a castle with a woman who was tempting him.

"She was beautiful. . . . But of course I just couldn't go through with it." He sounded almost disappointed in himself, or perhaps sad. I felt the shadow of midlife pass over us, the weight of responsibility, and I sighed. Yes, of course he has these dreams.

"Well, I'm glad you didn't go through with it," I replied. Then we pushed it aside, as adults must, and pulled back the comfort of the blankets to rise and face our responsibilities, feet on the floor, kids to be fed and gotten off to where they must go, us getting to work. Midlife.

Later that day, while I was packing, I got a phone call out of the blue from a photographer friend, a celebrated artist whose work hung on the walls of some of the world's great museums.

He had just driven across the United States, from west to east, taking thousands of pictures, calling people he knew, if even vaguely, in each place he went. Now he was a few miles away from me, in the town of Paterson, photographing a famous waterfall in one of America's most famously broken-down Rust Belt towns.

"Want to have a coffee?" he asked.

Why not? His photos were brilliant—particularly adept at capturing the things beneath the surface, the vicious, the weird, the funny, the sad—and the ironies of American life—the details of normal that are suddenly not normal at all—whether meat-eating rituals of backyard barbecues, a set of ten perfectly painted red toenails, or a glimpse of a peeled banana about to be eaten, held up in the hand of a driver, the other hand on the steering wheel . . . going where?

Inside a Jersey diner, we took our seats at a vinyl-covered booth at a Formica table. He ordered a hamburger and talked on and on about himself the way many artists do—where he'd gone, what he'd accomplished, what he thought. When I told him that I was going to Italy that very night and the purpose of my quest, he offered without hesitating. "I've spent a lot of time in Italy. I think some of the food there is overrated. We've got better in northern California." And for some reason I couldn't identify—perhaps my inner skeptic—I was very glad to hear this. We went back to talking about New Jersey.

"The pure products of America go crazy," I said, quoting a poem by the great William Carlos Williams, author of the poem "Paterson." But my photographer friend had never heard of it, and he didn't seem to care. He was merely a visitor to my Rust Belt territory, a foreigner to our particular layers of irony, our immigrant history of the factories, and the rhythms of our densely crowded place.

What would my outsider eye find in Genoa? Would I fall prey to the tourist images and stupid Italy love? Would I find my recipe?

I sipped my coffee. Beneath all this civilized talk was a terror inside me, this rapid heartbeat flush, this panting. This thinking that the plane was going to go down and I would die and my children would be orphans because their mother couldn't be happy enough with the life she had— and a pretty good life at that.

But instead of revealing any of this, I asked the important question. "How do you get your photos?" This is why I came to have coffee, I suddenly realized, to ask this very question.

My friend lifted the lid off his hamburger and poured ketchup on the brown disk within.

"Chance," he replied casually. "Serendipity. I just have to be ready to be there so I can get the shot. I've learned to change my thinking every ten minutes so I can go this way or go that way, to get the shot."

A COUPLE of days later, and I was standing at the door of an apartment house in Sampierdarena, Genoa, ringing the bell. Maria Carla came down to meet me. This was no old-world mama, *please.* Maria Carla was an elegant woman with blond curls, in her early sixties, wearing a lovely sundress and a fashionable choker around her neck. She and her husband, Guido Guigoni, ran a paint shop downstairs. They had one child—a highly educated daughter, Alessandra, who was a food anthropologist and, through email correspondence, had introduced me to her family and arranged for this day.

I awkwardly produced my memorized Italian phrases to introduce myself in the formal way. Maria Carla listened patiently while I mangled my way slowly through it, nodded with obvious relief when I was done, then led the way up in a small elevator, which she operated, to the apartment where she and her husband had lived for decades and raised their daughter.

The doors opened, and we stepped directly into the dining room, airy with high ceilings, terrazzo floors, antiques, and pleasant images framed on all the walls—an orderly and gracious home. The table was set with white linens, crystal glasses, and fine plates. The plan was that we would make and then eat ravioli. Some friends of the Guigonis would arrive later to join us.

I had come with a long list of questions, but Maria Carla immediately took charge, and I didn't have a chance to ask any of them. She handed me a starched white apron and put me to work chopping carrots. And so began my first ravioli lesson.

The Guigoni kitchen was modern and bright, with a lot of light and a worktable in the middle of the terra-cotta tiled floor. It was a cheerful place with pretty teapots and plates placed about, jars of spices lining the open shelves.

I hardly had any idea how to proceed. I'd read only a couple of recipes for ravioli, but what little I knew is that three main theaters of operation existed, three smaller stories that made up the larger epic:

1. the filling (*ripieno*);
2. the pasta (*sfoglia*); and
3. the sauce (*salsa*), which for these Genoese or Christmas ravioli (as the Guigonis call them) was called *tucco* (in Genoese), a meat sauce.

Because the filling was the hardest and the most time consuming part, we needed to get this under way immediately.

Maria Carla opened up white, wax-paper packages of beautiful-looking meat—fresh, thick cuts of bright flesh, evidently bought that day. She had beef, tender pork, and veal—"less than 20 months" she stipulated about the veal, an important detail. I commented on how fine the meat looked. "In the trattoria, you'll get organ meat in your ravioli," she quipped, one hand giving a quick swirl in the air above her head; a phrase in the language of Italian gesticulation.

Indeed, she was lavish with her ingredients, not only the finest cuts of meat but also the wine, butter, and herbs. She gave me a mezzaluna—the half-moon-shaped knife—and asked that I cut the carrots and celery. I was awkward with this tool, so Guido took over, competently rocking it back and forth over and over again until the vegetables were neatly minced nearly to pulp. These vegetables—along with aromatics like onion, garlic, and a few dried porcini—went into a terra-cotta dish with the beef and veal, to slow-cook on low stovetop heat. The pork, however, was a lean cut and cooked more quickly in a stainless-steel pan with lots of butter, a bay leaf, finely cut rosemary, and a tablespoon of pignoli. Every so often, Maria Carla extravagantly splashed in white table wine and a sizzle of steam flew up.

Maria Carla turned out to be—as promised by her daughter—an excellent cook who worked entirely from memory. What I admired most was not that she used the best ingredients and attended to the smallest details, but that she was confident and in control. She knew what she wanted, and so there was no hesitation in her gestures. She gracefully went about her work. No measuring tools. No written recipes.

She'd made these ravioli perhaps hundreds of times. She'd learned from her mother and her mother before her, which meant, if I'd calculated the ages correctly, we were in striking range of my great-grandmother Adalgiza.

We spoke through a translator, an older man I'd found through a professional group. Despite efforts to keep appropriately in the background, he was an awkward barrier. When I heard my words relayed in his Italian, I felt immense frustration, as though I should have simply understood, as though I was *on the verge* of understanding, that somehow I should have just been able to flip a Romance-language switch in my brain and convert all my French to Italian and start speaking instantly. And yet I couldn't.

MOST ITALIANS see food as part of their cultural heritage, and Maria Carla and Guido were no different. They showed me a ravioli cutter that was one hundred years old, passed down through the family. They seemed to understand fully what I was doing. "There are many requests these days," they explained. "Writers and scholars nowadays want to interview older women for their recipes."

Here, in Maria Carla's kitchen, there was a foot in both worlds—the past and the present. She was a bridge between the old and the new. Yes, there were two mortar and pestles displayed on her cupboard, but a food processor stood proudly on the counter. During our day together, Maria Carla comically blew that machine a furtive kiss every now and then, to make me laugh. *"Je l'adore,"* she said, and giggled with pleasure at her own small defiance.

Now, while the meats braised, it was time to move to theater two: the pasta.

Because Guido was gracious and friendly, and because men help with Christmas ravioli ("After all, it's so much work"), he disappeared and returned with a large pasta board—about two by three feet—wrapped in plastic. Out came the electric pasta machine.

There was a pause. "Would you like us to roll out the dough with a rolling pin?" asked Guido with a genteel air, being as hospitable as possible. He appeared worried about my answer.

Maria Carla threw up her hands. "Well, if you want this, I can't do it. I don't remember anymore." And with that she attached the motor to her pasta machine.

THIS WAS modern pasta—with a luxurious four eggs plus an extra yolk, and all worked into the soft flour sifted to a fine white powder that Italians favor for fresh pasta. "Double zero," she said emphatically, pointing to her bag of flour. When my great-grandmother lived in Italy, I doubt she had these luxuries, such light white flour, so many eggs. But then again, I knew so little about Adalgiza and her kitchen so long ago, I had no idea.

Maria Carla mixes the sfoglia.

Maria Carla made me knead the dough with her *push, push, push and fold* rhythm that became unforgettable. It was a large hunk, and my arms tired. But finally, it was satiny smooth, its stretchy glutens all worked up and ready to rest, which it needed to do, for at least a half hour.

Back to theater number one. The filling. At this point, Maria Carla announced that having known full well that the meat would take half the day to cook, she had braised a complete extra batch earlier. She miraculously pulled out a plate, and sure enough, there was the pork, beef, and veal, all slow-cooked to tender perfection and ready to go. A meat grinder came out, and Maria Carla and Guido fussed over it with exasperation. (The old one had lasted decades—this new one was such trouble!) But finally, it was all set up and the meat got trimmed of fat, and piece by piece went into the canister, past the revolving blade, and pushed out, transformed into soft little worms of meat that would become *ripieno*.

Now came the *borragine*, "borage" in English. This leafy green vegetable that gives a purple flower was a staple in Genoese ravioli. Once gathered wild in the mountains, it is now farmed, Maria Carla explained. And I thought back to Schenone ravioli with its frozen spinach as a memory of this *borragine*, which Adalgiza would never have found in Hoboken. This batch here grew in a pot on the Guigonis' sunny terrace, picked this morning. After being boiled and squeezed dry, it was sent through the electric grinder, and then into the bowl of meat for the *ripieno*, turning the whole mixture distinctly green.

More flavors and textures followed. Maria Carla mixed in a couple of crusts of bread she'd soaked in milk, eggs, marjoram, salt, pepper, and nutmeg—a hint of the Middle East spice that once came through Genoa's port—and a couple of generous handfuls of *Parmigiano-Reggiano* cheese. She tasted it, then added salt, a little pepper. Then she had Guido taste as well. They fussed with the seasonings a bit more. Once they were satisfied, theater number one was put at rest. The *ripieno* was ready to get stuffed into pasta.

BACK TO theater number two. The pasta had reposed nicely and its glutens had had a good rest. Now it was time to turn the dough into thin sheets of pasta. Maria Carla cut the hunk into six smaller pieces. Hunk number one was on deck now, and Maria Carla pressed it into an oval-shaped disk, which she fed between the revolving motorized rollers of the pasta machine. When it came out flattened, she folded it again and reinserted it. It became flatter yet. Time and again she did this until the pasta was in long, thin strips, four inches wide and two feet long, miraculously smooth and even.

Guido Guigoni with the family's hundred-year-old rotella *on the left and a new one on the right.*

She laid the long strip out on the pasta board. I followed my mentor's lead and used my fingertips to pick up the creamy mixture and drop small olive-sized dollops in a row about an inch apart. Maria's hands flew—dot dot dot dot dot—all in a second. Mine were clumsy, plodding along. We folded over the top of the dough and used fingertips to gently press each *raviolo* (singular for *ravioli*) closed. Then with the *rotella*—the ravioli cutting wheel—we cut a frilly line along the length, and then, one by one, each small square. A logic and shape emerged from the hunk of dough and meat. Ravioli was born. I felt suddenly aware of all the space around me. The air began to tingle. It was all so simple and logical, yet so irretrievable as well. Would I ever be able to replicate this at home the following Christmas? I was quite unsure.

WE SPENT THE DAY making 380 Christmas ravioli in the midst of summer. Maria Carla's friends arrived, Ebe and her husband, Nanni. Ebe, who spoke some English, presented me, most graciously, with a cookbook called *La cuciniera genovese,* originally published by Gio Batta Ratto in 1863. In heavily accented English, Ebe explained that this copy was the eighteenth and most recent edition. "For us Genovese," she went on, "this is the bible."

Then, with her other hand, she produced a battered and marked-up

Filling and cutting ravioli with Maria Carla.

copy of the same title, except a 1920s version that had been passed down through her family for eighty years. I was thrilled and wiped my hands carefully on a dishtowel before I leafed through both books. Here were recipes for ravioli, *torta*, pesto, polenta, mushrooms, meat, and many sauces. These were all the dishes I wanted to know.

"Of course, this will only be of use if you read Italian," she ruefully noted. I thanked Ebe profusely and reassured her that I was studying the *bella lingua* and would carefully read these recipes. Then I returned to the pasta board with Maria Carla—a strip of pasta dotted with *ripieno* awaiting me. I folded over the top piece of ravioli and set about my job, pressing shut, cutting frilly edges. Maybe I'd gotten the hang of things.

"Careful, careful!" Ebe gasped. Apparently, when I pressed down the dough to seal each raviolo closed around its dollop of meat, I was leaving an air bubble inside. "If air is in them, they will break in the water!"

I took this advice into my heart, like a talisman I will carry with me the rest of my life. And I tried, honestly, but my fingers did not obey and could not make the proper shape. After a hundred or so they got a little better.

Now that the ravioli were well under way, I took the opportunity to ask the women some questions. "Were there any Genoese meat ravioli that had soft fresh cheese in them?" Of course, I was sleuthing around for a clue, any clue that might explain the cream cheese in Adalgiza's recipe—some scrap of evidence that our cream cheese was worthy. No, they shook their heads confidently. Just hard cheese. *Parmigiano-Reggiano*.

"Did you ever use a press?" I described the ravioli press in detail, but they looked at me with bewilderment. Nope. They shook their heads. They'd never heard of any such thing.

Meanwhile, the phone rang. It was Alessandra calling us from her home in Sardinia to see how things were going between her mother and me. We are colleagues of a sort, but have never met in person. We connected via Internet through a Listserv group of food professionals. Alessandra had responded to a query I posted, asking if anyone out there knew anything about cream cheese in Genoese ravioli. She now assured me her parents were happy that I would learn from them, and that I should feel comfortable. As I hung up with her, I marveled to myself that because of modern technology—the Internet—I have met these people in the search for my ancient preelectronic origins, my noncommercial past.

"Was your mother an old-fashioned woman?" I asked, imagining Maria Carla as a child, learning this recipe at the knee of a woman with an old rural memory.

"No, she was quite modern," Maria Carla answered. "And of the middle class. When Alessandra was born, my mother had hoped for a son because she believed boys would suffer less. The idea was to educate her as a boy so she could survive." And indeed Alessandra is far from home, in Sardinia, finishing her Ph.D., the one to break tradition.

NOW THAT the ravioli were done, Maria Carla scurried our little party out of the kitchen, off to the sitting room, while she finished the preparation. I realized that we never got to theater number three, the sauce. Perhaps Maria Carla worried it would be too much for me.

Soon we were called to the table, and Guido poured wine. Maria Carla carried out the ravioli in a big bowl, covered in a tomato sauce, liberally sprinkled with *Parmigiano-Reggiano* cheese. We posed for photos in front of our ravioli.

And then we began, each with a generous bowl.

It is difficult to describe the taste. To say that the ravioli was wonderful, well, this certainly was not enough. To say that the pasta was soft, and the meat inside was rich and melting in the mouth, bitter and sweet with hints of nutmeg and marjoram perfume too, and that the sauce held the tang of tomatoes and also an earthy depth from being cooked long with porcini-scented meat—no, this was not enough either.

What is more honest to say is that I was aware of myself as the outsider, the interloper who could not speak the language but had shown up here ignorant and unprepared. Perhaps what I tasted most in my mouth was a gratitude that these people had welcomed me into their home and their kitchen, had shared this family recipe, and had taught me this flavor I'd never had but so deeply craved. They did it because their daughter asked them. But they did it also because they were generous. Beyond my gratitude, I tasted some mystery and amazement at the possibilities of life, that I had somehow found my way to this table.

After the ravioli, Maria Carla served the braised meat, sliced on a platter, and then a salad of chicory and green radicchio, cut in fine bright green strips. After the salad, she brought forth a fruit bowl containing many kinds of carefully cut fruit. The finale was a *pandolce*, which I knew to be a festive holiday cake and a symbol of Genoa, with its raisins and pignoli and citron, the dough baked golden with a sign of the cross slashed on top.

"Twenty kilos," she said. "I made twenty kilos of *pandolce* last Christmas."

I calculated that this probably came out to about forty round cakes, which she gave mainly as gifts. "But I kept a couple back," she said cleverly, "for moments like these." And I understood her words, without a translator.

Later in the kitchen, over a mountain of dishes to be washed, I remarked on all the work it took to make ravioli that are consumed in but a few minutes.

"And you have a job too," I noted. "You work in the store. Would you ever buy ready-made ravioli from the *pasta fresca* shop on Christmas?" (I was referring to the little storefronts that sold a variety of fresh pasta of a quality that would be a precious luxury to most Americans.) Maria Carla shook her head vigorously.

"I'd rather eat spaghetti with garlic and olive oil," she said, again a characteristic wave of the hand in the air. And so that settled it.

"But still—all this work." I pressed further. "Why do you go through all this trouble?"

She looked me in the eyes and replied, "For my pleasure." Then she shrugged, as though to say, "Isn't it obvious?"

"*Per mio piacere.*"

CHAPTER 5

So This Is Ligurian Food

THE TOURIST IS ALWAYS AT A LOSS, always a bit of a fool—clutching guidebooks and observing through the artifice of distant telescopes, seeing and hearing only the exteriors of things. I wandered blinking in the sunlight, entranced by the sounds of the language and simply letting myself be shaken by the vibration of roots that went far beneath the surface, complicated long histories I could not understand.

The story begins at Genoa's port, with its ancient layers, its grittiness, its eye toward the Mediterranean Sea. Here we cross paths with Greek, ancient Roman, and Arab worlds during much earlier eras of globalization. Olives, wine, and wheat traveled along these water routes. Migrations began and ended. But it was not until the Romans were long gone that great power arose here. During the Middle Ages, a time of glory, Genoa became a rich maritime empire. Yes, Adalgiza's ravioli comes from this place of trade routes and water, with access not only to the rest of Italy but also to Europe, Asia, and the Arab world too.

But the story also begins in the mountains, with the ancient Ligurian people who were here thousands of years ago, allied not with water but with wood and stone. It's a story of steepness and difficulty, of chestnuts and mushrooms and gathered greens—a life so difficult with its harsh coast and lack of flat land that classical writers described Ligurians as a famously tough people, owing to their impossible terrain.

On a hot afternoon, I took the bus from center city up a hill on the outskirts of town and hiked along woodsy roads smelling of pine and earth. If culture arises from geography, I saw it there—the slope of mountains and hills pouring down to the cluster of city buildings, then the port, and then the immense blue facing Sardinia and Africa beyond. I was searching for the panorama.

In photos from the era of Salvatore and Adalgiza, I had seen wooden ships and a complex clutter of sails and masts in the air above. Dozens of small rowboats lay on the beach, bottom up. Today, the port was a massive industrial place. Immense cranes filled the horizon, ready to lift and lower steel containers from ships. Nearby, an alternate tourist version of the port lured visitors with a huge floating aquarium, galleries, Internet cafés, and shiny bright piazzas.

I sought a table at a hillside trattoria where I could gaze down on this marvelous vista and placed an order for Genoese lasagne. The waitress brought a bowl of wide, delicate, fresh noodles, not layered and baked in an oven but loosely arranged like a pile of fallen leaves, simply tossed with pesto, which was invented in Genoa and remains the region's most important and most symbolic sauce. Here it was creamier, greener in color, and more delicately aromatic than any I had ever known. For me, who grew up with a life drenched in marinara sauce, the complex smell and flavor of basil were an unexpected luxury to the senses and a joy. In the markets, I brushed by bunches of basil arranged like flowers with roots in pails of water, and the intense perfume rose up and swirled by me. I felt as if it might lift me up off the ground.

I wanted to move from the general to the specific. These were the beginnings. This was my starting place. The color green. The smell of perfume, the view of mountain and sea—all with my newcomer's ignorance, working from panoramas, looking from the outside, hoping to reach in.

MUCH OF WHAT the world loves as Italian food today is not "tradition" but modern invention.

When Salvatore and Adalgiza left Genoa, there was no "Italian food." Italy became a unified nation only in 1861, and the new national identity was still barely formed. My great-grandparents were not Italians but Genoese. I am certain they mainly ate local foods.

In any case, during the nineteenth century most people living on the Italian peninsula did not eat much pasta or meat. They subsisted heavily on corn polenta, barley, chestnuts, vegetables, and wheat as they could afford it. Pasta was a luxury.

This is why millions left—especially those in southern Italy with its legacy of poverty and hunger. But in northern Italy too, scarcity was a central part of life among those who lived in the mountains and those who lived in cities and worked in factories. Even middle-class families had to devote huge parts of their income to food.

I am sure that scarcity sent Salvatore away on his journey to America. He was thirty years old and had already been working long and hard enough to know the limits of life as a mason. He could see his future— the same as his past—and he wanted more.

By 1920, nine million people—about one-quarter of Italy's citizens—lived outside the country, writes historian Carol Helstosky in her book *Garlic and Oil*. Ironically, she argues, it was this exodus from Italy that finally helped create more abundance for all Italians. There was more food to go around for those who remained, and those abroad used their new wages to import the foods they desired but never could afford—dried pasta, olive oil, tomatoes, and cheeses— from back home. This external demand provided the capital to help build the Italian mass-produced food industry, which ultimately helped create a stronger, wealthier Italy and a new concept of unified Italian cuisine based on tomatoes, pasta, parmigiano cheese, and pizza.

It is an odd idea to imagine that immigrants had to leave home to eat the food of home. In this way, Italians around the world fueled an imagined culinary tradition. It was what life "should have been," writes Helstosky.

What should have been but what was not. . . .

THESE THOUGHTS CAME to me as I headed to the large medieval neighborhood of Genoa searching for authentic Genoese food. I was like Italian-American immigrants before me, using the benefits of capitalism—affluence and education—to rewrite my past. I was not raised with Ligurian food or the warm Italian family I would have loved to have. Yet here I was to claim something.

And so I entered the serpentine maze of ancient stone streets and dark alleys—called the *caruggi*—that rose up from the industrial port. In contrast to the clean and new, wide-open spaces of the touristy port, the *caruggi* were intimate and cramped, a jumble of narrow tunnel-like streets. It was easy to get lost and find yourself in a dismal, dark alley of garbage Dumpsters, decayed stone, and graffiti-covered doors leading up to, you can only imagine, bleak and overcrowded apartments. Then you'd turn again and emerge into a festive bazaar of shops, artisan studios, bakeries, Mediterranean grocers, and cool bars, strings of lights beckoning. Long ago, it was a region of seafaring people and merchants. Today, the apartments are taken up mostly by the new immigrants from Latin America, eastern Europe, and Africa—feared and distrusted by some Genoese.

I was eager to find the *friggitorria* (fry shops) that once served Genoese "fast food" to the sailors and fishermen and other people of the port—ready-made dishes like dried codfish stew made with potatoes and oil, anchovies marinated in lemon, pesto-tinged minestrone, or a strange oily-looking flat bread called *farinata*, made of chickpea flour, oil, salt, and water crackled by the wood-oven fire.

The old dishes here were based heavily on vegetables and techniques that could stretch and transform the materials at hand—the cheap, small fish, the small portions of available meat. Many of these old foods could still be found in the simple eating establishments with signs: *cucina antica, friggitoria,* or *cucina casalinga* ("home cooking").

Slowly, I began to discover a kind of Italian food I'd never known. I found it in the medieval tastes of heavy vegetable pies bound together by cheese and egg. I found it in a litany of stuffed vegetables: onions, mushrooms, peppers, zucchini, and even the delicate orange petals of zucchini flowers. I found it in the alluring and delicate ravioli-like dish of lettuce wrapped around a small dollop of meat, cheese, and herbs, floating in a delicate broth. A concept emerged. A culinary theme. How very often one thing fills another: I searched trattoria menus and old cookbooks for more evidence, and I was rewarded: Stuffed sardines. Stuffed *baccalà*. *Focaccette*, a deep-fried pocket bread filled with cheese. I found the stuffed theme in Genoese *cima*, a veal breast stuffed with a mixture of nuts and herbs and breadcrumbs, then sewn shut.

In these dishes, the presence of hands was always there—shaping, forming, filling. The effect was transformation, ephemeral little sculptures, and endless possibility for variation, according to region, according to season, according to economic means. You might have embellished your ravioli or *torta* with lavish herbs, meats, and cheeses, or the simplest thin bits of gathered herbs and homemade cheese. But the concept remained, no matter. You began with something simple. You ended with something much more. And always, there remained a certain secret, a certain intrigue, as to what might be inside. Always that unknown question that could never be transcribed by a recipe, but only by tasting, and maybe not even then.

Is this why our ravioli traveled so long and so far and survived so many generations? Because of its flexibility? Because of its transformations? Because of its potential for mysteries? And in these transformations, the possibility of bringing people together for a happy time, a celebration?

I DID NOT fall in love with Genoa. This was no verdant Tuscany, no ethereal Florence, no fashionable Rome with dazzling energy and street life vibrating around fountains and piazzas. Genoa did not care about impressing you. It was a real place, a hardworking port town that just went about its business.

People were quick to tell me that the Genoese are reserved people. That they keep to themselves and do not welcome outsiders. That they are careful with their money. I could never say. But I did sense something impenetrable in the tidy piazzas, a certain restraint—a certain businesslike order even in the streets that thunder with motorcycles, a certain feeling that *we have our ways of doing things here* whether you like them or not.

All along my travels, I was looking for the spinach *torta* of the Schenones—the vegetable pie we ate all our lives, the one that even my mother and my Irish-German grandmother made. The one that was toted to family parties for generations. Here in Genoa, *torte* (plural for *torta*) were present in great variety. But I did not see our spinach version—not exactly—so by my third day in Liguria, I finally entered a *friggitoria* and ordered a slice of something that seemed close enough. It was called *torta di bietole*, beckoning from a giant pan. *Bietole* is a leafy green that is similar to chard. No, it was not our *torta*, not even the mother of our *torta*. It was too different. But perhaps it was the grandmother of our *torta*, and in any case, I was running out of time. It would have to do. And so I was served a slice of this pie—built with a layer of greens, then a layer of white cheese like ricotta, all held between a leaf of pastry crust on top and bottom.

Ravioli for sale at a pasta fresca *shop in Genoa.*

I brought fork from plate to mouth. My first thought was *old . . . very old*. Before Columbus, before tomatoes—medieval old, with lavish oil and dough and no fear of calories. Second bite. Wait. There was something here—a creamy, almost lemony tang. Another bite, and I realized. This tang came from the cheese, which was not ricotta, oh no, but something more like yogurt.

I asked the girl behind the counter for the name of the cheese by pointing dumbly at it.

"*Presh-in-syu-a*," she said, smiling proudly.

It was a word I could hardly pronounce, despite several efforts and her coaching. So I ask her to write it down for me. *Prescinsêua*. And with this slightly sour taste in my mouth, my heart started beating more quickly.

Was it *prescinsêua* that Adalgiza remembered when she decided to put Philadelphia cream cheese in her dishes? Had I discovered the true cheese?

A thrill rushed through me. I took a last gulp of wine and jumped up from the table, energized by my discovery, filled with new purpose to continue my search through this strange old city. I had found a link. Perhaps it was possible. Perhaps I could find my way.

AN HOUR LATER, I arrived at the Mercato Orientale, the city's biggest market and a fabulously lively place, where purveyors of fruits, vegetables, herbs, spices, meats, and cheeses set up stalls beneath one huge roof. It was hard not to become distracted by the porcini mushrooms and pignoli, the bins of glorious tomatoes, the exotic cardoons, and crates of artichokes, long stem and leaf—all marked with handwritten signs of pedigree, whether Sicilia, Toscana, Piemonte, Sardegna, or *nostrani,* which means local, or literally "ours." But I kept focused. I knew what I was looking for and headed to the nearest cheese monger.

I did not want to try to pronounce it, so I did not ask but rather just searched over the overwhelming array of *formaggio*: goat cheeses in gray ash molds, big yellow wheels of cow cheese in golden rind, plastic packages of creamy *Crescenza*, crumbly *Parmigiano-Reggiano* ready for grating, mozzarella soaking in water. I looked and looked until finally, there it was. I finally spotted a small plastic container—much like yogurt—

labeled *prescinsêua*. (Later, I would sneak into the off-limits area of the hotel kitchen and find a spoon, so that all alone in my room, I could meditate on its sour flavor and creamy soft consistency—somewhere between milk and cheese. I would ponder whether this was the flavor in Adalgiza's memory, or whether the tastes of the past are irretrievable.)

Having paid for my purchase, I triumphantly clutched the container in my hand and turned away from the counter. But wait. My eye caught something strangely familiar. I did a double take. A quick scan of my database. A flicker deep in the mind. An icon. I looked again.

There—just a few inches away from the *prescinsêua*—I saw it in a flash of silver foil: Philadelphia brand cream cheese displayed in a neat row of little four-ounce squares—a small show of glory.

CHAPTER 6

The Herbs of Liguria

O<small>N THE TRAIN RATTLING FORTH</small> through tunnel after tunnel, mountain after mountain, emerging again and again to the sight of the sea. Dark, light. Dark light. Bougainvillea. Oleander. Swallows diving.

Two days left in my journey. Which way to go? To the west of Genoa is the Riviera di Ponente with its string of resorts leading to San Remo and France. To the east, the Riviera di Levante. Despite my predilection for France, I boarded a train for the east and soon was chugging along past a string of towns with pastel buildings, red-tiled roofs, and lyrical names: Recco, Camogli, Rapallo, and Portofino, and not far behind them, the Mediterranean flashing its sun-sparked waves.

Less than an hour after leaving Genoa, I descended with my suitcase in Santa Margherita Ligure, a buzzing and fashionable Riviera town, with fleets of motorcycles zooming along the waterfront and yachts in an aquamarine sea, encircled by mountains covered with evergreen cedars and silvery olive trees. The sky was as blue as forever.

Here was the Italy of our dreams. Who could not fall for it? Who could not fall for such beautiful people?

Walking from the train station along the main waterfront street, I passed a string of luxury hotels, cafés, bars—and much bare skin on display. Sparkle and energy and beautiful people in spades. I suddenly felt like a frumpy anthropologist, focused on the lives of the dead. Quickly,

I found the way to my little hotel room where I put on nice clothes and makeup so I could fit in with the gorgeous Italians.

The Milan journalist Beppe Severgnini describes the extraordinary Italian talent, love, and perhaps weakness for beauty in his book *La Bella Figura,* named after an expression that means "to make a good appearance." He describes a common pitfall of Italians: they will take far too many risks to put forth a good impression, sacrificing much because beauty is so very important.

If such a generalization could possibly be true, well, then in this I sensed my own lineage. My father had always possessed this weakness for beauty and appearances—he loved clothes, design, good looks, beautiful music. And I did too. So did his Italian friends, who dressed so sharp.

In my hotel room, I flicked on the television set to see the image of a breaded and stuffed chicken filling the screen. A fork slid through, and it began oozing with cheese. A busy woman smiled at the camera. Then came the close-up of the frozen, boxed product. The voice-over said something like "Ready in minutes and the kids love it."

Snapping off the television, I headed out of my room and back to the waterfront to stroll along with the lively vacationers, listening to their language, its trills and melodies and rolling *r*s. At 9:00 P.M., after a day of holiday, sun, water, and focaccia, the Italians were slowly reappearing on the scene, showered, dressed, and ready to eat dinner alfresco along the water. There was chattering, wine, and cigarettes. There were *telefonini* (cell phones) and *gelaterias* with long lines of young people flirting with one another. There were more zooming motorcycles. It was vacation, and there was an undeniable mood of happiness that seemed to say *Life is good. Our food is good. Our country is beautiful.* Bands of handsome young men sauntered about in strappy sneakers and fashionable cropped pants. They were laughing and looking for girls. The girls showed off their midriffs and strutted and laughed, looking for boys. The middle-aged women emerged looking like bronzed goddesses. After wearing skimpy bikinis all day (no matter the age or body) and sprawling their bare selves over the big black rocks along the coast, they arrived now in marvelous clothes, heeled sandals, makeup, and shiny jewelry. The older men were here too, walking amidst it all with their wives. There was a certain look—

immaculate creased pants (often of a bright color), the generous belly of the fifty- or sixty-year-old, a sweater thrown over the shoulders at night, the fine shined loafers. There was a certain confidence, a certain pride in the walk, a certain Italian style.

Portofino harbor.

Some of the men took a good look at me—and then they glanced away. All my young life my good looks had given me power and made me prey, but I had recently turned forty and things were different now. I was too old and too strong for anyone to bother. No worries of men following me and terrifying me as they did when I was a girl of twenty-one in Rome. I could be a lone traveler, a lone woman, with no problems.

And with this new power of age, I fantasized that I might fall through the cracks of reality into another world, where I might have some other kind of life. A mirror existence that was separate from my own, that would hurt no one I loved, but a life that was free. A life where I'd have the time to start over again and find what was truly important.

For women, it is the eternal problem. Wanting to have a family and a home. Working so hard to achieve it and then wanting to escape. Back and forth, back and forth. How to resolve it? There was the beautiful

Croatian great-grandmother, the bigamist, who ran away from family in search of love. There was Adalgiza who'd crossed an ocean to keep it, chasing after her husband who'd fallen astray. Her ravioli was a gift that came as part of this certainty, this gesture of holding a family together—whether for love of her husband, her children, or for her own survival I cannot say. But I do know that it is very hard to hold a family together, and she was determined.

I SEARCHED out a promising but simple trattoria off the beaten path. It was here that a plate of *pansotti* was put before me. Perhaps I was especially desirous, but I believed I had found the food of my dreams. *Pansotti* is a descendant of the *ravioli magri*—filled with herbs and cheese—for Lent or lean times. This modern version was large and triangular, generously filled, corners pinched together and pasta so delicate that the *pansotti* seemed to flutter on my fork. Inside, I discovered at the center a soft mixture of greens and tangy cheese. But it was the sauce on top that sent me somewhere very near happiness—it was called *salsa di noci*—walnuts crushed finely, mixed with parmigiano cheese, garlic, herbs, and oil, perhaps a little milk. Food, when it is wonderful, jolts me to the present—the place where happy people and children exist. This sauce was extravagant. It was earthy. It was complex and simple.

And so my journey deepened beyond the search for simply an original recipe for Christmas ravioli. Inside these little stuffed triangles was a message from another place. The mixture of greens and herbs is called *preboggion*, or more accurately, the memory of *preboggion*, a mix of greens that grew wild up in the mountains and valleys known as the *entroterra*. Those mountains began just a couple of miles inland, but a universe away from the glamorous Riviera.

Preboggion—a Genoese word without an Italian translation. It referred to edible weeds like sow thistle, wild beet, pimpernel, dandelion, balsam leaves, nettle, and borage, most of which were believed to have healing properties. *Preboggion* went into stuffed pastas, *torte*, rice dishes, soups. Today these herbs come from farms, but long ago the men and women of Liguria gathered these wild greens. I've heard that some still do. I looked up to the mountains and wished I'd planned on renting a car so I could have traveled to the interior, beyond the shiny coast.

I didn't know then that Salvatore came from those mountains and surely lived on those greens and nuts gathered from those very hills. I regretted that on this trip, I'd stuck to the well-traveled routes, beautiful though they were.

OF COURSE, these were all just ideas. They were just things I'd read in books. Things people told me. What writers write. What culinary experts codify. The ideas of the kitchen—like the idea that the Genoese have a perfume kitchen built on herbs. Herbs in the *pansotti*. Herbs in the *torte*. Foods of the mountains. The smell of marjoram and basil, wild sage, and other edible grasses and greens. Food lyricism flows so readily.

But was this really knowing?

In New York, I'd discovered ethereal ravioli filled with greens on the menus of great chefs, though the herbs of course had been cultivated and harvested in northeast American farms. And I began to wonder where cuisine really begins—with earth and sea and all the foods nature gives us? Or does cuisine begin with luxuries—our ideas and desires of all we want to have and be?

My husband, with bloodlines that go to northern Germany, always feels religiously called to mountains and rivers, deep green, shady places, smelling of damp earth and evergreen. He is a fly fisherman at peace by cold waters where trout swim and pine needles lie underfoot. And though he works in New York City every day, he is never so happy as when he is near mountains. I spent many years following him along woody riverbanks in search of trout, happy to do it.

But for me, there has been the lifelong yearning to be around lemon trees and olive groves, to see a big bright blue sky and treeless rocky vistas, scorched dry by hot yellow sun. From a young age, I had a natural taste for the foods from these places. I was a lover of vegetables and nuts, herbs, dishes like frittatas and vegetable pies. I took to squid and sardines, and all the pungent olives and anchovies I could find. I was in love with the smell and taste of chestnut. These were foods I was never fed, yet craved nonetheless, and discovered on my own.

When I was twenty-one and went to the French Riviera, it was the first beautiful place I ever saw. Life changed at that moment. The sight of the red rocks of Saint-Raphael and the Mediterranean Sea gave me my first hope that I could be happy. I felt reborn, far, far away from the oil tank vistas of my childhood, far from my working-class roots. Free of home, I felt at home. I hadn't expected this, or chosen it. It simply happened to me.

I didn't know then that the Schenones were just a hundred miles or so eastward, facing the same sea and bright light. I did not realize that the French Riviera was once part of Liguria, and the town of Nice was once called *Nizza*. I didn't realize Liguria was so close or that my ancestors did not say *ravioli* but almost certainly *ravieu*, which is the word for it in Genoese dialect and filled with French influence.

Now that I was older, being near the Mediterranean brought the same sense of recognition, and brief moments of passion and joy. But after years of being a mother at home with young children, the freedom of travel was almost too much. Now I was cut loose and weightless—as though on the edge of one of those steep mountainous cliffs, about to fall. I suddenly feared I might lose my way, to not have a home to return to, to be without family, to be forever searching.

When I returned to New Jersey and stepped out of the cab, my boys were waiting behind the screen door. Gravity took hold again, thank god, when I saw them standing there in pajamas, impossibly beautiful boys, who didn't ask to be brought into this world, but came because I brought them, children who inherited histories and destinies and genes they did not choose. They called out my name and hopped up and down as I walked up the front steps, as though on the verge of breaking if we didn't hug and link together again.

Soon, I was back in my routine of days, organized around children and work, and driving around the suburbs in my car, doing errands, bending down each night to collect all the plastic Legos off the carpet, making bagged lunches for my boys.

During the first few weeks, something strange happened inside me. Whenever I ventured out of my town, even for just a few hours, there was that fast heartbeat under the surface again, that watchful eye on alert, that voice saying *Get back home to your children*. I could not bear to be away. Nothing was right unless I was home.

And yet, I could not stop dreaming of the colors of the Mediterranean while I drove my children to their suburban destinations, helped with homework, and ventured beneath the fluorescent lights of the grocery store late at night. I asked myself whether this search for ravioli, this search for the ancient, was really desperation for something beautiful to help me transform the confines of domestic family life?

A view from Cinque Terre.

CHAPTER 7

Rolling the Dough I

THE FAMILY STORY is a mess. My father doesn't remember much. The cousins disagree on when and why the Schenones came. I reach out to my aunt, she does not return the call. My youngest sister and I are not talking again. I said something to insult her. I didn't mean to. But it seems to happen easily, and half the time I'm not sure why.

My middle sister, Lisa, is more like me. She likes New York. She likes travel. She's got a career in the media business. I understand the path of her life, and she understands mine.

But with my younger sister, it's different. She does not leave New Jersey much. She's never left the country. And though she has had her stints in school and careers, she does not get her life's passion from such things. Her real life's work is at her evangelical church. She runs a youth group there and teaches Sunday school. As the years have gone on, she's become increasingly devoted, studying her Bible in the literal way. She dresses more simply than she used to, wears less makeup, and leads a pared-down life. Her friends are mostly all from the church. Whenever she has a problem, they are there. If she needs something, they come. If someone is sick, they pray. They are, in a sense, her new family.

And so there is much now that she and I can't talk about. Does she believe I will burn in hell because I am not saved? Does she vote for politicians I hate? We try to stay off these topics, but one day I make mention of our differences, and she says, "You don't approve of my religion."

It's hard to answer. I try my best. "I'm glad if you are happy."

"You don't approve."

And it's hard to disagree. I don't understand this kind of Christian way.

SEARCHING FOR RAVIOLI is a much easier bit of the family story. It runs along on a different plane entirely, it travels the globe, and it travels across the United States. I find a trail of ravioli tools that belonged to either Adalgiza or her daughter Tessie. In Washington State, there's a cousin with Aunt Tessie's handmade cheese grater. Another has a ravioli press made from the wood of Adalgiza's wedding bed. In Florida, there's a wooden-handled ravioli cutter that belonged first to Adalgiza and then to Tessie. In Wyoming, a copper ravioli lifter Adalgiza brought from Italy. Here in New Jersey, cousin Kay's daughter Valerie has a rolling pin. And of course, we—meaning, my parents—have the famous falling-apart ravioli press that once belonged to Aunt Tessie and maybe even Adalgiza. It is a secret society—the keepers of Schenone ravioli tools. I discover that all these cousins hold these ravioli tools quite dear.

Now that I've undertaken this quest, I ask my parents to entrust the relic to me on temporary loan. I want to see it again. I offer to bring it to a carpenter for gentle repair, and while I'm at it, I plan to have a replica made for myself.

I can hardly wait to examine it newly after all these years. When it comes into my hands, I immediately note that the squares are remarkably small, only about one square inch. How delicate! How civilized compared to the giant hockey-puck ravioli they sell at the Italian specialty shops around here.

I begin to visualize myself using my replica to stamp out dozens of small and refined ravioli. I will keep my freezer full of them, so that whenever people want to drop by, there will be no problem at all. "Sure, come on over. We'll have ravioli. Get the water boiling." Our house will be full of people. My sons will be popular, their friends begging to eat at our table every night. And each year at Christmas, my sisters and I will come together for ravioli day and take the necessary time for the necessary rituals of dough and meat——expertise and magic finally memorized into our fingers. This is what I want most of all.

This fantasy floods over me while I hold the ravioli press in my hands. But wait. There's a catch. How silly of me. A ravioli press is expressly for making ravioli out of big sheets of *hand-rolled* dough.

This realization forces me to confront an unpleasant matter regarding my electric pasta machine and its steel cylinders: it simply will not do the job. Oh sure, the results are great—and in some ways amazing. With the aid of a pasta machine, you can produce strips of pasta so perfectly thin that you can practically read a newspaper through them. It is a great tool, not to be shunned. But Adalgiza and her daughters had no such thing. They rolled their dough out on a big board—a process that approaches art, particularly in the stretching of the dough, which is a choreography unto itself requiring sure movements of pulling and extending and flipping so that the dough slaps the board and grows.

I conclude that if I want to know the true ways of my ancestors, I will have to get myself a big board and a rolling pin and learn the old way. Sure, I may decide that a machine is a fine enough substitute, but only if I learn the original way too. And while I'm facing the facts, I might as well just admit right now that no matter how wonderful Maria Carla's recipe is, it can never be mine. Not exactly, anyway. I need to find my own version.

As for learning to roll pasta by hand, who in the world would teach me? I could try to find a chef in New York. I could seek out one of the still-living grandmas in New Jersey who do it with a broomstick. But my inquiries indicate that most chefs and cooking-school teachers use pasta machines these days, and that the grandmas have died off, alas, taking the knowledge to their graves. I hear the same elegy and regret again and again: "Ah, she was amazing. She could roll out that dough like nobody's business. But none of us thought about learning until it was too late."

So I turn to one of my muses, Marcella Hazan, Italian cookbook author for Americans. In her *Essentials of Classic Italian Cooking*, Marcella (who is in the kitchen with me so often I speak to her by first name) says that both machine and hand-rolled pasta will give results far better than you're likely to find in any shops except those, say, around Emilia-Romagna. But she pulls no punches about the superiority hand-rolled pasta has over what you can produce in a machine.

> *Pasta rolled by hand is quite unlike the fresh pasta made with a machine. . . . The color of hand-stretched pasta is demonstrably deeper than that thinned by machine; its surface is etched by a barely visible pattern of intersecting ridges and hollows; when cooked, the pasta sucks in sauce and exudes moistness. On the palate it has a gossamer, soft touch that no other pasta can duplicate. But learning the rolling-pin method is, unfortunately, not just a question of following instructions but rather of learning a craft. The instructions must be executed again and again with great patience, and mastered by a pair of nimble, willing hands until the motions are performed through intuition rather than deliberation. The machine, on the other hand, requires virtually no skill to use. Once you have learned to combine eggs and flour into a dough that is neither too moist nor too dry, all you do is follow a series of extraordinarily simple, mechanical steps and you can produce fine fresh pasta inexpensively at home, at the very first attempt.*

Gossamer. I am after gossamer. So I tackle the hand-rolled method as Marcella describes it, but no matter how many times I study her diagrams I cannot quite carry off what she is telling me to do. After each attempt, I find myself with torn, uneven dough. Ditto with Giuliano's *Bugialli on Pasta*, with an admirable thirteen diagrams. I still don't get it. Nor is the famous Lidia Bastianich much help either. She takes a different tack in her *Lidia's Italian-American Kitchen*, not providing a single diagram or picture of the "hand rolling" process. Instead, she supplies instructions in a single paragraph—a clear tip-off that hand-rolled pasta is impossible to teach in a book.

Perhaps it is just me. Perhaps my hands are simply too old and not "nimble" enough to learn.

I call my mother on the phone. "Mom, how did Tessie do it that day you watched her make ravioli? How did she stretch the dough?"

My mother pauses to think. The event, after all, dates back to circa

1972. After a long while, she ventures with a soft voice, "She wrapped the dough around the pin and flipped the dough. The circle got bigger and bigger each time, each flip, until it was a big round circle—very thin. Then she spread her meat filling over one half of the circle. Then she folded the other half over the top, like a cover. Then she placed her ravioli press on top and pressed it into the dough. This sealed them shut, but it also gave her a pattern. When she lifted it, she could see the checkerboard lines imprinted. She went over these with her ravioli cutter."

Bellissimo. But these memories will hardly get me there.

In fact, there are no instructions that will ever work. Rolling pasta dough must be learned person to person—there is no other way, at least for me. And since this is a family recipe I am seeking to reclaim, I will have to find a Schenone of true ravioli lineage to teach me this art—this skill, this mystery of flat, thin dough stretched and slapped to delicate submission—hand to hand, side by side.

I look again at my sketchy family tree, reviewing once more the direct mother-to-daughter routes where ravioli-making skills are most likely to have traveled. Aunt Tessie had two daughters. Surely these women would be good prospects. But two seconds on the phone with Lillian and I hit a dead end. "I never learned it. Never made it. My husband liked lasagna instead."

Years have passed since my first conversation with Tessie's other daughter, Adele, out in Washington State, and now she has succumbed to dementia and other illnesses. Her daughter Linda provides round-the-clock care. Even in Linda's email, I can hear her depleted voice. "There'll be no ravioli in this house this Christmas. Try my brother Michael and his wife. They make ravioli all the time." Indeed, this leads me to a most remarkable discovery, that the most ardent inheritor and follower, the most devoted practitioner of Adalgiza's ravioli, is Michael's wife—and to clarify the connections, though her name is Chris Bacigalupi, she is the Polish-American wife of Tessie's grandson. And yet, she's the one who makes Adalgiza's ravioli to this day, at least once a month, she explains. "I like to have it on hand in the freezer. I give it to people as gifts." She has made Tessie's ravioli for fund-raising events at the big city high school where her husband is principal. How pleased Adalgiza would be.

Chris got her ravioli lessons from Tessie when her husband Michael had gone to Vietnam and she moved in with her in-laws. Tessie the resident grandmother in the house found an eager apprentice.

"I was her strength in the kitchen. I was her arms," Chris explains to me by phone. "I asked her to teach me the ravioli, and she did."

I turn to the family tree again. One last mother-to-daughter line remains—and this is Millie, daughter of Lena, daughter of Adalgiza. I call Millie on the phone. She is another octogenarian cousin of my dad's whom I haven't seen since my wedding. Millie now has a pacemaker and a terrible arthritic hip. From the first word, it is clear that she is tired, and that life with pain is hard. But she tries not to complain.

"Hey, what are you going to do?" she asks in the school-of-tough-knocks way that Hoboken people do. "I'm eighty-two. You can't have everything."

As it turns out, she is the person I am looking for. A hundred years after immigration, she is still making ravioli every Christmas, and she does it with her daughter Susan. They are not ravioli devotees, like Chris. Rather, they do it once a year and only once, but faithfully, each year.

I certainly surprise Millie when I ask if I can come this year.

"Um . . . yes," she replies. But then she pauses. She wants to talk to Susan about it and get back to me. I hang up the phone. Will she really call? It is only September. Ravioli making doesn't happen until December, and so I'll have to wait.

IN THE MEANTIME, I do what I always do when at a cooking impasse. I go running over to my dear friend and neighbor Lou Palma, an Italian-American in his early seventies who has been a mentor to me for many years now. He is a home cook of the highest order, a bon vivant, and a natural talent in the kitchen he shares with his wife, Susan, in this New York suburb I moved to seven years ago. Over the years, it is Lou who has become my most loyal friend in town. My contemporaries are too busy and stressed for much fussing around the kitchen. But Lou is semi-retired and devotes many hours each week to his kitchen avocation. Along the way he has adopted me as an acolyte and makes it a point to check on me regularly, like when he calls to say he's on his way to Corrado's market for fresh ricotta and do I want any? Or to tell me about red peppers on sale for ninety-nine cents a pound. Or perhaps when he's just come back from fishing and drops by to share a piece of striped bass. He also calls just to give me a hard time.

I answer the phone and hear, "*Che cosa!* Where the hell have you been?"

And I know it is Lou.

"After you left last week, I spent an hour cleaning up after you. Listen, I know you're as busy as a one-armed paper hanger. But why don't you come on over with the kids next week and I'll show you how to make the best pizza on earth."

Indeed, Lou has taught me many things I desired to learn—how to make fresh sausage, gnocchi, escarole and beans, how to preserve tomatoes for winter—but mainly, a certain clear and straightforward way to think about cooking that is creative, but also very practical. In our friendship, he brings the skills, the experience, and the vivid memories of his mother's cooking from southern Italy's Campania region—dishes all cooked by heart, nothing ever written down. Since I am the researcher and seeker, I bring new ideas every once in a while, and even rope him into some of my projects, such as hunting down a specific flour with a certain gluten level, or maybe a foray into homemade cheese. But I am clearly the winner in the bargain.

When I came back from Italy and made ravioli that first Christmas, I naturally ran right to Lou's house to show him. The next week he went out, got himself a pasta machine, and invited me over to practice and try various batches so we could figure things out at a deeper level—dough with and without semolina flour, dough with more and fewer eggs. Ravioli with individual hand-sealed packets. Ravioli made in a silver form. Dough from the thinnest setting on the machine. Dough from the second thinnest. We always cook at his place rather than mine, because

Lou's kitchen itself is a work of art—perfectly designed and spacious, a calm, well-organized place with fine equipment and beautiful surfaces of wood and stone.

Now when I tell him that I want to try to make dough rolled and stretched by hand, Lou rolls his eyes at the prospect. But we go about mixing flour and egg and water and kneading.

"You're never going to beat that machine, you know. Never."

But I insist that we give it a go. "Rolling pin, please," I demand, holding out my hand.

He offers a French-styled dowel. Fine enough. I tear off a hunk of dough and start rolling and stretching awkwardly, recalling the diagrams from a book. It does not go well. I quickly get holes and tears.

"Jesus Christ. Give that thing to me." Lou takes the pin and pasta from my hands and suddenly is wrapping and flipping it around the rolling pin with some very impressive moves clearly remembered from some other era—moves he didn't even know he had.

"My mother and the old ladies of the neighborhood in Brooklyn used to compete," he exclaims. But alas, he fails too. We get inelegant, thick, chewy dough.

This brings us back to our old disagreement about tools. Lou, being a mechanical guy, likes tools quite a bit. He uses a heavy KitchenAid mixer for his dough, he's got a smoker in the garage, he's got grinders and sausage presses and even likes to invent his own homespun gadgets like gnocchi imprinters and broth siphons, and a rigged-up fan inside the fridge for aging beef. Me, however, I'm not very mechanical by nature. I don't have that kind of mind, and I don't have that kind of space for tools. But it's more than that. I'd never want to use a stand-up mixer to knead my dough. I like the feel of the dough in my hand. I mean, isn't that the point?

We turn back to the pasta machine, however, because we've got no choice, and that day we produce several dozen delicate mushroom ravioli filled with a mix of cremini, oyster, and portobello sautéed in olive oil, wine, and garlic, along with some bread crumbs and *Parmigiano-Reggiano*. Lou's idea, of course. They are divine. In fact, when I taste them, I can hardly believe that food can taste so wonderful.

Often with ravioli, the pasta seems unimportant—just a container for the all-important filling, which is what matters most. But here, the pasta is so soft and delicate and light that it somehow carries the earthy and sweet taste of garlic and mushrooms off to the moon.

Over the next few weeks, I want to make them again, but am busy editing magazines, writing articles, taking care of the kids. Lou, meanwhile, sets himself to serious ravioli making. He won't give up until he's got it nailed. Soon, he's got hundreds of ravioli in the freezer and has left me in the dust.

Lou Palma at the pasta machine.

"Bravo, Luigi," I say.

But I do not relent, and gently remind him that this is still just *machine* pasta, and we can't go acting like we've conquered the real thing. We have this conversation when I show up at his house with Aunt Tessie's wooden ravioli press. He is duly impressed. It is a tool, after all, and a lovely object that has been made by hand. A skilled carpenter, he quickly makes me a copy with squares measured exactly to size—a little less than an inch square. He repairs Tessie's ancient press, which I promptly return to my parents, so it can once again hang on their wall.

And Lou also makes with great care a beautiful big round pasta board and—ever generous—gives it to me. He does not simply cut out a piece of wood, but makes it in panels so it won't warp. But as to my plans for hand rolling, he is doubtful.

"You're never going to beat that machine," he says. "Forget about it."

CHAPTER 8

Hoboken

THE WORDS "SALVATORE AND ADALGIZA" are written on the page in a younger, more flowing handwriting that once was my own. "Salvatore and Adalgiza Schenone."

My father never told me these names, never told me much. But his Irish-German mother did. They were northern Italians from Genoa, she explained. He was a tile man from the hills. She only told me any of this because I asked. Schenone was not her name; it was her husband's name. And Schenone was not her own history. She was born Frances Patterson, a mixture of Irish and German roots, but we called her Grandma Schenone, not Grandma Frances, for the simple reason that by some crazy coincidence, my Croatian grandmother was also a Frances from Hoboken, and this helped us keep the two of them straight.

I AM sitting on a bench on Washington Avenue in Hoboken with Grandma Schenone. She is dead now. But no matter. I have willed myself back to fifteen years ago—that day when I took her down to Hoboken to ask her some questions about her life in that ridiculous city where all my ancestors arrived and mingled together their improbable mix of cultures. We are together again, she and I, and I am busy scribbling down everything she says.

"The Italians were icemen, peddlers, garbage men," my grand-mother says. "Oh, so poor," she sighs. "My husband was different. He worked in an office, a bookkeeper. He was so neat. So nice. He was a baby when they brought him from Genoa. They counted his teeth to fig-ure out how much his boat fare cost."

She pauses to think and retrieves what she was looking for. "Their names were Salvatore and Adalgiza," she declares, and smiles with the memory. "Salvatore called me his Irish daughter." She looks into the distance with her wrinkled eyes as though trying to see him. "He bought a little house on Willow Avenue in Hoboken."

"Which house?"

"Gosh, Honey, I can't remember."

WHEN YOU DRIVE into the mile-by-a-mile-square city of Hoboken today, you see a prominent sign that says "Welcome to Hoboken, birth-place of baseball and Frank Sinatra." It is such a ridiculous sign, such misplaced pride. Hoboken's sloganeers missed the point entirely in choosing to juxtapose these two most unrelated bits of history. First of all, though it is possible that baseball in fact was invented here, some his-torians disagree. And second of all, though it is true that, yes, Frank Sinatra and his miraculous voice were born here amidst the tenements, he got out as soon as he could, and more or less stayed out.

A more honest sign might say "Welcome to Hoboken: Mile-Square City Where Millions of Immigrants Built American Industry." But Hoboken's image-makers could never do this. The town is, by nature and necessity, a grasping place—insignificant in size but with a remark-able geographic destiny, located next to the cultural mecca and economic engine of New York City. Like many people and places in America, it has survived by constantly recrafting itself in the great American tradi-tion of continuous self-improvement and re-creation, always trying to measure up. However, there has been an odd twist to the formula: The new layer does not completely override the previous, and some previ-ous eras hang on. The result has been that rich and poor, overeducated, undereducated, honky-tonk, and corrupt still overlap one another blithely, both erasing the past but also coexisting with it.

In Hoboken, the story begins—as all American stories do—with Indians and their land, then the Europeans who took it from them; first Dutch, then English, then German, then Irish, then Italian, who have left, perhaps, the biggest mark in a long while.

For a long time, Hoboken was a pastoral refuge on the Hudson River, a densely green place, just a short ferry ride across from New York City. It had lush fields, gardens, and trails where you could walk and enjoy the fresh river breezes blowing up Castle Point even on the most sweltering summer day. At a mysterious carved-out rock in the cliffs, called Sybil's Cave, you could buy a drink of mineral water for five cents a cup.

An 1868 engraving of Manhattan Island. Hoboken is on the near shore.

When the pastoral dream comes to an end, when the mineral water is found to be toxic, this is when my family arrives, ready to work, ready for the factories. Except they are not my family yet, but four different families. This is where my story always began. It only comes to life at the docks and ships of Hoboken, or in the factories and construction work. It continues on with my grandmothers and aunt standing on conveyer belts making Jell-O or pencils, and with the grandfathers of the family working in the bottom of ships, or in a rubber factory, or in the building trades. The women struggle tooth and nail to gain office skills so they don't have to make Jell-O or pencils forever. The men save money to buy out the boss, and they do. But many of them drink too much or die too young.

And so it passes over the decades, that these various stories somehow come together to produce my sisters and me and a vast collection of more than a dozen cousins. And so our families grow and multiply and disperse.

But even when my sisters and I are safely transplanted to a quasi suburb amidst oak leaf, concrete patios, and aluminum-sided homes, there continues, in the far back streets of Hoboken, far from the fancy brownstones near Stevens Institute, the life of "the shop," where my father's family construction business carries on for decades, with my uncles and grandmother. It is a place where none of us daughters ever went and even my father avoided, though this business was partly his own. We avoided it because after the shipping business died and the factories closed in the sixties and seventies, Hoboken was no place you wanted to be.

WHENEVER MY MIDDLE SISTER, Lisa, and I talked to my dad about Hoboken, he had little good to say.

"Old sins," he muttered, and shook his head. "All those buildings have old sins. Nothing up to code. Old plumbing. Decrepit stairs. Waste pipes sending sewer gases up to the attics. Oh, the old wiring in those walls—and god knows what else." (God knows what? I'd wonder. Rats? Skeletons? What do people hide inside walls?)

This was in the late 1980s and my sister Lisa and I took a big interest in Hoboken. We were young and unattached, the real estate was cheap, and Manhattan was close. Artists and rock musicians and Wall Street people were moving there for the easy commute to the city. My sister and I liked this old place that was part of our roots. Despite the suburban upbringing our parents gave us (for our own good), we had some pride in that town. We liked the way all the unmatched parts mixed together out in the open, out in the streets—the old *nonnas* wearing black dresses and white tube socks and black sandals sitting on lawn chairs on the sidewalk, the Italian guys washing their hot rods in the street with the music blasting, the Irish longshoremen who still came and went to the union hall, the Latino women who walked up and down Washington Avenue speaking Spanish, and dressed oh, so glamorously. Lisa and I offered our own overlap contribution. We were part of the new. We were part of the old. We thought about buying a place.

"Old sins," said Dad. "Nothing up to code."

My father is a journeyman with a love of craft—a plumber and mechanical contractor who wants things built right. Don't even mention all that chromium in Hoboken soil from the factories that once were, or the lead in the drinking water, or the stink of beer down by the Clam Broth House, near the waterfront—and never any parking for your car, *just* never. Then there were the rotting wood piers sitting there all those decades after the shipping business collapsed, just sat there all those years because the city was too corrupt, too mismanaged to do anything.

My father had a right to say all this because his family business was there, the source of his life's work. His mother and oldest brother went down to Hoboken each day to run the "shop," while my father and his youngest brother worked in the field, traveling all over New Jersey in their pickup trucks loaded with pipes and fittings and big scrolls of inky plumbing plans, working with the guys from the plumbers' union hall.

Like thousands of other Hoboken descendants, we made an upward migration over generations. After Hoboken, my grandparents moved up the hill a mile or so to better towns like Weehawken and Union City—still in the urban ring with brick houses all clustered together. But these houses were not connected. They were freestanding and better than Hoboken in a better family neighborhood. When I was seven years old, we progressed even further to a three-bedroom 1920s colonial in the barely suburbs of a gritty town called Hackensack—a half hour away from Hoboken and its old sins. Straddling the line between working class and middle. Here my parents raised my sisters and me.

My father rewired our house himself, put in new ceilings, replaced all the doors, installed wall-to-wall carpet over the wood floors, erected aluminum siding, paved new concrete paths around the house, and reinforced the main floor with extra wood beams because it bothered him the way the house shook when children and dogs ran down the stairs. He planted rosebushes in a neat row, no climbers or messy rambling varieties, but the kind that grew straight up—five perfect rectangles cut into the lawn, five perfect bushes, tended methodically, to bring forth luxurious peach-, red-, and cream-colored blooms each June, for twenty-five years. Pruning and feeding them after work, bending over those bushes wearing his work boots and permanent-press work clothes from Sears, with that faintly damp plumbing smell on them, like metal mixed in a river bottom.

"In the city, there's rich and poor," he once explained to me. "But in the suburbs—well, we were all the same." He was talking about the 1970s, stating this as though the fact of "everyone being the same" was a self-evident truth, an obvious benefit beyond reproach. I did not agree then or now, having found our suburbs lonely beyond compare. I have always loved the city or village where I can hear voices on the street or travel on foot to the center square. But I understood him to mean middle class. Fair and democratic. Private. Tabula rasa. A fresh start.

AND YET, we never escape the past entirely, no matter how hard we try. Most strangely, my husband got a job in Hoboken, and we had our first child there. Despite the "old sins," my sister Lisa opened a computer-graphics business in a Hoboken storefront when she was twenty-four. And I, for a brief while, worked with her, making computer-generated slide presentations for companies on Wall Street. One Christmas, she held a party in the office for all her clients, friends, and family. She was sure to invite Grandma Schenone too, who with her Irish-German descent had Hoboken's working-class history imprinted in every wrinkle of her face and bony hands. The night of the party, Grandma arrived in festive spirits, wearing one of her characteristic flounce skirts and gum-soled shoes, sporting her short, gray hair curled in a permanent, and sparkly rhinestone pins attached to her blouse. She was in her late seventies then, but still loved a party and any social event to do with family.

"My lans!" Grandma said when she saw the surreal electronic equipment before her, the extraordinarily good-looking young people dressed in sophisticated black, the lavish spread of antipasti and wine, and perhaps, most of all, the sleek and sophisticated postmodern office space my sister had created. She was awestruck, and a bit bewildered, as though she'd landed on an alien planet. But clearly she was proud of her granddaughter.

Who wouldn't be? What a magical creature Lisa was that night, the hostess and owner of this dazzling affair, with gorgeously arrayed flowers, votive candles, and catered food. A beautiful young entrepreneur—"and only in her twenties!"

Later, Grandma Schenone casually mentioned that she knew this space well.

The party was loud, and we were hardly listening.

"Oh, sure. It used to be a bank," she said in her singsong voice. We nodded politely. Yes, of course. She knew everything in this town—everything that once was.

"And I used to work here as a clerk in my twenties."

We stopped and looked. "Here? Here? You worked in this very place?"

"Yes. Right here." She gestured to the space in which we were standing. "Then I got a job a couple of doors down. That's where I met your grandfather."

Then we looked at her as she laughed her still girlish laugh, happy to pull a surprise on us. "You know, I'm an old Hoboken girl."

⚶

NOW, A COUPLE OF DECADES later, Hoboken still has some Italians who didn't sell their row houses, preferring to stay and run bakeries and food shops and other businesses in town. They also organize annual

"Italian Festivals," carrying life-sized statues of patron saints on their shoulders through the street.

But Hoboken has largely been transformed into a high-priced utopia for the young who are willing to share a small space with many roommates— or the very wealthy New York professionals who buy luxury apartments in high-rises or refurbish the grand Victorian brownstone buildings to their mahogany-balustrade glory. My husband and I thought about buying a place in Hoboken and raising our family there. But by the time we got around to it, the prices had quadrupled, and we couldn't afford it. The old rotted wooden piers had been replaced with bike paths, observatories, and bright grassy parks with gazebos that look out on the Manhattan sky-line. New condominiums and restaurants were lining up at the water's edge—all built up to code, or so we think. If there are sins hidden in the walls, they are different kinds of sins than ours, and some future gener-ation will find them. For me, there is no going back.

My grandmother is gone now, and so many others too who would be able to tell me things I want to know. I wish I'd asked her more about the quiet handsome Italian man from Genoa with whom she fell in love and his parents who spoke only broken English but managed to buy a little brick row house on Willow Avenue. I wish I'd asked her more about the ravioli that Adalgiza and her oldest daughter Tessie cooked. The only Genoese recipe my grandmother had of theirs was the spinach *torta* that she toted to family parties for decades.

Still, on scraps and note cards, on the backs of old envelopes grabbed during family parties, I casually scribbled down details I heard of my grandparents' lives and placed them in a file labeled "Hoboken." These scraps and threads of stories revealed eccentricities, hardships, and rev-elries that seem beyond comprehension today, as though of some lost race of people: a woman who got paid for sexual companionship and childcare ("Hey, she needed to earn a living, too."); a good job in the rubber factory; brothers who sold fruit on the corner; limbs shriveled from polio; bad uncles who preyed on little girls; many singers and musicians, including a guitar-playing uncle missing some fingers, an aunt who played piano for the silent movies, the Italians with man-dolins, and their sons with jazz piano and guitar. More still: a grandmother who embroidered Adriatic memories on empty sugar sacks from the Jell-O factory and turned them into tablecloths; an underweight baby wrapped and warmed in an oven (he survived); underground tunnels and liquor smugglers during Prohibition; money for secret payments carried in cannoli boxes, tied with a string.

Lyric Theatre, Hoboken, date unknown.

I have kept these notes all my life under the impression that they mattered. Without the past, the present was always empty for me. Now that I am searching for ravioli, I take out this folder again and begin sorting through these bits along with old newspaper articles, pages of Hoboken history photocopied from books, and loose-leaf sheets covered with blue ink. All of it is messy, and hard to decipher—jotted quickly to keep pace with the old ladies' voices.

I sort out everything from Frances Schenone and give her a separate file. Reading through it, I am amazed at how well I can hear her voice again and how I can see her before me, with her dowdy flowered dresses and girlish flouncy walk. And now that the world has changed all the more, now that we here in New Jersey have become all the wealthier and more developed, all the more technologized and credit-cardized, my notes seem all the more like an archaeologist's relics—bits of bones, old jewels, and shards of broken pottery.

Irish father. Orange Ireland. Drove a six-horse team truck. A drinker. Came home drunk. Broke my mother's dishes and holy pictures that she collected each week for a nickel. Hit her for not having steak on the table. Put in jail.

People (family) slept in the living room. Railroad flat.

No money around.

Brothers drank and fought and made their money peddling fruit and vegetables on street corners.

In Hoboken—hundreds of taverns by the waterfront. Seagoing men from countries all over the world stopped in Hoboken. Loads of single-room boardinghouses. Loads of taverns. Drinking men everywhere.

Mother—a janitress. Mother took in laundry. Got job at night working in arsenal. Had to support family. My father was gone.

And then, in the margins . . . something more fluid. A phrase I remember her saying.

You could cover it all in one word, Honey. **Poverty.***"*

I can hear her voice saying the word "poverty" with emphasis. And then:

You kids have so much today. You're so busy. So many things to do.

But I don't need my notes here, for this would become my grandmother's mantra as her life came to an end, and as dementia began to creep over her mind. She could only repeat a few things over and over—thoughts and beliefs that had seemed to harden into grooves her mind repeatedly got stuck on. "You kids have so much today. So many choices. You're so busy." It was as if she were desperate to remind us, again and again. Any problem you had. Any challenge in life, my grandmother would answer with these words. "You kids have so much today. You're so busy. So many things to do."

My notes are fuzzy on her courtship with my grandfather, a man named Louis Schenone. An easygoing northern Italian with good manners. With Louie, she could put together a new life, a hundred times better than what she'd had. She could leave that apartment she shared with her rough-and-tough brothers, have children, have respectability, have vacations at the Jersey shore, have enough.

Now that I am looking for ravioli, these days I am back sitting on that bench, happy to be with her again, taking notes.

She is trying to help me, trying to explain what life was like. She rattles off the names of the many Catholic churches in Hoboken—which ones were for the rich, for the poor, for the Irish, for the Italians. At some point, she recalls a terrible fire, and the horse-drawn fire trucks racing down Washington Street in the middle of the night.

Her eyes, with drooping lids, look off, seeing this other time, this event.

"Horses?" I say.

She snaps from her dream state and sees my incredulity, my straining naïve face, trying to imagine the preposterous image of horses racing down Washington Street, pulling a firetruck. She looks at me and sees that I cannot see.

"Oh, Honey, you could never really know it," and she gives up trying to explain.

I am hearing these words so many years later, searching for Salvatore and Adalgiza's old house on Willow Avenue. Because of Cousin Catherine, I know where to find it.

It was always a poor street, my grandmother told me—all the struggling people crammed in together. It was a long walk from the waterfront. Homes were cheaper the farther away you went.

The block is now filled with Bradford pear trees planted neatly in front of tidy renovated apartment buildings and reappointed brick row houses that sell for a million or two. Well-dressed people walk up and down the street. It is a humid summer night, and I walk through the thick warm air until I find it—number 120 Willow Avenue, a wide, brick building that once held apartments filled with Schenones.

The building clearly has been reconfigured over the years, with an awkward newer entranceway tacked on to the front. A new incarnation is clearly on the way—the house is vacant and uninhabited, a work site left empty by contractors for the night. How unsettling and eerie that they left all the windows open, as if I could nearly climb inside and wander around through those rooms, as if all the old secrets were free to fly out and away into the balmy night.

I stay there, very still, listening to the air, and I try to imagine Salvatore and Adalgiza, not as ghosts, not as names on paper, but as people who were once very much alive.

Perhaps Adalgiza first met him when she was going to the market back in Italy. Perhaps she was just walking down the street, preoccupied in her thoughts, when she looked up to discover him right there before her, staring at her—Salvatore with his dark eyes and mustache, his big broad back and muscles. He was not a tall man, but strong and compact, and so handsome, that for a moment, anything seemed possible . . .

Or perhaps she was out in front of her home, tending the garden, early in the morning before the heat—watering the beans, thinning out her basil. Maybe Adalgiza heard his footsteps, strong and confident, along that road, while watering her vegetables or flowers—there was something to the rhythm of his walk—something so determined. She looked up, and there he was. Did she know that something was happening to her life—something enormous?

Talking was forbidden, of course. He could not ask her name. Adalgiza was only twenty years old, and everything was arranged for her marriage.

Perhaps Adalgiza frequently found reason to be in her garden at the exact same moment early each morning, and as a result, geraniums and roses grew into spectacular blooms, and her basil, tomatoes, and beans grew in perfect form. Suddenly all things in the world looked more interesting and beautiful, and the air nearly vibrated each morning.

Meanwhile, Salvatore continued to pass and look. How could so much be said with no words? Well, perhaps words were forbidden, but no one ever said anything about singing. A few weeks after the whole thing began, Adalgiza was lying in her bed one night when she heard the sound of a mandolin. Was it possible? She rose from her bed to look out the window. (How had he known which window was hers?) There he was looking up at her, singing in a sweet deep voice about love.

She got out of her bed. There was really no choice—no choice once a man like this starts following you and watching you and singing to you. Your life is written. "He is the man you'd leave home for." The man she'd defy her father for. Give up her parents for. Give up her village and her life. Follow across an ocean if she had to.

And so she walked outside into the night.

CHAPTER 9

"In Lumarzo, All Persons Are Schenone"

ONE DAY I RECEIVE AN EMAIL from a woman who has found me through my web site. She says her name is Marialuisa Schenone, that she lives in Genoa, and wishes me well. "Your family must be from Lumarzo," she writes, "because in Lumarzo, all persons are Schenone."

Actually many Schenones from around the world similarly find me and write. Schenone is not a common name in New Jersey—I've never met one who was not my relative. But now I get emails from Liguria, from France, and from all over the United States. These Schenones all want to know more about their own roots, whether I can help them, if we are related. My favorite email: "I am Ligurian man. Tell me your origins immediately."

And I ask myself the question, is it vain to want to know your roots? People in the United States frequently put great effort into researching their family trees back and further back still. But at what point is this an egotistical labor? At what point do we blur into the larger pool of humanity?

My son comes to this discovery at age eight. One morning I find him up and pacing barefoot across the kitchen floor before breakfast. "Mom, did you realize that everybody is really related to everybody? I mean . . . if you go back in time—back and back—we all must come from the same two people—the first people."

Still, I take out a map of Liguria and look for Lumarzo. Did the Schenones come from there?

Marialuisa and I develop a correspondence. "Lumarzo is located in Valfontanabuona (Fontanabuona Valley), and it is among the meadows and chestnut wood," she writes. "I have my mother (88 years old) living there and I go Lumarzo almost always. My mother has always made RAVIOLI and I eat with pleasure. I can send you many Genovesi recipes."

Still, I want more certainty. One night, I check the Ellis Island ship records using the Internet and plug in the name Amianto for my great-grandmother. And just like that, I find them. I find the passenger list showing Adalgiza in the fall of 1907 on a ship from Genoa to Hoboken, with four children in tow—Tessie, Lena, Mamie, and the youngest of these, my grandfather, Luigi, a two-year-old baby. Their destination: Hoboken. Their town of last residence—Recco, Italy, about fifteen miles from Genoa, along the coast.

To my utter delight, I learn that Recco is famous for its food: a beloved style of focaccia with cheese, a little pasta called *troffie* made of chestnut flour, and *pansotti* filled with *prescinsêua*. It is a town with several old family trattorias still going strong dating back to the era of Salvatore and Adalgiza. How could I have not visited there?

I call Catherine to tell her.

"I could have told you that, Honey. Yes, of course they came from Recco. You didn't ask."

When I share this information with Marialuisa, she insists again about Lumarzo. "I think your great-grandfather is from Recco but more precisely from Lumarzo because in Lumarzo all peoples named Schenone." Lumarzo is indeed just to the north of Recco—maybe fifteen minutes by car. But what about by foot or donkey?

Marialuisa writes to me about old Genoese foods, describing the dishes her mother cooks such as *farinata* (chickpea bread), minestrone (made with water), and *cavoli neri* (black cabbage boiled with potatoes and pigskin, seasoned with olive oil). Marialuisa takes care to note which dishes are the truly old ones and advises me to learn dialect, supplying not just Italian but also Genoese names for the typical dishes: a cornbread from long ago called *focaccette di granturco* in Italian but *fûgassette de gra-*

non in Genoese. *Castagnaccio* —a rustic chestnut cake in Italian—is *patonn-a* in Genoese. Pesto is *pestu*. And *sugo* (gravy) is *tucco*. But when you say *tucco*, you're really not talking about just any gravy, but rather the distinct Genoese tomato sauce built upon a slow-cooked, pot-roasted beef—the curiosity that Kay told us was in Adalgiza's pot.

"In Lumarzo (Schenone's country) are many chestnut trees," writes Marialuisa. "And many years ago was in use chestnut flour, still my mum make gnocchi al pesto (old recipes) using half white flour and half chest-nut flour . . . very good!!!! We also eat fried mushrooms, I think also your grandparents liked mushrooms 'porcini.' They spring up in Lumarzo into chestnuts wood."

Not long after this, a big box arrives in the mail containing an immense quantity of dried porcini mushrooms so large and white they seem nearly fresh. I put my face in the bag and inhale the smell of the earth—pungent, dark, and still alive with the earth of Lumarzo.

The connections continue. My father's *berodi*—the pigs'-blood sausage his father loved—is easy to find in the butcher shops of Val-fontanabuona.

"Ask your father if he eat polenta made of corn. Here in Lumarzo it was very much in use. I love."

And indeed, my father confirms that he had polenta when he was a boy, baked in large pans—a favorite his dad used to bring home from Adalgiza or Tessie because his Irish-German wife had no clue about it.

"You know," my father adds reflectively. "Now that you bring up these things . . . I remember the Schenones used to roast chestnuts in the oven and then crack them open and eat them. I never would have remembered this if you didn't ask me."

How gratifying to unearth this chestnut memory—it feels far more conclusive than birth certificates in proving that some bit of my DNA goes back to the hills over Recco where chestnut trees grow and porcini spring up after the rains.

But what of ravioli in Lumarzo?

Marialuisa sends an email reciting a technique that sounds like Tessie and Adalgiza's. "My mother draws paste with rolling pin, after she spreads the stuffing on half paste disk and covers with other half; after she pass over another rolling pin that is checkered. Sincerely this method is use only to oldest women because I don't know anybody who draws paste anymore, including me."

On my previous trip home from Genoa I became the source of great laughter at airport security when the guards opened my carry-on bag for inspection and discovered long wooden rolling pins inside. I'd purchased them in the *caruggi*—one for me and one for Lou. Vigorously, the guard shook his head no. When I asked why not, he pulled one rolling pin out of the bag and began to swipe the air with it, demonstrating its potential as a weapon should I decide to hijack the plane. This turned heads and got all the male guards and nearby passengers cracking up. The male guard offered the pin to the female security guards who rolled their eyes, saying *Don't look at me. I have no idea how to use that thing!* My flight was leaving, and the security guard would not relent—so those rolling pins of mine wound up in the trash of the Genoa airport.

ॐ

ALL OF Marialuisa's letters close with a warm wish for my entire family, regards to my parents, and kisses for my kids. Her daughter Laura (yes, the same name as mine) and her mother, Giuseppina, also send me best wishes. "My mother wants that I go to the church to find out about your family origins."

Naturally I reprieve her of this task. "I hope to come some day and do it myself," I explain.

And she replies, "My mother awaits you in Lumarzo. She will make ravioli when you come."

CHAPTER 10

Rolling the Dough II

Ⓘ N THE MIDDLE OF NOVEMBER, I come home one day to find this
message on my telephone answering machine:

*Laura, this is cousin Millie. My daughter Susan and I are going to make ravioli on
December 6. You're very welcome to come.*

It is exciting news. Adalgiza taught her daughter Lena. Lena taught
her daughter Millie. Millie taught her daughter Susan. And now they
will show me. My heart kicks up a beat when I confirm that they do not
use a machine but roll it out the old way. Eagerly, I mark the calendar
with the appropriate date and turn once again to ask my husband for
clearance.

"Okay, Honey? This is my chance to learn how to flip and stretch."

"Of course," he replies.

I will disappear for an entire Sunday, and he will manage the kids,
who, quite frankly, are not in a tranquil period. Thank goodness he does
not know yet that I want to go back to Italy so I can see Recco and visit
those Schenones in Lumarzo.

It has been a year and a half since my ravioli day with Maria Carla, and
a full year since my first solo ravioli voyage. Will my cousins teach me
something new?

Meanwhile, I have amassed a small collection of reprinted Genoese cookbooks from various eras. I hope these might guide me a little—some are dated from the time that Adalgiza left. That said, cookbooks are troublesome. They are prescriptions that tell how life *should* be lived, not necessarily how it *was* lived. But they provide useful clues, and so I eagerly read all the old ravioli recipes.

As it turns out, ravioli is a big world in Genoa. In various books, I find Genoese recipes for artichoke ravioli, potato ravioli, fish ravioli, orange squash ravioli, green herb ravioli, spinach ravioli, and many variations on "lean" ravioli. But it is "Genoese Ravioli" that remains at the center of my search, for this is the Christmas ravioli, and now is the time of year.

In order to read these recipes, I have been studying Italian for some months and now have acquired some feeble skills. The discouraging fact is that at forty-two, I may have sprung a leak somewhere in my brain, as everything I memorize seems to trickle out. Still, I persist, putting the same things back in my head again and again, and within some months I get the gist of fifty or sixty percent of what I read in recipe books. The rest is tedious work, dictionary in hand, one word after the next.

BEFORE GOING OFF to Millie and Susan's, I dig up the all-important strawberry-bordered recipe card and take a review of the Schenone recipe. It really couldn't be simpler in concept: uncooked finely ground beef and pork, frozen spinach, eggs, cheese, salt, and pepper. That's all. This raw mixture is then spread over thin pasta dough.

Then I turn to Ratto's *La cuciniera genovese*, that cookbook "bible" given me by Ebe in Genoa.

The differences between this old Genoese classic and our Americanized version are—to say the least—well, significant. Where our Schenone recipe calls for frozen spinach, the Ratto recipe calls for escarole, borage, and fresh marjoram. Where our recipe simply calls for ground veal and ground beef, Ratto's calls for lean pork, lean veal, marrow, sweetbreads, veal udders, and brain—cooked in butter then worked into a paste by mortar and pestle. Whereas my Schenone relatives call for parmigiano and cream cheese, Ratto calls only for parmigiano. I am happy to note that Ratto, like my relatives, insists that the circle of pasta must be very thin.

Cream cheese question aside, varieties of meat aside, the most unsettling difference is that in our family recipe, the meat is raw: and this confounds me beyond words because now I have read dozens of old and new ravioli recipes alike, and each and every one calls for the meat to be cooked first, then ground, then mixed into *ripieno.*

It's not that I'm closed-minded. Indeed, I'm sure there may be some raw ravioli recipes in this world, and I know that Asians almost always make their pork dumplings with raw meat that cooks in the boiling water. Furthermore, Italians are not afraid of raw meat and the finest cooks serve thin slices of highly seasoned, high-quality raw meat, in the form of carpaccio. No, I've got no beef against raw meat. But still, I just can't seem to find any precedent in the written canon of Italian ravioli.

Shyly, I reach out to two of my Italian cooking heroes.

"I checked my many cookbooks for you," responds Marcella Hazan. "But I cannot find documentation in any region of Italy for a single raviolo filled with raw meat."

Giuliano Bugialli is not very encouraging either, and can tell me of no ravioli filled with raw meat. "When you try to come out with very authentic and classic recipes, the sources from mothers, and aunts, are not so good. You'll find authentic recipes for the family—but not authentic recipes for Italian cooking."

This statement bothers me. But I believe it is mostly true.

SO THEN how did this come to pass? Did Adalgiza or Tessie, upon arriving in America, suddenly realize they'd better speed things up and take shortcuts like American cooks? Perhaps they were seeking their own American dream of liberation from the kitchen. Or perhaps they were simply innovative people. Maybe one day Adalgiza was at the butcher when the sight of ground "hamburger" meat, with its soft creamy consistency, sent a lightbulb on in her head. Why not? Imagine how much time would be saved. After all, each thin little raviolo contained just a small bit of filling. The boiling water would cook it right up in a few minutes.

As for the cream cheese, most formal Genoese ravioli recipes do not call for any fresh cheese. Meat ravioli was a wintertime dish before refrigeration; fresh cheese did not come with abundance until the spring when the grass grew and the cows began grazing and giving lots of milk. But I conclude, quite simply, that Adalgiza fell in love with the Philadelphia stuff.

I imagine her standing in her kitchen in Hoboken, the wood table in the middle of the room, a coal stove, and a picture of the Blessed Mother on the wall. She brings a spoon to her lips, and there it is—that thick consistency, that sweetness and faintly clabbered undertaste.

"*Non male,*" she thinks. Not bad at all.

In fact, each time she tries it, the taste grows on her. It's like home-made fresh cheese, but just fattier and richer and sweeter. Before long, she can't stop herself, and she's using *Feeladelfia* cream cheese whenever possible: in *torta,* in pesto, in stuffed vegetables. And why not in ravioli too? In America, you can do as you wish.

IT IS THE DAY I am to make ravioli with Susan and Millie, and after a long drive down the Garden State Parkway, I find myself knocking on the door of a sweet little house on a back street in a quiet neighborhood near the Jersey shore. A blond, blue-eyed woman of middle age appears— she's got sleeves rolled up and sticky flour all over her hands. This is Susan—another great-granddaughter of Adalgiza. She is fit and attractive, wearing no makeup, a white T-shirt, and blue jeans. She nods for me to open the door myself on account of her doughy hands. "We've just started. Come right on in." Then she calls her husband and says, "Come meet my cousin, Laura."

It is the kind of home I think of as ideal, where indoors and outdoors flow together. The house is built directly on the bank of a river, and just next to the kitchen, sliding doors open up to a wooden deck with steps leading down to a dock and a small boat. From anywhere in the family room, you can see water and sunlight and trees. The kitchen shares this view and flows with no walls into the family room, so that the cook can socialize and doesn't have to work in solitary confinement.

After scanning about me, my eyes fix on eighty-two-year-old Millie, who leans on the kitchen counter to help hold up her body. She is changed since the last time I saw her, wearing a smart dress and heels at my wedding. Now an excruciatingly painful hip gives her trouble standing and walking, but she hugs me with unmistakable good cheer. "Laura, I didn't know you even knew I was still alive," she jokes. Millie's spirits are high. Today is ravioli day, and a great day because she spends it with her daughter whom she clearly adores.

(How strange that all those years ago I told my father I wanted a small and intimate wedding—simple, no fuss, and certainly no long lists of distant relatives. "You don't want to invite my cousins?!" he replied with complete shock and outrage. "I never heard of a wedding where you don't invite cousins!" I relented, and they came. Now, fifteen years later, I'm desperately seeking out those same cousins and the thin threads that bind us.)

Susan steps up to the kitchen counter and points to a silver bowl filled with the green mixture of raw meat and thawed spinach, evidently mixed by a KitchenAid. "This is the ravioli filling," she explains. "It's all ready to go." And her sticky hands go back into the lump of dough, still eggy and messy, needing to be pulled together. I am delighted to see a jar of nutmeg on the counter. This was not on the Schenone's recipe card. "Oh, yes," she confirms. "We've always used a little nutmeg." Then Susan sets about the job of mixing dough and apologizes. "I don't have a big ravioli board, so we do the ravioli a little at a time." In fact, her board is shockingly small—no more than two by two feet, not even a pasta board really, but a very large cutting board. "We manage," she explains.

Once the dough is satiny and well rested, Susan reaches for the rolling pin. I'm expecting the long Italian stick, but she pulls out an American rolling pin, with handles on each end—well designed for pies but not typical for pasta. Back and forth, back and forth, she vigorously rolls over the dough, pressing down hard.

Millie provides the expertise and judgment suited to her age and experience. "No, Sue. It's not thin enough yet." Or, "No, it's not even. You've got a thick spot here."

I'm waiting for the flipping and stretching. But then suddenly I realize that, no, it's not coming. My heart sinks a little. The old techniques of rolling pasta have been lost. Susan's motions are, in effect, like the pasta machine, pressing and pressing down further until the dough is flat and thin.

And yet, I am entranced and, in some ways, humbled. Stretching or not, these two women have a certain choreography that is undeniable—a confidence and cheerful vigor that come with the repetition of an act that is carved into a very small, very special part of their lives.

Casually, I pose the question. "Didn't you ever use a big board and do the flipping, stretching thing?"

"Oh, my father used to do that for my mother. He was big and strong and could really flip a huge piece of dough," replies Millie, making no indication at all that this old way was superior. "We had a huge board back then."

"It's ready now, Sue," she declares. "The dough is thin enough." And with this, the two women step into place, side by side, spooning out the creamy mixture of spinach and raw meat over half the dough. After the other half is folded on top, Millie does the most shocking thing. She hands Susan a long metal ruler.

"What's that for?"

"To make the lines," replies Millie.

Susan uses the ruler edge to press down first vertical lines, then horizontal ones to achieve a checkerboard. Mother-daughter ravioli cutters come forth, and so they cut along the ruler-pressed lines.

"Don't you use a press?" I am nearly in a panic but trying not to show it.

"What do you mean a press?" Millie asks, a little dismissively.

I proceed to describe the beloved wooden tool that belonged to Tessie, about how she came to teach my mother, about how it hung on the wall.

"Oh, that's a bunch of baloney. They didn't use no press." Millie shakes her head and continues. "My mother was Tessie's sister, *she* used the long skinny wooden thing inside the bottom of a window shade."

"But wait," I persist. "It looked like this." I walk to my bag and produce my Aunt Tessie replica, the one Lou made me. Millie and Susan study the tool with respect but make it clear that this is some kind of curiosity they've never seen before.

Millie disappears a few moments, returning with a stack of empty shirt boxes from Macy's. She puts down a layer of wax paper and a sprinkling of cornmeal. "We always use gift boxes," notes Susan, pleased with the quirkiness of this ritual. "It's just what we always do." Then she takes a dough scraper to carefully lift up the ravioli and place it in the box. She lays them out in careful rows. Ravioli are delicate when raw. If you're not careful, they can break or stick together, and then you've got a lot of mush for the garbage.

"Forty on the bottom," Millie announces.

(My father once told how the Schenones always talked about ravioli quantitatively. "Hey, here's three hundred for Louie's family, three hundred for Al," Tessie would say. And then to another hopeful, "Did you get your hundred? No? I'll give you two boxes of fifty." I've heard that Adalgiza and Tessie could make three thousand ravioli in a single day—but could such a thing really be possible?)

"Okay, Sue. Done," Millie announces, sealing a box shut. She writes the number 100 on the top with a flair of happy accomplishment. Into the freezer it goes. She also records the number on a sheet to track the day's tally.

And so the work proceeds. Because of the small board, they carry out the full procedure—flour, dough, kneading, spreading, cutting, boxing—many times.

A couple of hundred ravioli into the project, we take a break and sit down to lunch in Susan's dining room. I learn that Susan is a high school Spanish teacher who spent some years in Spain. As she helps maneuver her mother in and out of the chair, I get the sense that Susan is often looking out for Millie, who lives in a retirement community not far from here. They have a long history of taking care of each other. Millie was there for Susan too, all those years ago when Susan left her first husband, and Millie helped raise that boy who is now a young man, doing just fine, and the apple of her eye.

"Back to the *tadjo*," Millie instructs, for this is what they call the ravioli board. Later I will search for all possible words in Italian and Genoese for the name of the board you make pasta on—*spinatoia, madia, meiza.* (It will take me years to discover that *tadjo* comes from a Genoese word for cutting board.) In any case, we return to work and after many batches, finally, they let me help a little with the kneading and rolling and even encourage me to try the Aunt Tessie replica press (humoring me, I suspect). Meanwhile, Susan's husband is stringing Christmas lights from their deck out back. Evening is getting near. When he is done, he flips them on, and then he comes inside and photographs us ravioli makers: Millie at eighty-two, Susan at fifty-two, and Laura at forty-two.

By the day's end—cream cheese or not, raw meat or not—I am certain that these two women are true ravioli heroes. When I say something to this effect, they are pleased but amused. "We just keep it going," they answer modestly. They have little more to say on the topic of ravioli. No other ravioli tales to share. They don't know much about the family history. Millie's mind is still sharp for the present but not for the distant past of Adalgiza's kitchen. When I ask, "Why do you use raw meat? Who started using cream cheese?" they each reply nearly simultaneously, "I don't know. This is what my mother taught me." Susan adds, "I make these each year because the kids would kill me if I didn't."

THESE ADVENTURES come to a sudden and guilt-ridden halt when my cell phone rings and I hear the voice of an irate husband on the other end.

"Are you coming home? I mean, is this going on all night?"

"Uh . . . I was just packing up." This is a lie. I meant to pack up, but I'd lost track of time. "Is something wrong?"

"Yes, something's wrong."

Our nine-year-old boy returned that day from a sleepover at a friend's house. All day he has been difficult and anxious and exhausted because the parents left them to go to sleep when they wished. They never did. Instead, they stayed up most of the night doing things they shouldn't have, playing violent video and computer games when everyone else was asleep. He has just confessed all this to his father. My husband suggests I am perhaps paying too much attention to ravioli and not enough to my kids.

I pack up my things and hug my cousins good-bye. I am grateful and lucky to have been with them but must leave instantly. I have no idea when I will ever see them again.

Before I depart, they give me a box of Schenone ravioli as a gift—this one has no number on top, but it's quite heavy, and I'd say there's a good sixty inside.

THAT NIGHT, while my husband and I are fretting and worrying about our boy, I take out a few of Millie and Susan's ravioli. I boil them up and drizzle them with olive oil and parmigiano, then give some to my husband to taste. "This is what I was doing all day," I sigh, and place the bowl before him. He takes a mouthful, then slowly chews.

"Damned good," he mutters. "Very damned good."

IN TWO WEEKS, it is Christmas—and it seems impossible to boycott the holiday this year. My father was only moderately interested in my ravioli the previous year, perhaps because they came by way of distant Genoa. This year, things are different. We have been talking for months about Schenone ravioli, and now he is thrilled that I visited his cousins and have a box to share—these are from Genoa via Hoboken, an entirely different thing, the true and authentic version in his mind. He has not tasted them in thirty years. In fact, he is so excited that the week before Christmas he calls me several times just to check and be sure. "Are the ravioli really on track for Christmas?" Yes, I reassure him. Millie and Susan's box are not enough for everyone, so I'm going to make more. Ravioli will be the center of our feast. "He can't stop talking about it," my mother confides.

I am determined to let go of Maria Carla's glorious wine, butter, and flavor-infused recipe. I'm going all-out Schenone this year: raw meat, spinach, and cream cheese. This is my inheritance, is it not?

But the question remains—pasta machine or rolling pin; to roll or not to roll? This is the obsessed person's question. But before I go off to ruminate a few days on esoteric matters, my husband injects some reason.

"We've got to plan things," he implores. And he's right. There is shopping, which takes enormous time. We've got to buy presents for my family and mail packages to his. The children have holiday events. There is cleaning and cooking and an already overly booked daily existence with two parents working to pay the mortgage. We sit down with a calendar and schedule our remaining days before the holiday. When to make ravioli? We look and look for a free day, but there is none. We look again, and juggle. Finally, we set my ravioli day down in ink: it will be the day before Christmas Eve.

৯৯

THAT MORNING I wake up early, and immediately after feeding and sending the children off to get dressed, I pull out my big board and assemble the ingredients. I begin to roll as I watched Susan and Millie do. After several hours, I've got about a hundred ravioli lined up drying on tin cookie sheets.

"Anyone want to try?" I call out from the kitchen.

My husband and sons come running. The water is boiling and I plunk a few in. But within seconds, it seems, I am watching their faces fall with disappointment.

"Hmmmm . . . ," says my husband carefully. "They taste a little . . . "

"Yuck!" My son cuts him off. "Too much spinach." He spits a chewed up raviolo back on his plate.

God help me. It's already three o'clock.

My husband takes the children out on last-minute Christmas errands. But for me, there's no other choice but to begin again and redo with one less box of spinach. I doggedly clean up and start over. But I'm spooked by this failure, and suddenly begin to feel crushed by doubt. I cannot go through with raw meat after all. In a frenzy, I pull out a mezzaluna and begin finely chopping some garlic, onions, and carrots, which I sauté in oil. To this *soffritto*, I add the chopped meat and lavishly splash in some wine and herbs and cook it slowly in some spontaneous and strange improvisation of a little Maria Carla and a little Schenone—fine cooking technique applied to ground beef and veal. When the meat cools, it has shrunk considerably, but I just go on ahead and add the spinach and cream cheese and mix it all to a paste.

The boys will soon be home in need of dinner, so I foolishly rush and spread the *ripieno* too thickly. Upon applying ravioli press to dough, the filling oozes messily out of the edges and I must go over each one carefully with my fingers, doing microsurgery to seal them shut. No, it is not a pretty scene.

Six o'clock. My husband returns home, finds the kitchen impassable. He makes a loud dramatic sigh, shifts his weight from leg to leg, and goes stomping out again, taking the children out for dinner.

At 7:00 P.M. the dough is snapping back at me as I roll. I cannot get it thin enough. I let it rest again so its glutens can settle down. Then, with desperation, I go madly running for the pasta machine and hook up its hideous but reassuring sound. *Mmmwaaahhh*. As usual, I get perfectly thin sheets of pasta. Lou's voice echoes in my mind. "You're never going to beat that machine, Laura."

Perhaps he's right.

At 8:30 P.M. I've only got about seventy-five small ravioli—not quite enough. I call Lou and tell him how lousy it's going. Plus, I'm out of meat. Ever ready and supplied for any emergency, Lou discloses that he just happens to have some extra *ripieno* in the fridge. Do I want it? I am embarrassed. I am ashamed. But I eat my hat and say yes because Christmas is nearly here. I creep out to his house and come home quietly with a plastic container of his aromatic well-braised and ground *ripieno*. This is *not* Genoese by any stretch. It has no green herbs. It is reddish in color, with some tomato in it. I do not care. I quietly put it in the refrigerator and make plans to get up early.

The next morning, when my husband walks down to find me at it again, he rolls his eyes, then swiftly exits in disgust. The children are waking up. They need breakfast. We say no. Go play in the other room. One brother slaps the other, followed by crying and promises of revenge. My husband looks at me: "We've got presents to wrap. We need a trip to the grocery store and dry cleaners. We must clean up before tonight. What's your plan?" he implores, standing over me in the kitchen with his tall body and worried dark eyes. He is a handsome man, a good man, a smart man, the love of my life. We have been together seventeen years. But every fiber of my being is focused on completing the ravioli. Ravioli is all I can see. Ravioli is all I can do. And so I desperately want him to leave the kitchen and disappear. I try ignoring him and his question. This strategy doesn't work.

"What's your plan!" he repeats emphatically.

"To finish," I reply calmly. "But unfortunately, I must run out to the grocery store for more eggs. . . . I'll get done as soon as I can."

He shakes his head in utter despair and walks out muttering, "You're out of control."

Two hours later, he returns. "I am nearly done," I swear. "I'm about to fill the last batch." And it is true. I nearly am done, but it's too late.

"This is ridiculous!" he fumes. "I gave you the whole day yesterday." He throws up his hands. He stomps. "It's Christmas Eve. I'm alone here. You go on and on and on. It's never enough. Aren't we enough for you?"

We argue, and it is bad. I make the mistake of defending myself. "I didn't know how much time it would take," I explain. "I'm not good enough, not quick enough, to make it alone. I'm almost finished, I promise!"

(Later, when I tell his mother how mad he gets, she laughs and offers, "My ex-husband wouldn't have cared if I spent my whole life in the kitchen.")

He storms out, and I scurry about to clean up as fast as I can. I cover the *ripieno* and put it in the garbage. I throw the last hunk of dough in the garbage. We go to bed on Christmas Eve, speaking little at all.

"YOU GOT the ravioli?" my father says smiling at the door. He is merry and bright. It is the next day, Christmas afternoon, and we are loaded with packages, entering their fourteenth-floor apartment. "Yes, I've got the ravioli," I reply. As usual, the music is so loud on the stereo that we must shout at one another over "Jingle Bell Jazz." My dad likes it this way.

"Yes, yes. I've got a couple of hundred ravioli." And I've got a meat sauce too.

And so the day unfolds with food and presents.

I don't know quite how it happened. Perhaps because my mom is tired from her Parkinson's disease, or for some other reason I don't understand, she has not prepared a lavish spread this year. We do not have enough food for a hundred guests. Rather, she has ordered a very simple antipasto from a local Italian shop. She has also prepared a pan of chicken, a salad, and a couple of desserts. That's all. But of course there's the ravioli too.

There are also fewer presents this year than I can remember. My younger sister Andrea and I—having patched up our problems some months earlier—get on splendidly. We were brought together in the emergency room over my mother's bed six months earlier, instantly apologizing in that setting of life and death. That's all behind us now, and we are all together.

I cannot deny the great enthusiasm for the ravioli. "Let's see. Let's see," they say, peering into the kitchen. My parents and children and sisters and in-laws come to the table eagerly. My husband—understandably worn down by the spectacle—is genial and pleasant. I am worn down too. But there is pleasure now—great pleasure, I cannot deny it. We've got three kinds of ravioli: Old Schenone ravioli (Millie and Susan's), Laura Schenone ravioli (a mix of Old Schenone plus Maria Carla), and Lou Palma ravioli (no spinach inside, inspired by Lidia; yes, he likes her too).

All go into the boiling water together and get served up in my mother's huge bowl, mixed in sauce, sprinkled with *Parmigiano-Reggiano* cheese.

It is amazing how quickly they go. Days of effort, and they are gone in a few minutes. Bowl after bowl gets served, and soon everyone is trying to distinguish which kinds are which.

"This is the Tessie kind!" declares my father. "You got it, Laura!"

I shake my head. "No, that's mine . . . I cooked it with wine."

"I want to taste a Lou Palma," says my brother-in-law.

"More *raviloli*," cries my youngest son loudly.

"Really wonderful," sighs my sister Lisa.

"Awesome," says the brother-in-law.

"Mmmm," says my nephew.

"Oh, man," says my father. "Oh, Aunt Tessie."

And then, after a silence, "These ravioli almost caused a divorce," mutters my oldest boy.

Forks halt in midair, followed by silence and raised eyebrows.

"May I have a word with you, please?" I quickly take my boy away from the dining-room table and into the kitchen to have a serious mother-to-son talk about privacy, about my love for his father, about respecting his parents. By the time we return to the table, the clatter of eating has returned and everyone acts like it never happened, even though all have taken note, no doubt. But the ravioli adventure goes on.

"*This*," my father pronounces, holding a forked raviolo high in the air, "*this* is the exact right shape! The exact right size!" He tries some more. And then some more. His face appears flushed from the excitement. "This one is it! This is Tessie's. . . . No. No. This kind."

At some point, my father goes to the kitchen, takes down the ravioli press from the wall, and actually brings it to the dining room. He compares its form to the ones I've made. "Yes. Yes. Just like this," congratulates my father. "You got it, Laura. You got it."

He tastes another, it is Laura Schenone ravioli, and he says, "Oh, yes, this is it." And then he has a Lou Palma and adds, "Hey, this is not bad either."

When I step into the kitchen to get something, I bump into my mother. She is rolling her eyes and muttering, "He doesn't know *what* the hell he's tasting, does he?"

The only person who does not eat is my youngest sister Andrea.

She sits at the table with an empty plate. She is blond haired with her big gray saucer eyes, the most beautiful of the three daughters. She tries to make genial conversation. But inside her body is a misery of stomach problems. Scar tissue grows around her intestines, a chronic condition no one can explain.

If there are certain people who seem to absorb more pain than others, then in our family it is Andrea—somehow vulnerable from the moment she was born, often in one kind of trouble or another growing up, hit by bad luck, bad events, wrong people. And though she's doing fine now—happy in a second marriage, proud mother of a fine son, living a life guided by the Bible—the scar tissue continues to grow inside her. She never knows when it will happen, but every few years there comes a day when everything stops working and she must be rushed to the hospital. The scars get removed but always silently grow back in the darkness inside her, plastering her intestines shut, threatening to wrap around her organs. No wonder she takes little interest in my ravioli adventures. Eating brings her misery and fear. She sits at the table, doing her best, happy it is Christmas, happy to be here just the same.

COMING HOME in the car, the kids quickly fall asleep in the back, their bodies warm and full, their dreams all sated by Christmas. My husband and I are happy this year, driving home through the dark down the Garden State Parkway. We made up first thing this morning. We always do.

About a year and a half ago, we went for marriage counseling. The therapist told us we had a lot going for us beyond love. We like each other. We joke together. We share a worldview. "There's a blinding anger

I get to see in some couples," said the therapist. "But you don't have that." And he added, "No one's easy, you know. No one's easy once you get to know them."

I repeat my apology again to my husband. "I know that I have these obsessions," I say. "I know that I'm not easy . . . I'm really such a bitch . . ." But he stops me and says it's okay. "That was a nice day with your family. A very nice day. You found a way to share something with them. You should really be happy, Laura, because your family has hung together all these years. That's something."

CHAPTER 11

The Summer of 1957: When Aunt Tessie Came to Cook

M Y DAD DOESN'T REMEMBER Adalgiza's ravioli. He remembers Tessie's. Ravioli was her thing. All those years, Aunt Tessie brought ravioli to everyone in the family. She lived a widow's life most of the year on the West Coast with one daughter, and spent long visits in New Jersey with the other. Every time she came, she packed her rolling pin and press, and all the family gathered for the results. Everyone expected ravioli.

She was my grandfather Louie's sister. My father remembers her coming the summer of 1957—the summer after his father died. She came to help Grandma Schenone take care of the kids, to cook, to try to make things better. (Thank god Adalgiza was dead—gone just two years earlier—and didn't have to know her son had gone so young.)

Tessie came to help the family pull itself back together, that summer in the rented bungalow on the Jersey shore. Three months of water and sun and freedom after the worst winter of their lives. A time to recover.

MY FATHER doesn't remember his Genoese father much.

He was thirteen and they were living in the New Jersey suburbs in the small, quiet, and clean town of Maywood. I used to imagine the scene.

It was dark, and my dad was at the gym with a circle of boys, waiting for his ride after basketball practice, dribbling the ball on cement. Bounce. Bounce. Bounce. One by one, each boy got picked up and went home, until my dad was left standing alone in front of the locked gym that January night, his toes going numb in thin Converse sneakers. An hour passed, but my grandfather did not come. Could he have forgotten? What had gone wrong?

Finally, my father gave up waiting and began to walk home. His sneakered feet hit the frozen sidewalks, along sticks and stems of bare privet bushes, the basketball going up and down with each step. Bounce. Bounce. Bounce. When he turned the corner to his block, he saw the ambulance that was in no rush because it was too late.

And it was over. Just like that. His mother and sister and brothers were thunderstruck. His father was dead, snatched away at the age of fifty-one. No time for a last word or a good-bye—just brushed away, out of this life.

Death never arrives at the right moment. You can go over that again and again, until you go crazy, thinking of all that might have been if it had come a year later, ten years later—twenty. All that might have been.

It's not the right time to leave the world when you're fifty-one years old and have four children, from nine to twenty-one. Surely not after you've just spent years working and saving enough money to finally buy a business. But this is exactly what happened. Six months after buying out his bosses, after achieving this American immigrant-turned-business-owner dream, my grandfather came home one night, lit a cigarette, sat down on the couch, had a heart attack, and died. Just like that.

GRANDMA SCHENONE goes a little crazy for a while. She keeps that cigarette butt in a special place—the last thing that touched his mouth. That's what I've heard. Her husband is dead. She has the children, a business. What will she do?

Even in normal times she is a tough mother. The kind of mother who tosses your clothes out of the window onto the front lawn if you don't clean them up. The kind of mother who throws mashed potatoes at you if you're bad at the table. A mother who sends a crying eight-year-old son back to the bullies on the skating rink—then leaves him there, to toughen him up and learn to stand up for himself. A mother who will develop a habit of frequently moving the family, selling one house and moving to another, with little notice to her children.

She is a strong woman, and in the months following her husband's death, my grandmother pulls her forty-six-year-old body out of bed and decides to carry on his business. So she heads down the New Jersey Turnpike to the men's world of Hoboken construction. She brings her oldest son, Louie, the one with her dead husband's name. She expects—and requires—that her younger two sons will follow. And they do. My father and his two brothers will spend thirty years building their father's business by laying pipe all around New Jersey. They go down into the trenches and provide the underground waterways beneath one public-works project after the next—municipal offices, hospitals, prisons, and schools—helping to build the infrastructure that takes New Jersey from the Garden State of farmlands to the most densely populated territory in the United States.

As my father comes of age, my grandmother seems to get tougher. She is perhaps the hardest, most confusing kind of mother, able to be both harsh and loving. I saw this too, when I grew up and she came to our house for Sunday dinner, insulted my parents, then came up to my bedroom, rubbed my back, and sang me to sleep. The grandmother who, when she saw my first baby on my breast and smiled with joy, exclaimed in her trill-filled voice, "Oh there's nothing in the world like nursing a little baby! You hold them so nice and close to you."

That summer of 1957, after her husband's death, she is the kind and good mother. She knows that her kids need to heal by the ocean, need to ride the waves, walk along the sand, find kids to run with, and let the hot glow of the sun warm them back to life after that cold miserable winter of so much crying and sadness. The Schenones were always happiest at the ocean. My grandfather had loved ocean fishing, I am told, and going to the Jersey Shore, so now my grandmother rents a beach bungalow with a screened-in porch and calls on her husband's sister, Aunt Tessie, to come and help, to cook and supervise the children, while she and twenty-one-year-old Louie go to Hoboken each day to pick up the pieces of the plumbing business.

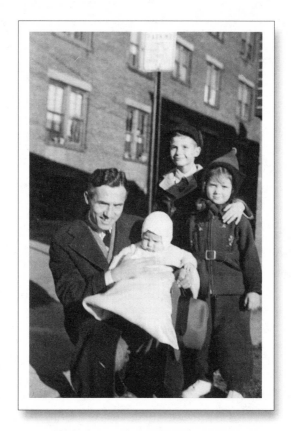

My father as a baby, held by his father,
with big brother and sister standing near, 1943.

(Years later, we are at a casino in Atlantic City. My father is way ahead at the blackjack table, confident and cool, alive. A winner. He's moving about the casino like liquid gold. When he sees me playing some amateurish game and the numbers come up 5 and 7, he quietly utters, "Good numbers, fifty-seven. The summer of fifty-seven.")

This is the summer when he's a sharp, slicked-back fourteen-year-old, rocked out and in love with the guitar, in love with music. He has a smooth tenor voice, and before long he'll be standing in a circle on the sidewalk with his friends singing doo-wop a cappella on street corners, in tiled bathrooms, under the boardwalk—wherever there is an echo to help the harmonies vibrate. He'll have a band and a shiny electric black Guild guitar and gigs to play. But for now, it is the summer of his life. Tessie is easygoing, and a wonderful cook. A "soft" Schenone, she never raises her voice, and my dad is free to leave in the morning and run free all day, so long as he makes it back by 10:00 P.M. each night.

On the boardwalk the arcade jukebox plays all night surrounded by teenagers—sometimes twenty bodies deep, bare-skinned and full of energy for the music, for one another, for life, for the little bit of freedom they taste in the salt air and their skin. My father finds his place in this crowd. They are a force together. They don't do drugs. They don't drink. But they do music, and their power comes from their numbers and the thrill of being young on the beach at night.

It is the summer of the guitar and Linc Wray's million-record hit "Rumble," playing on that jukebox in Manasquan. There are no words to this song. Just electric power-chord guitar and rhythm, and breakout bad solo, the Bixby arm electrified tremolo. All vibration and sexual trance—a song banned on the radio because even without lyrics—maybe because it has no lyrics—it's too fierce, too outrageously defiant, it offers too much escape. This is the song my father chooses as his own.

And this is the time when rock and roll is still dangerous, before Elvis has come back from the army a changed, diminished man, before Frankie Avalon and the teen idols have whitewashed the stuff clean of its black rhythm and blues, its Little Richard arrogance, its rockabilly groove. This is the summer when my father finds out which side he is on.

True, he still wakes up to the grim truth each day. *He's gone. I'm never gonna see him again.* But he can push it away now and go out as the outlaw, barefoot, bare chested, free to run under Tessie's easygoing watch. Three months to be happy.

Too short and not enough. At the end of August, the kids thin out on the boardwalk. The air gets dry and clean, and the humidity lifts its druggish cloud. The shape of life retracts, snapping back to its old forms. The summer bungalow is swept clean and closed for the season, and my grandmother brings the kids home to get ready for school. She hands my fourteen-year-old dad over to the Catholic boys high school run by the Irish Christian brothers.

THERE'S NO WAY it's going to work with my father and the brothers. He's not academic, that's bad enough. But he's got a "Rumble" attitude. He's what they call a "rock"—slang for a tough guy—a greaser with a turned-up collar. That's what his mother calls him when she yells. And he likes the label just fine. A rock. He's not about to change. So comes the hard smack to the head for the wrong look, the rubber ruler to whack the hands, five blows (screaming skin and bones), but not a tear from my father, not an apology, not a flicker of remorse. There's no kid more stubborn. Five more whacks. Still no tears.

"If you didn't fit the mold, they set out to break you," he grudgingly explains all these years later. When I declare my outrage and call it "brutal," he cuts me off with a shrug. "I wouldn't say brutal." My dad is still a tough guy, still a rock, now with his silver hair long and smoothed back in a ponytail, tattoos covering his body—on his back a colorful mural from shoulders to waist of Lucifer, the angel, tumbling from heaven to the orange tones of fire, and on his arms a blue and green shamanistic face and a lion. All those needles laying the ink into his skin, changing his skin into a scream, a work of art, a panorama of stories, never fully explained.

"Nah, not really brutal." He brushes it off.

"Not brutal?"

After two miserable years with the Christian brothers, a stroke of luck finally arrives. Grandma Schenone decides to move again. She comes home from Hoboken one night and makes an announcement to my father. "Go down to Union Hill High School and register yourself. We're moving," she says. And that is that.

It is a strange reverse migration, back to the urban ring, the brick-and-cement world of grit and tough, five minutes away from Hoboken.

My grandmother is the widow carrying on her husband's plumbing business. She doesn't want to make the half-hour drive each day to work anymore from the suburbs. And so they all go back again.

WHEN MY FATHER shows up for his first day at Union Hill High School, *everyone* notices. That's how my mother tells it. Surely in a school like that kids would care less. But he turns heads. That's what my mother says. He is the new kid who looks like no one they've ever seen. He's different from the guys who talk like truck drivers and wear crummy slacks and football jerseys to school. My dad arrives Day One cooler than them in a dark sports jacket, hair slicked back, shoes shined to a pitch. That's how my mother tells it.

Before long, an Italian guy named Johnny finds him and takes him in. Johnny has a smooth, silky voice—a lead singer in the making. He knows a drummer and a guitar player too, and soon they are playing music together, standing on the stage, doing the school show—playing rock and roll. They are all working-class, immigrant kids who come from nothing much. But they do the *oohs* and *ahs* of doo-wop, songs with silly nonsense sounds like *ooooh weee shom ba diddly oh*—free of words so that the sound and vibration can let loose and the harmonies can fly. This is back when rock and roll was still for dancing and had that raw kind of joy. Everybody is moving in the gym.

Of course, they do the ballads and slow stuff too. How can they not? That day at the big show, it's "You're Mine." And after the first few verses, Johnny steps back from the microphone and my slicked-back father in his dark jacket, with his guitar strapped on, steps up and does his Elvis-style talking lines. "I love you so much, my darling."

That's when the girls start screaming. You can barely hear the next lines.

"I swear by everything I own I'll always—always—want you."

They jump out of their seats and scream louder, electricity jolting straight up to the ceiling. The girls are out of control.

My mother, who is a dancer and choreographer for the show, is back-stage, fussing with costumes and timing and last-minute runs. But she wants to see her friend Johnny sing, so she's run to the back of the audi-torium now, and when the girls start all of this screaming about my rocked-out father at the microphone, she wonders, *Is this guy for real?*

Some months after this, a few chance meetings later, they go out. When he sings, he devastates her. There is something so beautiful in him, so impossible. And she understands also about dead fathers and difficult Franceses from Hoboken—because that is her life too. A young gentle father, gone too soon. A difficult Frances. They are the same. They are opposites. And before long, it is serious and fast, headlong love.

Soon she is pregnant, and they are married in a quick ceremony in winter, to which Grandma Schenone wears black and cries loudly through the whole ceremony. Once they are married, they settle into a one-bedroom apartment with a bed, a dresser, and a table, and the rock-and-roll dreams are over. Just like that.

By nineteen, my father is in the union, in the family plumbing busi-ness. He and his band still play gigs in nightclubs on weekends. They're trying to cut a record. My mother goes and drinks a Coke at the cocktail table while her belly grows bigger and bigger.

A couple of months before the baby is due, my dad gets invited to go to Europe to do a summer gig. Amazing but true. Europe. Who could imagine? But I am scheduled to be born in August.

"You tell him that if he goes to Europe, you won't be here when he's back," commands Grandma Schenone. She has no problem with saying no.

But this is not my mother's style. She simply requests that he not go because she doesn't want to have the baby alone.

And that's what happens. My dad doesn't go, and I am born one hot August night after a thunderous race down Kennedy Boulevard to the hospital in Jersey City, forty-five minutes after my mother's labor began. No one expects it to happen so quickly. My father deposits her and turns to go home as fathers did back then, waiting for the call when it's all over. He no sooner gets out of the hospital door than he is sum-moned back.

"Your baby is born. Go see her in the window."

He turns to see the Filipino nurse who is holding me, pointing and mouthing the words through the glass, "She looks just like you."

My parents, 1967.

For a while, my dad keeps his band and plays in clubs on weekends. For some years, we have electric amps and guitars and microphones around our apartment. When guys come to jam, our whole apartment is filled with glamour and vibration, and the coolest groove. I am so proud of my father that when I look out the window of my bedroom into the dark sky—my eyes set on the glimmer of the Empire State Building while holding a pretend microphone up to my mouth—I see beauty and energy shining upward, and I believe that anything is possible. Anything. But by the time I'm four or five, all this fades away, and there are years when everything is tense in our apartment, when my parents are only in their early twenties with two little girls and another on the way, and my father lays quietly on the couch with his back to us, and my mother explains to me that he is sad. For a while he is gone, and then he is back again, and the new baby sister is here too. It is Christmastime, and my father is wearing a brown suit holding tinsel in his hands, and I am nervous around him, and my mother is nervous too.

Time passes, and we move away from the row houses and iron railings and Madonna statues in cement front yards where the old ladies sit all day in lawn chairs, and the Cubans who have fled Castro walk up and down the block rolling their rs in rapid Spanish, and we kids in the neighborhood are outside all the time, running loose, playing on the sidewalks and in the asphalt lot across the street.

When I am seven, we leave this noisy world of street life and boulevards and crowded lives and little stores with sawdust on the floors. We leave and go to the new house in the suburbs, to a quiet block. This is our upward mobility. My parents chose the best town they could afford. It is not a pure Anglo-Saxon town—there are still plenty of immigrants here, and African-Americans too, and Jews. There are rich and poor and lots in the middle. My father sits on the edge of his bed and still plays his guitar once in a while, and he tries to teach me too. And so we all grow. He takes up running and lecithin powder instead of music now, and spends hours each week lifting weights and running, until his chest and shoulders are bulky and as hard as rock.

And all the while, all these years and decades, my father goes to work with his family, and seems to manage his stress by going to the gym or running on the streets each night. Twice, he leaves the business briefly to work for other companies. But each time, he returns to the family business, as he believes it is where he belongs.

At the end of each workday, he comes home and goes straight to the basement to undress because my father is an immaculate man, and his work clothes are dirty from the grit and dust of the job. He scours his hands in the utility sink with a special soap that comes in a tin container for men who work with their hands. Then he comes up for dinner.

He goes out with his friends on the weekends—the Italian men who became his real brothers, men with names like Donaruma, D'Amico, and Rosi—the friends who became a kind of family after his father died and after everything went wrong. It is from them, perhaps more than his father, that he learned his Italian style, and the rules of *la bella figura* when he was young. Now, when he goes out with these men, he wears finely woven wool pants, perfectly creased, shined Italian shoes, and gold chains. He likes suits and ties, chesterfield coats, a silk handkerchief in the pocket.

The few photos I've ever seen of my dad's father, Louis Schenone, show a well decked out man. Sharp trousers. Pressed white shirt. A jacket with a handkerchief in the breast pocket.

But my father never tells us anything at all about his dad, and he seldom talks about work, with the exception of occasional stories about annoying architects on the jobs, a few anecdotes about men in the field, or the occasional recounting of hazards, injury, or even death—when a spark from a welding torch hit the eye, when a steelworker fell from so high up and hit the ground with such a thud that everyone knew . . . Like his mother, my father can be warm and loving. He takes us to the beach where we are always happy riding the waves, where some magic seems to always be in reach for our family. He makes sure I have a record player and a guitar, and we sing together. We have some songs we do well, and these are our best times. He comes to his daughters' recitals and sports events. He makes these efforts because he wants to do right. But much of the time when I am growing up in that house, there is an aloofness in my father that frightens me, an inward tension building that I always fear will explode again. I have seen it explode before. We never know when it will come, and so we learn to live with a certain amount of fear. My mother is the information channel, his publicist and intermediary. When he is quiet, distant, or remiss, she tries to communicate his good intentions. But for decades, my dad is a closed door when it comes to his life and the family business. He is a roadblock to the past because it is really not any of our business. He doesn't understand that his story is partly mine—because he is my father.

It takes me years, until I am well into adulthood, to ask. One day, when I am in my twenties, he and I are driving in rural North Jersey at Christmastime in his pickup truck, a tree strung up in the back. I ask him what his dad was like. He pauses, hands on the steering wheel, eyes focused on the road. "He was never severe or harsh. He was not a hard man. He left all the child rearing to my mother." And then, in his ever-understated way, "The Schenones were not harsh people." This is all he says, and this is a lot. Not harsh.

"Were they a happy family?" I press.

"A happy family?" He pauses and laughs a little. "I never met a happy family." He says this with defiance that haunts me for years, like he won't be a sucker having hope. No, he won't get caught believing in happy families.

CHAPTER 12

Preparations

A COUPLE OF DAYS before my second journey to Liguria, I bring my four-year-old son with me for an afternoon in New York City. My passport has expired after ten years, and I need to pick up the new one in person. So I bring him along, and we make a day of it, afterward heading to Chinatown for lunch. Traveling through the city in a taxi heading east, he requests my cell phone, saying he'd like to call my mother to say hello.

"Hi, Grandma," he says, as calm and confident as a stockbroker on his way to Wall Street. "I'm in a taxi in New York. I'm on my way to lunch but I just wanted to say hi." As parents do in certain moments, I see his life far ahead of mine, moving with great speed to places I'm never going.

On the sidewalk, heading toward Shanghai Café, we pass through the streets of Chinatown, with its little cheap storefront shops with sidewalk displays of incense, trinkets, and bamboo, and restaurants where jelly-fish and duck blood are on the menu, along with some of the greatest pasta inventions the world has ever known. China and Italy, after all, share the legacy of pasta glory, and these two cultures above all others created the biggest and most illustrious tradition based on the simple but versatile invention of dough, rolled and shaped into endless shapes and possibilities. Here in New York, they have long occupied two neighborhoods side by side. But while Little Italy has diminished over the last forty years, Chinatown has grown larger and more vibrant, absorbing immigrants from other parts of Asia too.

By chance, it is the day of the Chinese New Year festival. The street is filled with families and children throwing little pop firecrackers on the sidewalk. Men parade wearing traditional dragon costumes and dancing along with huge fierce and beautiful heads, colorful and awesome, nearly shoulder to shoulder with vendors selling firecrackers. It is a thrilling kind of mayhem. The streets are shut down, and thousands walk on foot. Women wear bright red jackets of embroidered silk, popping forth with color in the midst of gray winter streets. Chinese mothers and children in from the suburbs huddle close and smile for pictures, posing at the camera as the fireworks go off about them. There is magic. The day is warm for winter, and everything feels alive and gleaming bright and extraordinary.

I almost leave, thinking it will be too much. But my boy is not at all afraid of the little firecracker explosions and crowds. Instead, he is as awestruck and as thrilled as I am.

At the small, bustling Shanghai Café, our dumplings are big and wrapped in thick dough served in a round bamboo basket with a lid. Inside each one is a delicious meatball made of pork that has a homey taste—but the real event is that when you break open each dumpling, there is a surprise: a bit of soup that comes gushing forth into the bowl. I am not sure how to eat them, and work at each one bit by bit. There is a heaviness to them and a messiness that is decadent and wonderful. My boy enjoys opening the packing to eat the "meatball" within and discards the pasta. (I later learn that this style of dumpling is actually known as the Shanghai method, a little tablespoon of soup in each one. Steamed dumplings, by contrast, are Cantonese.) I take this happy afternoon to share the news with my boy that his mom is going to go away for a week.

It is on the bus home to New Jersey that my son tells me about his other parents. We are driving along Route 3. "Mom," he announces, "did you know I came into this world in a taxi?" he asks.

"No I didn't, Sweetie. What was it like?"

"Well, I was wearing diving shoes. Reenie and Peenie were my parents." He is deadpan honest, but with a hint of mischievousness in his eyes, which change from gray to green. "But I left Reenie and Peenie, and I came to this world."

"I'm so glad you came," I offer.

But he ignores this, continuing on. "I came to this world because I wanted a house with a playroom." Then he pauses and looks up at me, his eyes on mine—straight on.

"And because Reenie and Peenie were dead."

THE NIGHT I leave for Italy I have stocked the freezer with frozen foods that my husband can easily heat up for himself and the boys.

Reinforcements are on the wall: a day-by-day schedule of babysitters, children's activities. In yellow marker, I highlighted all of the direct actions my husband must take. He laughs. "I really don't know if that's necessary." But I can see he's relieved I've done this. My international cell-phone number is printed out in large letters. I make sure the car is serviced. I even have a handyman come to fix the broken sink because I know that every little drip, every little ache and pain and malfunction will be intensified by my absence. Yes, all lids clicked shut on all the boxes. Sleepless nights of preparation.

When people ask—as they always, each and every time, do—what I'm going to do with my children while I go to Italy, I've got my story ready. "They have a great dad," I explain. "We have great babysitters. I'm here fifty weeks a year, at the door when the school bus comes." Finally, all is ready, and the night arrives for my departure. It is not until this moment that all my carefully laid plans fall to pieces.

My oldest boy starts to cry. This surprises me because I have traveled before. He knew I was going to go for weeks and gave not a hint of protest. Now, tears. Not little ones either, but big huge sobs, and most disturbing of all, a panting, like hyperventilating, which I recognize as fear. Once the oldest one is crying, the younger son takes his cue and starts. Soon, a symphony has taken hold. In my ever-shifting balance of whom to worry about most, I focus on the older one and pass off the little guy to the trusty babysitter, who is now physically restraining him as he tries to jump out of her arms to hurl himself at me with every ounce of raw four-year-old determined self. My oldest boy, at nine, is a quiet, soulful one. Now his face is twisting before me into vulnerable shapes I haven't seen in years. The adults are swiftly losing control here, while the clock ticks forward. There is nothing to do but catch my plane. I am already late.

"Mommy's got to go," says the babysitter, trying to helpfully intervene with a firm voice and the power of rational facts. "Planes are not like cars. The plane won't wait." But all this does is bring a new burst of heaving sobs, and my son throws himself on the carpet in the middle of our living room.

I get on my knees beside him. "I can't go with you crying like this."

The clock is ticking. The plane is leaving in two hours. I am already a half hour late. We are all quiet a moment as panic builds.

"Can I go?" I ask him. "I can't go unless you say I can." It is true. I cannot leave.

He looks up from the floor, his face red, covered with tears. "Go!" he cries at me. It is an angry imperative. I pause. "Just go!" he yells even louder, his face all the more twisted. And so I leave.

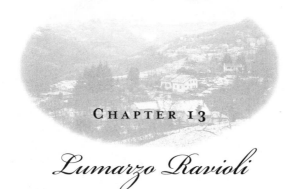

CHAPTER 13

Lumarzo Ravioli

BRIGHT AND EARLY, Marialuisa Schenone is standing in the lobby of my hotel in Genoa. There she is before me, the woman who insists she knows the town my relatives are from and has arrived today to take me there. She is a tall, strongly built Schenone in her late fifties, I guess, with dark hair and big, dark eyes. She's casually dressed, wearing jeans, hair pulled back. Standing in the lobby, we look at each other shyly. Are we relatives of some kind? We walk toward each other, a little awkwardly, shake hands and kiss on the cheek.

In a calm slow voice, she says, *"Oggi parliamo italiano"*—simply that we will speak Italian today. Clearly a communication disaster lies ahead. Marialuisa has written in English but evidently does not speak it very well. And I have the Italian speaking abilities of a three-year-old. I think back longingly to all the squandered months when I could have been memorizing verbs. Well, there is no choice now. I step into her car, toss my bags in the back, and place myself in the hands of this Schenone I've just met.

The city of Genoa fades behind us as she pulls her little car into the dingy outskirts and then onto a small highway. Soon we are ascending into the hills. The leaves are treeless and covered with a thin layer of snow. It is February and an unusually bitter cold day for Genoa, below freezing. This snow is a rare event, she explains. It only comes once every several years. Then she smiles and points to the bare trees that cover all the hills around us. "*Tutti castagni*," she says, which means "all chestnuts." And she smiles with pride.

We are headed to Lumarzo, "where all persons are Schenone." The Fontanabuona is one of many valleys that create the mountain culture here, the *entroterra* that is at the heart of Genoese cooking, the backyard to Genoa and the ports of Liguria, with the wild foods of the mountains and hills of long ago, the *preboggion*, the pillowlike porcini mushrooms springing up beneath the trees. And most of all, the chestnuts of fall. The sweet, starchy nuts were gathered, roasted, smoked, hulled, dried, boiled, mashed, and turned into breads, pastas, and porridges (the original polenta here). Chestnuts were the staff of life when wheat was too expensive or scarce. Chestnut wood—hard and durable—made the furnishings of beds and chairs and tables in these mountain homes. Chestnuts made civilization possible. I wonder if any of these very chestnut trees—which have long lives, sometimes hundreds of years—were standing here in the time of Salvatore and Adalgiza.

Now, the motor of Marialuisa's car goes into high gear as we press on higher and higher in these rugged white-topped mountains, spiraling upward, through bare chestnut trees, past terraced farming hills carved into this rocky terrain. We come upon Lumarzo, finally. It is a small but sprawling village with white snow and red-tile-roofed houses spread across the slope of astonishingly beautiful and huge hills. There is a small town center with a bakery, post office, and a few little shops, as well as an ancient church with a bell tower.

Marialuisa stops the car and lets me get out to breathe the cold air of the hills and gaze out at the impressive mountains. I smell wood burning from a chimney nearby. Back in the car, she navigates switchbacks up the road and announces that we have arrived at the *cimitero*. I've never heard this word but quickly figure it out when she parks the car and I look inside the courtyard and see the headstones.

In the tradition here, the graves are not buried in the earth but are stacked on top of one another inside a mausoleum, each with a square headstone facing out, each with a laminated photo attached and protected in a frame. The effect is a long and tall memorial wall filled with dead Schenones. I am surrounded by hundreds of them, with their faces and names looking out at us.

"*Tutti Schenone*," she says. And she is almost right. More than half are Schenones. And many are Salvatores too.

WHEN WE ENTER Giuseppina Giuffra's home, she is standing at her kitchen table, bent over a little hill of flour on her pasta board, ready to crack an egg in the center. This is Marialuisa's mother. She wears a mismatched skirt and sweater, covered with an apron, and she has the curved-over back of an old woman. She is slow and deliberate in her movements, and her face is focused down on the flour seriously. But when we are introduced, she looks up and breaks into the warm, disarming smile of a girl. "This is Nonna," says Marialuisa.

Giuseppina kneading pasta dough in her Lumarzo kitchen.

"*Bisnonna*," corrects Giuseppina, which means great-grandmother. She authoritatively points a finger to the new baby across the room, held in the lap of a lovely thirty-year-old woman. This is Laura, Marialuisa's daughter, who, lucky for me, speaks English quite decently.

Giuseppina lives in a small house on the side of a hill. Many Americans would be tempted to say that this home does not really contain an actual kitchen, but rather a cooking area (two narrow marble counters and a sink) installed in the corner of the single main room that serves as both living and dining rooms. Off to the side, a small closetlike room holds the stove and refrigerator.

The main room is cheerfully decorated with small trinkets, photographs of cats, wood-carved mallards, and a couple of earthy-looking primitive art replicas. A small couch is pushed against the opposite corner wall under a steep staircase—almost an afterthought. It doesn't look like anyone sits there much. Rather, it is the dining table and chairs, set next to an entertainment center and television, that seem to be the true center of the home, the true gathering place. A rocking chair at the window, perched by a radiator, faces out toward the backyard and hills.

Giuseppina rattles off her recipe. "*Sfoglia*—½ kilo farina, 3 eggs, some water. *Ripieno*—300 grams pork and 300 grams veal, cooked slowly in onions, olive oil, butter, and marjoram. Then add: escarole, borage, 4 eggs. That's it," she says.

But of course, this is not it at all. This is just a list of ingredients. I step closer to pay attention. Laura does too. Giuseppina is not giving a lesson; she's just doing, and we are free to watch. And watch I must because Giuseppina's hands in the dough are a sight to behold. Right away, I see she has something in her that relates to dough like I never have. She kneads it so gently and casually that her hands almost seem part of the dough. She is working, and maybe sweating a little, but she is utterly relaxed. She has done this on hundreds of occasions, no, probably on thousands. There was an era, they tell me, when she made ravioli every Sunday because her husband liked ravioli so much. The people in the family all confer a certain reverence on this skill of hers. Neighbors and family members drop in throughout the day and comment, "She's good at it," and they nod knowingly. In fact, as it turns out, no one else in the family really knows how to make ravioli. What will they do when she is gone, I wonder. Will anyone else make the ravioli?

"I want to learn," says granddaughter Laura, as though reading my mind. She nods to the dough in Giuseppina's hands. "But she is not a good teacher."

"You're not too bad," says Giuseppina, looking toward her grand-daughter. "But your mother . . . " She shakes her head.

"My mother prefers to work in an office," explains Laura. "But I'd like to learn."

Giuseppina working with the pin.

When the dough has finally taken its rest, all its stretchy glutens relaxed enough for handling, I cannot help but be excited. Giuseppina takes hold of her rolling pin—about two feet or more of dark, worn wood. I take a step closer, regretting now that I do not have a video camera because she is moving ahead so quickly. And somehow, though I've been watching so carefully, I'm not sure how she does it, but she's got her dough wrapped around her rolling pin. Slowly and steadily she goes.

With the dough carefully wrapped around her rolling pin, she pulls it back on the board toward her, almost dragging the pin against the board, so as to stretch the dough as it goes, then with a flick of the wrists she flips the dough over the top and it makes a slap—and each slap makes the pasta bigger. She has a rhythm—pull, pull, flip . . . pull, pull, flip. And there is a sound, *shh shh slap.*

Meanwhile, her hands are simultaneously stretching the dough side to side along the pin. She unrolls the dough from the pin and turns it, then rerolls the pasta in the same way around her pin, changing angles and sides to keep an even circle of dough, growing bigger and bigger, and thinner and thinner.

I ask her if I can try. It is a little bold of me, I know. This pasta board is Giuseppina's theater. And I can see that the request disarms her a little, but she gives me that girlish smile of hers, so I step up to the board. The others watch. Awkwardly and slowly, I do it. Pull. Pull. Flip. And I try to stretch the dough sideways too, like Giuseppina did. I succeed, and she nods in approval.

Of course I can do it. It's like someone gives you flowers and a vase and says put them in. Giuseppina went and got the flowers, then made the vase. Giuseppina hands me everything all ready to go—dough, already perfectly soft and pliant, already wrapped around the pin, already three-quarters of the way there. But I do memorize the rhythm and write it in my book: Pull, pull, flip. Pull, pull, flip. Giuseppina returns to her board and continues. Soon, she has her perfect circle of thin dough, and she covers one half of it with *ripieno*, which is smooth and creamy, colored green from the leafy herb borage. She spreads it out evenly with a spoon. Then she covers it with the other half moon of dough and takes out a ravioli rolling pin with squares indented all around it. This is her press. She rolls it over her creation, imprinting neat, even rows of squares. Then she cuts them with her *rotella*—an old wooden-handled ravioli cutter she says is a hundred years old.

Her ravioli rolling pin is brown with age—she estimates she's had it for forty or fifty years. But she concedes it is a newer invention. Before this tool, in the old days of her mother, they had to shape them by hand, one by one, square after square.

And what about a press? I ask. "Have you ever heard about a wooden press to stamp them out?" She shakes her head no. The mere thought is strange. Then I go on to ask about *ripieno crudo*, and whether she has ever filled her ravioli with uncooked meat.

I watch her cringe, like she's been struck. "*No, no*," she shakes her head immediately, and a little "*tut, tut*," for shame. How embarrassed I am for even asking.

We look out the window and they tell me about the trees on this land and the surroundings: medlar, cherry, plums, persimmons, figs, pears, and apricots.

"Do you know anything of your ancestors?" everyone asks.

"No—just that my great-grandfather Salvatore was poor. And that he was a mason."

Giuseppina laughs. "In Lumarzo, everyone was poor."

AFTER WE DESCEND from the mountains, Marialuisa drives me along the coast past the jewel necklace of Riviera towns. We take the pin turns and spirals. On this dark, winter night, we pass through the deep dark blue of the Mediterranean below us and the shapes of the mountains above. I feel as though somehow I have known them a long time, as though they are a calm place deep inside me—a place I have both lost and yet have always had within myself, somewhere deep in the physical roots of my body—skin, stomach, chest, bone.

My real home in New Jersey I associate more with my brain. It is a place of highways and crowds. To raise children and work there, extremely complex navigation is required each day. A tangled knot of family and personal history, a million highways of neurons and dense signals of memory, habit, love, and bleakness of the landscape to decipher. I hold its images somewhere behind my eyes—concrete sidewalks of Hoboken, the tiles inside the Lincoln Tunnel on the way to New York, banged-up metal car fenders, the enormous black steel-girded bridge of the giant ugly Pulaski Skyway going over the swamps and toxic industrial wastelands to New York. The landscape of commerce and its garbage dumps. Not far away, the promise of a better life in private houses where the doorbell rings and the aunts and uncles and grandmothers stand in porticos holding plates of something they made, and summer barbecues in intensely green patches of summer yards. New Jersey is my Croatian grandmother telling me "Now, Honey, pick each string bean one by one to get the best—no handfuls." It is those deep pits where my father and his brothers laid pipe, and those small kitchen refuges where we had so much coffee and cake. Those few tomato plants growing along the fence, next to the asphalt driveway. The crashing waves of the Jersey shore. Everything is a tangle.

Here, this piece of Liguria feels like another place inside me. It is primitive, buried in my chest or body, it is water and mountain side by side, all open and calm.

I am exhausted from having been with strangers all day trying to function in Italian. And so we go along with few words in Marialuisa's car and the winding paths above the sea. Have I left my roots to come here? Perhaps not. After all, Marialuisa is a Schenone.

CHAPTER 14

How Deep Do You Want to Go?

CHANCE. SERENDIPITY. An ability to quickly change directions. That's how my photographer friend told me he finds his photographs. But first we have to have an idea, a direction. I have cast a wide net—reaching out to experts, cookbook authors, friends of friends, and complete strangers—anyone who can help me find my way.

It is in this way that I first meet Sergio Rossi, who arrives at my hotel early in my trip, and early in the morning too. He is the director of the Genoa chapter of the Conservatorio delle Cucine Mediterranee, an organization devoted to conserving the culture and foods of the Mediterranean. I'd written him from home to ask if he might talk with me about ravioli and other Ligurian foods. He understands something of my quest. He has relatives in California. "They still make the ravioli too," he explains. "It means a lot to them."

In the lobby of my hotel, we shake hands. Sergio is a gray-haired man in his mid-forties, dressed casually in jeans and a pullover sweater. He's arrestingly sincere and soft spoken, but he has a seriousness to his face, and a bit of weariness, making it clear that he only wants to spend time on what's important. We go into the breakfast room and take a seat. Sergio gets right to the point.

"What is it you are looking for?" His tone contains a gravity I did not expect.

I try to explain about Adalgiza and the ravioli press on the wall—my search for an old family recipe. The cream cheese. Hoboken. ("What is Hoboken?") Suddenly it all sounds a bit foolish—a bit thin. Perhaps even absurd.

He looks at me cautiously, trying his utmost to understand.

Clearly I must do better.

"I want something authentic and true," I continue. "Something real. I want to find what was lost. The recipe they gave me is not quite right. I want to know what it was like before they left here—the authentic and true Genoese ravioli." And in my mind, in the space of a breath, I hear the things I don't say: *I'm not satisfied with the history I have, and I want to rewrite it. I want something beautiful from this beautiful place, something that can redeem me.*

Sergio nods. I see an adjustment in his face. However ridiculous I may seem, he will allow that I am serious, that I might perhaps be helped to understand things I was not raised to understand.

He takes a deep breath. "There are many levels," he begins. "You need to decide how deep you want to go. There is superficial knowledge—you travel across things, horizontally. Then there is vertical; you go down." He pauses. "For example, you might say even the simple word 'pasta.' But 'pasta' has many meanings in Italian." And he goes on to explain that pasta means spaghetti, yes, but it can also mean dough, it can mean the pastry in *torta* or focaccia, it can mean the dough in sweet cakes and pies. "Pasta, pasta, pasta, pasta," he recites like a mantra. "They all mean different things."

The breakfast dishes are cleared away from the hotel eating room, and the travelers get moving, off for their day, while the hotel managers look toward our table, confused as to why we don't move. But Sergio continues to talk in his earnest way, as though these are spiritual issues that cannot be held to the schedules of earth and simply take the time they must.

"Take care," Sergio warns. "*Prescinsêua* cheese may mean one thing in the city, but to some *contadini* in the country it may mean something completely different."

"How deep will you go?" He presses me again to consider.

"I want to taste," I reply. "I want to know what these dishes should taste like. I want authentic. I want to know what my great-grandmother made before she left."

Sergio shakes his head slowly. "There is no one taste. Each village has its own way. Each family has its own way. Things vary even within a family. I can share with you *my* tradition, but not *the* tradition. However . . . if you spend time, you should eventually be able to recognize for yourself what is authentic."

"What is your tradition?" I ask.

He hesitates, but then goes on to tell a little bit of his story. He is from an old restaurant family from the rural mountains north of Genoa. About a hundred years ago, his great-grandparents started a trattoria there, and it continued down the generations to Sergio's mother who grew up working in that kitchen, and to Sergio himself who also began there as a child and continued on as an adult working in the family food shop in the city, spending most of his adult life getting up in the middle of the night to make sure that the *torte* and bread would be ready the next morning.

"The taste memories are in my blood and in my soul," he explains gently. "If you come into my house and I cook for you and feed you from my special plates and glasses, well that's nice. But it's a better thing entirely if I serve you on the everyday plates."

For information about "the old dishes" from Adalgiza's time, he suggests I turn to three main sources: the old trattorias that have been in families for generations, the kitchens of families, and the old cookbooks. "But be careful of the old cookbooks," he warns. "Yes, Ratto's *Cuciniera genovese* is called the bible here. But it has mistakes in it. All cookbooks do." I nod. Yes, I understand this. I have studied old cookbooks.

Sergio simply imparts the information as though it's not about him, not coming from him, but rather coming *through* him. He has a distaste for those who do fake food history, those who dig up a medieval recipe and say here's what your grandmother used to make. And he has little interest in food fashionistas and righteous organic farmers and other food advocates who want to criticize or correct the ways of the *contadini* in the hills.

I realize that I have come upon someone who is willing to be a guide, if I am smart enough to see it.

"Remember," he explains of the nineteenth century, "the rich had meat frequently. They ate the farmed animals with soft flesh. But the poor ate meat less often. They had to use their animals for work, and those animals got muscular so that by the time they were slaughtered their flesh was too tough. But if that tough meat was mashed up with a pestle, it became soft with flavorings and made creamy—good for a *ripieno*. Good for the poor and people who didn't have teeth. Everyone can eat ravioli."

And of the tomato meat sauce called *tucco* by the Genoese? Sergio reminds me that tomatoes came relatively recently from the New World. They were not in wide use in Liguria until the nineteenth century. Before this, ravioli were eaten with a sauce or broth made from the juices of the meat only.

I ask more about his organization.

"Every day we try to save traditions," he explains. "If we don't have people there in those mountains, then we don't have agriculture."

It is true. In Italy, abandoned mountain towns are scattering across the landscape. Young people have moved to cities for education and jobs, leaving behind villages with tiny populations where there are only funerals and no new births. In the vertical landscape of Genoa, unplanted mountain soil washes downhill toward the sea if there are no roots to hold it together. "We want to revive the agriculture in the mountains," Sergio insists. And this is no small ambition.

Sergio and I make plans to meet again over the coming week. He suggests places to visit, people I should talk to, books to consult. In the meantime, he offers his cell-phone number. "If you get lost, call me. Call me any time. It's no problem, really." And finally, a warning. He takes out a map and points out some streets. "Be careful around here in the *caruggi* at night."

THE WINTERS in Genoa are supposed to be mild. The Mediterranean Sea to the south brings warm weather, while the Apennine mountains to the north buffer the region from the severe winds of northern Europe. But during my visit, this arrangement is not working well at all, and an unusual cold snap has descended.

"*Fa brutto*," the cabdriver mutters, pointing his finger out the window and shaking his head at the frigid weather. He lets me off at Piazza Ferrari where the enormous fountain is turned off, quiet, and the cold bites as miserably as it does in New York. The Genoese wrap themselves in big puffy parkas and walk quickly with heads bent beneath the rain.

Down Via San Lorenzo, past the church of zebra-striped white and *pietra nera*, a local black stone, I am soon among the helter-skelter narrow streets of the *caruggi*. My mission is to find a place called *Sciamadda*—the Genoese word for "fire." No luck. I have forgotten my map and the notebook where the address was written. *Sciamadda*—on this February day, it would be especially welcome. I'm dressed in many layers of clothes but still shivering. Hung over from jet lag, I wander fuzzyheaded through these baffling streets. I'll never find it, I think to myself . . . and yet, somehow I do. Suddenly, I'm standing before a brown stone facade of a *friggitoria* with the sign "Antica Sciamadda," tucked into one of the small back alleys not far from the port.

A lively fire in the wood-burning oven inside beckons, and a sign on the window announces the daily special: *Umido di Stoccafisso*, the centuries-old stew of air-dried cod brought back to life and then cooked with potatoes, olives, and oil. Immediately, I know this is where I am supposed to be, this little shoe box of a shop, which has been around, in one form or another, since the beginning of the eighteenth century. Everything I want is here. I am overwhelmed by the sight of *farinata*, the chickpea crepe I have read about many times but never tasted, and I am delighted at the wide array of *torte*—vegetable cheese pies—displayed lovingly on trays in the window, like gems in a jewelry store. At this moment, I believe I would take a piece of this *torta di bietole* over any expensive jewels.

Wasting no time, I promptly order slices of *farinata* and *torta*, along with red wine, which comes in a glass the size of a Dixie cup, to clear up my fuzzy head. A few sips and the warmth of it all envelopes me, as I lean against the tiny marble counter, near as I can be to the *forno* with neat stacks of kindling piled beneath.

Farinata *in the wood-burning oven at Antica Sciamadda in Genoa.*

Having read descriptions of *farinata*, I was expecting it to be like the French crepe—a light, flimsy, soft thing. But chickpea is an elemental, hearty legume of the Mediterranean, and *farinata* is much more rustic and substantial, made of four simple ingredients: chickpea flour, water, salt, and olive oil, soaked together and baked in an enormous round pan, three feet in diameter, pulled in and out of the wood-burning oven with long metal prongs, reminding me of the earliests breads invented by humans thousands of years ago and cooked on hot stones. In fact *farinata* is quite ancient, traced back to the Romans and documented in a fourth-century cookbook. How can such a primitive food be so wonderful? The bottom of the crepe is soft and coated with olive oil, the top is crackled by fire and crunchy; the taste is a little like a potato pancake, but more interesting and earthy.

Next, the *torta di bietole*, with its thin sheet of pastry on top, cooked to a golden brown. What a thrill to taste the lemony *prescinsêua* again. I cannot help myself and begin talking to the shop owners in my poor Italian, asking questions about the cheese. Before I know it, they are bringing out a large bucket of *prescinsêua*, handing me a spoon so I can dip it in and taste. It is not a modern taste, I reflect, with its acidic yogurtlike flavor. "It is a fading tradition," they tell me. In fact, this bucket comes from the last commercial *prescinsêua* maker in Genoa.

"It's between milk and cheese," the baker explains, and he is right. It is loose, fresh, and tangy.

Inviting me behind the counter, they let me peer into the stone compartment in the wall, the wood-burning oven that is the heart of the *sciamadda*. They show how the kindling is placed on the side so that the fire will climb up the wall to the low ceiling and nearly singe the top of the *farinata*, creating a wonderful crackly crust. This oven, they explain, is a gem in itself, having been well seasoned by fire after fire, day after day, for one hundred and twenty years.

I taste more. A sliver of *torta di cipolline*—an onion *torta*, sweet and creamy. Then a small piece of slightly bitter *torta di zucca*—which is pumpkin. They are amazed at all I am eating, but I must go on. A little bit of the *stoccafisso* in a golden broth—perhaps similar to what Adalgiza made in Hoboken after soaking the air-dried cod in the basement many days. Another little thimble glass of wine, and I can only look at the *polpettone*—literally "meatloaf," but a trick of a name here because in Genoa it means a vegetarian loaf made of potato, string bean, egg, and cheese—and the sweet *torta al miele*, made with honey.

Meanwhile a group of middle-aged Italians squeeze themselves beside me in this tiny shop. They festively order *torte* and drink wine, while standing at the counter. Clearly they grow merrier with each bite, and a sense of well-being begins to fill the shop as they laugh, eat, and drink from their little glasses of wine.

When I finally stumble out of Antica Sciamadda into the gray stone paths of the *caruggi*, I feel so full and warm and happy that I go the wrong way and pass some prostitutes down by the elevated highway built near the water in the 1960s. Turning back, I come upon a cluster of tough-looking motorcycles guys in a dark alley. They look up at me, with angry faces. I pass them, nervous for a second, but that is all. I continue on, and the narrow stone street turns this way, then that, then suddenly opens into a glorious courtyard with a seventeenth-century church. Beyond it is a square bordered by mansions, where one can peek at the grand painted ceilings and chandeliers built by the rich families of the Genoese empire. A few steps farther, a few more narrow alleys and turns, and I come to a street of tile-maker, mason, and carpenter shops, humming with the sound of stone being chiseled and wood being carved. The smell of focaccia drifts in the air.

I am happy to be beyond the reach of Italy's postcard beauty wandering these freezing cold streets. It all looks far more intriguing than it did two summers ago. Suddenly I am taken with the mysteries and charms of the *caruggi*. In fact, I am so exhilarated that I fear it will get the best of me, and that dizzy feeling may return—that I am so far from home, so wonderfully anonymous and free, I might never get back.

Later, on the phone call home, my littlest says, "IloveyouIloveyouIloveyou. Are you coming home the day after tomorrow?"

"No, Sweetie, just a few more days than that. IloveyouIloveyouIloveyou back." And then I keep moving and push on toward the coast, to Recco, the town that Salvatore and Adalgiza left.

DRIVING INTO Recco, I spot a sign at the entrance of the town with the word "Sinatra" on it. (Sinatra is a Genoese surname, and Frank's mother was born in nearby Lumarzo.) But it is more than this coincidence that brings comparisons with our waterfront city in New Jersey.

Like Hoboken, Recco is a small city with a fate intimately tied to its geographic location—a coastal town at the base of three mountain valleys—a place, therefore, of comings and goings, and exchanges of goods and people. It's not hard to imagine fishermen on their boats and farmers descending here on donkeys from the mountains above to sell their produce in the markets when Adalgiza lived here.

And it's immediately obvious that Recco is not like the other dreamy stratospheric Riviera resort towns near by. It's still a place for real people, with lots of practical stores where you can buy kids' shoes, inexpensive clothing, books, and hardware. Today, as in Adalgiza and Salvatore's time, it remains a crossroads. You can easily hop on the *autostrade* (the major highway) for a straight shoot to more glamorous or important places, whether Genoa, San Remo, or Milan.

It is the oddest thing that people respond with recognition when I say my name. "*Tanti Schenone in Recco,*" they reply. Yes, many Schenones here.

They ask if I have *parenti*, relatives, in town. Indeed, my distant *parenti* very well may be here—descendants of Salvatore and Adalgiza's brothers and sisters—but I am not searching for them. I am here instead to see my great-grandparents' city, to walk the streets they walked, to find the center of town and look at the sea from their point of view—the shape of the mountain to the left, the outline of the coast with its cove on the right— the point of view they once understood to be their own.

Aside from the shape of mountain and sea, almost everything else is gone, and this is because Recco was such an important hub of transportation that in 1943 the Americans and British bombed the town to rubble. Local historian Sandro Pellegrini tells me that ninety-five percent of all homes were destroyed, and most of the five thousand inhabitants fled to the hills. Within about ten years, many returned, with new people coming too. The town rebuilt itself in a 1950s style of functional modernity and generic apartment buildings—outfitted with twentieth-century luxuries such as elevators, parking places, and wraparound balconies—that just as well could be in Florida.

Recco in ruins after the Allied bombardment.

"*UNA GIORNALISTA AMERICANA*," calls out Gianni Bissou, leading the way into the kitchen, pushing open the swinging doors. This is Da ö Vittorio, one of Recco's oldest trattorias, established in 1895 and a place where Salvatore and Adalgiza quite possibly might have eaten. Moments ago Gianni and I were sitting at a table talking, near the fire. I was asking him questions about his menu when he jumped up spontaneously and offered, "Come on, let me show you."

"*Una giornalista americana,*" he repeats, and gestures for his chef to come. The chef, who has worked in this kitchen for decades, rapidly opens up refrigerators, sliding out trays of pastas to give me a close-up inspection of the output of his kitchen:

ravioli,

corzetti,

pansotti,

trenette,

troffie . . .

Gianni and his chef rattle them off. It sounds like a song. They seem charmed by their own performance, almost as though they can't believe themselves how ingenious and wonderful those old Ligurians were to have invented these clever pasta shapes—all these various geometries of dough and fillings—and a particular code of sauces to match. It's similar to the way some Genoese people will explain a word in their dialect as though they are letting you into a secret society. *Maggiorana* (marjoram) in Italian, but *persa* in the Genoese language, they explain, smiling with almost mischevious delight, as though to say, "See how wonderfully different it is from Italian! Such curious language."

"*Corzetti,*" exclaims Giovanni, and he picks up a delicate thin coin of pasta, imprinted with a pretty design. This esoteric specialty of Liguria, a culinary woodcut, is created by pressing a carved wooden stamp on dough. Gianni pulls down a ceramic jar filled with the wooden stamps for me to see. These have been collected by his family over the decades.

"And the sauce for *corzetti,*" continues the chef, who pulls out a bowl of parmigiano, marjoram, and crushed pignoli all mixed together. "*Molto semplice!*" ("Very simple!")

Corzetti *stamps.*

"Many uncooked cold sauces in Ligurian cooking," adds Gianni. "Walnut sauce, pesto sauce, *salsa verde.* Very healthful. Very easy to prepare. When I was young, I wanted the heavy foods—ham and lasagne, like in Emilia-Romagna and Tuscany. But now I'm happy with our Ligurian cuisine. People are returning to it. It's full of vegetables and olive oil. It's good for health."

Then we come to a tray of very small pasta called *troffie,* which is essentially the Genoese word for "gnocchi," except these are not round dumplings but rather thin little twists of chestnut dough no more than two inches long. Both Gianni and his chef express a certain reverence for this very local form, which is essentially a Recco version, sometimes diminutively called *troffiette di Recco.* They use the pasta machine to press out sheets of dough for all the other pastas, but not for *troffie.* No, a machine just *can't* make these right. To prove the point, the chef takes a little nut of pasta dough and tries to roll it off the side of his hand into a twist. The dough does not cooperate. It does not twist. No, this is not as easy as it looks.

"I have two old women who make them for me," explains Gianni. "You've got to see these old ladies do it," he says, shaking his head with admiration. "I can call them if you'd like. Perhaps we can go see them. They make it at their house."

Of course I would. Gianni makes arrangements.

When I return at the appointed time, we walk a few doors up from Da ö Vittorio to a small apartment building. During our short walk, Gianni is a trove of local lore and legend, happy to share his knowledge—that Ligurians are a very ancient people, that Genoa was once a huge producer and exporter of dried pasta because of its port, that *fedia* is a very old word for "pasta maker," and *fidellini* the name of a pasta. He adds other small observations. Did I know that the black stone in the tilework is *pietra nera*, a local stone? When I reply that yes, I noticed the stone here because Salvatore was a mason and tile setter, he's impressed. Perhaps because Italy is a country built of stone.

We arrive at an old apartment building, one of the few that survived the bombing, as evidenced by its tall ceilings and ornate details. Gianni rings the bell and we enter a small two-bedroom apartment with a large mahogany table in the dining room and a simple but well-organized kitchen with a table and wooden pasta board atop. The two sisters, Giulia and Meri Senarega, stand in dresses and aprons, wearing matching soft clogs. They are a little flustered and giggly about my visit, but full of hospitality, welcoming me to come see their table and pile of *troffie*. They have been making it for thirty years for Da ö Vittorio, five or six kilos a week—a job they took over from Gianni's mother.

Meri takes a small piece of dough, the size of a marble, and demonstrates rolling the *troffie*. One little piece at a time, each a perfect thin spiral off the side of her hand. And so her pile grows. It is incredibly slow work. And Gianni admits, he doesn't know what he'll do when they are gone as no one could replace them.

The sisters insist we drink some of their homemade walnut liqueur. And so we all take chairs in their dining room and sip this sweet elixir, which they explain has sat forty days in alcohol—achieving wonderful sweet strength. Oh, they make *limoncello* too. Do I like *limoncello*? They giggle again. We spend a lovely hour, chatting, and the sisters quiz me as to whether I know any words in Genoese. When I say *picagetta*—a word cousin Kay taught me for "dishtowel"—they find it hilarious. I tell them that I also know about *prescinsêua*. What kind of

American is this? When I ask if they gather herbs from the hills, they reply *of course!* and describe how they have always collected wild *preboggion* herbs and mushrooms. Each season has its mushrooms, they explain, but they especially love the special mushroom you find in spring. They describe going out in the rain in boots with an umbrella to collect snails too. And with this, one sister retrieves an old hand-written recipe book, from which they give me instruction as though I will go home and cook snails this night. "Wash them first in vinegar to see if they're alive or dead," they advise. "Cook them with celery, carrots, oil, garlic, wine, and tomatoes at the end. They are so good, you can eat fifty of them!" And they giggle some more.

BEING LOCATED in a transportation hub, Recco has long been a town—even in Salvatore and Adalgiza's time—where you could stop and get something decent to eat. But in recent years, Recco has come to vigorously promote itself as "the capital of Ligurian gastronomy." Today, a consortium of restaurants (including Da ö Vittorio) holds tasting events, symposia, and an annual food festival that draws thousands of people to eat the town's signature focaccia. Their particular kind of cheese focaccia—completely different from that which you find in Genoa—has become so famous that when you've barely finished saying the word "Recco," people reply as if on cue, "*focaccia col formaggio.*"

Salvatore and Adalgiza may have eaten here at Da ö Vittorio, but the menu would have been much simpler then, and they would surely be surprised by this cult of "*focaccia col formaggio*" in Recco today. Back then, *focaccia col formaggio* was not on the menu of trattorias, and, according to Gianni, it was mainly associated with the Day of the Dead celebrations, on November 2, when the *panificios* ("bakeries") gave it out for free. Today, it is advertised on trattoria and restaurant signs on every other street. "*Focaccia col formaggio*" is Recco's flag, as though it is from forever ago.

One of the focaccia giants here is a restaurant called Manuelina. Here I order the dish for the very first time. To my surprise, it is like a giant cheese ravioli—two crispy, very thin leaves of dough enclose puddles of an oozing bittersweet fresh cheese called *stracchino*—except it is the size of a small pizza and is eaten in slices. The crust is browned, and the cheese bubbles. It's true that once you eat it you can never forget it. And you really can't get it anywhere else. You have to come here.

Making focaccia col formaggio *in Recco, date unknown.*

People tell me I can see what Recco used to look like if I go up the road a piece to the neighboring fishing village, Camogli, which escaped the Allies' bombs. Here I find a quiet and beautiful old-style waterfront, lined with pastel stone buildings that are works of art to behold—not because of any special architecture but because they are covered in elaborate trompe l'oeil paintings, a local specialty. One building after the next beckons with imaginary windows, colonnades, shutters lifted halfway, and balustrade balconies you are certain you could enter. Even in alleyways, when you know the bricks are not real, you can't help but touch your fingers to the faux grooves and lines of imaginary masonry. It is all just beautiful illusion created with paint on a plain flat surface of stone.

At the waterfront, the beach is empty beneath the gray heavy sky. A cluster of people are gathered along the promontory, gasping and pointing at a giant white cloud, which is hovering suspended over a section of Portofino Mountain and pouring out a patch of white snowy mist. Snow only comes to the coast every few years. It is a remarkable event, and so crowds gather to watch the spectacle.

While I watch, I ask myself, how far in those hills was Salvatore? How remote? How poor? How comfortable was Adalgiza's family, in her seaside town?

I'll never know, of course. The past is irretrievable. We go searching as best we can for the ghost shapes that might lead us back to something real, but illusions and desires play tricks on us, just like those trompe l'oeil paintings on flat, ordinary walls.

SERGIO'S WORDS haunt me. How is it possible to get to the deeper level of origins—my own origins, and the origins of the old recipes too?

In the city of Rapallo, about twenty minutes east of Recco, I meet an earnest young man, Guido Porrati, who first tells me about the chestnut farmer up in the mountains.

I am visiting Guido in the specialty wine shop Parlacomemangi, a family business he runs with his father. In his thirties, Guido is passionate about his business. He speaks excellent English, and jokes that he learned it all from listening to Bruce Springsteen records when he was a teenager.

Located squarely in the stratospheric Riviera of wealth and palatial homes, Guido's shop is pristine—airy and bright, modern in design, all the walls lined with bottles organized according to region. He carries not only wine but many exquisite handmade foods, including cakes and breads and biscuits baked in the mountains by rural women. Guido runs the business with his dad—a former salami producer—and they've got another gorgeous shop down the street filled with meats and cheeses that make your head swirl when you step in the door.

"Of course we don't always agree, my dad and me. But we have a very special relationship," he says with clear admiration. When Guido joined his father in business here, he wanted his own realm of expertise and threw himself into the study of cheese and wine. His job is to go about the countryside, visiting farmers and producers so he can carry the best local products in his stores.

"We have to keep the old traditions alive because of the multinational food corporations. What we have here in Italy is a great history of food. But after World War Two, industrial production came, and families stopped buying real cheese. They immediately forgot what it even is. Now they choose bland round uniform cheeses in the supermarket. Oh yes, we are proud here in Italy that we are the land of the great cheeses and wines, but most people don't really know what they are."

Since the 1990s, a revival has been growing for artisan food products in Italy, as it has in the United States. "Now there's a lot of confusion," Guido notes. "Even the industrial producers are exploiting the old traditions—they tell you they're using artisan methods. But they're not—it's not the same."

I ask him about *prescinsêua*. I tell him I am on a hunt for authenticity. I want to know what is *real*, small-production *prescinsêua*.

"Go to Val d'Aveto," he says, referring to the very northern and remote part of Liguria, high up in the mountains, near a national park. "Up there, you can find farmers who still make *prescinsêua* in copper pots over a fire. It's a very beautiful experience to go see this. It is very beautiful up there. And the cheese is different from the industrial production you had in Genoa. The color is more yellow. And the taste is . . . how do I say? . . . ruder."

Guido has been to the United States and is proud to tell me he's infiltrated the megafood producers, visiting warehouses and supermarkets and producers, as if to explain that he is a spy who has crossed the line and seen the opponent's side. He has even visited the Mondavi wine empire to see for himself the industrial machine that moves millions of bottles each year.

"We here in Italy are in the roots of wine. You are in the future in California. These corporations study and set the fashion. . . . This is *not* what we want to do in Italy."

I admire Guido because he has such clarity about what is authentic and what is not. And it seems that he's never had to compromise. This is his advantage in life, and I hope he gets to keep it.

It is when I am about to leave that Guido mentions the chestnut farmer. He says there's a woman up in the hills who still makes chestnut flour the old way. She grows the chestnuts, picks them by hand, and dries them in a smokehouse for thirty days. "This is very interesting to see—very primitive," he explains. "Not so many people do this anymore. She's not far. Maybe you should go visit her and have a look." He pauses. "But she doesn't speak any English." He leaves it to me to decide about the language barrier. "Would you like me to call?"

I do not hesitate, and Guido picks up the phone. Moments later he returns, saying, "You can go there this afternoon. " He gives me directions and the woman's name: Franca Damico.

The story of pasta overlaps the story of chestnuts. In the old days, peasants who were too poor to afford wheat used the chestnut instead—chestnut for pasta, chestnut in gnocchi, chestnut in bread and cakes and porridges and gruels.

"She's way up in the hills in the Valgraveglia. You'd never find it. But if you drive close to a meeting point, she'll come get you. She says you should call her when you get to the town Conscenti."

Before I leave, I tell him I want to buy a bottle of wine I can bring home to my husband who's working in New York and taking care of our two children while I'm gone. I want something very typical, the real thing, I explain. It doesn't have to be easy. I'm talking to the right person. He suggests a few possibilities. Then a bottle catches his fancy on the rack. It is from the nearby Cinque Terre region—stupefyingly dramatic for its farming terraces built over generations by *contadini* who hauled up thousands of rocks to create a mind-boggling series of ledges where grapes could be planted and grown in the added brightness of sun reflected on the sea. The area is now designated a United Nations World Heritage Site. Since production is so small, Guido tells me that many wines are sold falsely as Cinque Terre. But this is the real thing in his hands. "This will be a wonderful experience," he says with certainty. "But you really will have to wait about three or five years to drink it."

"Three to five years?"

He nods.

I am no vinophile. I have succumbed to plenty of mass-produced California wine. I have never bought an expensive bottle of wine to save for so many years, but I go ahead. As I walk to my car, I try to imagine my husband and me that much older, opening this bottle, finally. And I wonder, by then, would my quests, and obsessions, my wanderings be over? What will those years do to us while the wine is settling into its mature and perfect peak?

IT IS AMAZING in Liguria how quickly the world changes from glamorous resort to isolated rural valley in just a few miles. Franca's farm is in the town of Ne (pronounced "Nay"), not far from the sophisticated urban center of Chiavari, along the coast.

After seven minutes or so on the main road off the highway, I make a turn, and suddenly I am driving amid a brown rural landscape of winter hills, passing run-down stone farmhouses and grim lonely roads. When I arrive at the town of Conscenti—a small square with a few businesses, a bar, and a bus stop—I call Franca on my cell. A quiet female voice fires away traveling instructions and other things I don't understand—except the disturbing fact that she evidently is not coming here to fetch me. Apparently—though it's hard to be sure with my level of Italian—I have much farther to travel to get to a fetchable point. A challenge is in store, as from what I gathered, it involves a long drive up many steep and distant hills.

"*Scusi signore.*" I stop a passerby who is walking along the square. Hand gestures can be invaluable. "*Dov'è Rue de Zerli?*" He obliges, pointing this way and gesticulating straight, and left, so it's clear.

But he looks worried and explains with furrowed brow. "There's nothing up there, you know. Nothing. . . . Are you sure you want to go there?"

"Someone's meeting me."

"Ah," he is satisfied and waves me off.

I advance along the road, farther along the stream, then take a left into a wooded dirt road and up a mountain. It is a long way when you have no idea what to expect or how long it will take. I steer the car along a series of narrow switchbacks, past empty winter vineyards cut down to the nub, through stands of bare chestnut trees. I am prone to a mild fear of heights, and now it seems I am driving up into the sky. The road is icy and extremely narrow, with no guard rails, and the way down is far. The trick, of course, is not to look down. The road goes zigzagging along, and so too does my heart, now exhilarated by the thrill.

Finally I allow myself to peek over the side. I cannot help but gasp. The vista is enormous—several snow-dusted mountains plunge downward from several directions to converge in a valley hundreds of feet directly below me. The terraced slopes are dotted by just a few farmhouses, all beneath the vastness of sky above and empty open space below. My eyes have trouble taking it in. I am not accustomed to so much beauty. And I wonder—as I have often wondered, having been born in New Jersey—how people who live in beautiful places bear it. Do they become habituated to beauty so it stops mattering? Do they even notice?

Finally I see the bell tower just ahead. When I turn in the lot, a small silver car awaits me. Inside is a lovely looking young woman in her thirties. *This is the old chestnut farmer? The keeper of the old rural ways?* I trail Franca's car farther up the hill and park beside her family's large stone house, home to her farm, which is called Rue de Zerli. *Rue* comes from Genoese and refers to a huge tree in this tiny locality. Zerli is not large enough to be considered a town, but this name goes back to the era when these mountains were filled with people and agriculture, and every place, no matter how small, even if just one house, had its own name.

Franca is a delicately built woman wearing jeans, a sweatshirt, and slippers, her hair pulled back in a clip. Soft-spoken and serious, she gives me a tour in a friendly and businesslike way. Here are the olive (*oliva*) trees, she points, and the chestnuts (*castagne*). It is unusual to see both together, as olives need warmth and low altitude, and chestnuts grow at higher levels. But here they both flourish, in a small but special overlapping zone of coexistence.

Since it is winter, Franca can only point to the sleeping rows of earth where she grows heirloom vegetables of the region, an old variety of red onion, a special potato called *quarantina* (recently saved from extinction by a local crusade), and old strains of beans. She also grows grapes for wine, fruit for jam, and herbs in between the crops. No space is wasted. Everything is planted on a sharply terraced hill, and she uses a unique system of rainwater collection that fills narrow canals, then flows down the mountain to irrigate.

On the way to the smoke room, we pass a barn with a large cow and a separate small guest apartment where tourists can come to stay. Agro-tourism, she explains.

By February, the annual chestnut harvest of October is long done, and all there is to see is the empty room where the smoking took place. Franca opens an old green door to a stone outbuilding that is connected to her house, and as we step inside this dark place paneled with wood, the floors covered with ash, the smell of smoke, wood, nuts, and earth-iness is so intense it nearly knocks me straight across the room. At Franca's direction, I look up to see wooden racks above me. This is where the chestnuts are laid out to slowly absorb the smoke from the coals below, some thirty days before getting sent off to be ground to powder.

We step into the main house to a comfortable sitting room where her products are displayed with a sophisticated Rue de Zerli label. She has bottles of olive oil, jarred chestnuts in syrup, marmalades, flour, and bags of dried herbs like rosemary and marjoram. On the back of the chestnut flour, a label describes the hand-harvested and smokehouse method and proclaims that her methods are not simply nostalgia for the past but a vision of the possibilities of the future. Franca has personally signed her name in pen at the bottom of each label.

"My whole life," Franca replies when I ask how long she's been here.

"And the family?"

"Generations and generations." Her mother and uncle work with her, and sometimes her sister, who holds a nursing job at the hospital, helps when she can.

"What kind of work do you do in this business?"

"Everything," she replies. "Even picking the chestnuts."

I don't want to leave Franca and her farm. I don't want to leave this beautiful place. But I have no more questions. I have run out of Italian words. All I can do is purchase some flour and oil, clutch them tightly, and step back out into the cold toward my car.

"I'm not just looking for nostalgia," I tell her. And she nods. It's important to me that she understands this. I'm not sure that I expressed it correctly, so I repeat it.

"*Si. Si. Ho capito, non è nostalgico,*" she replies.

But I'm not sure she believes me.

The valley is darkening in the late afternoon, and the emptiness here in the air feels enormous and astounding.

"Are you happy here?" It is a ridiculous question. How rude. As soon I ask, it I regret it.

Something shifts in her face. "It is hard work," she replies. "But I am happy." Surely I see something darken in her face.

"Are you married?"

She shakes her head.

"Really?"

"Do you see many men around here?" She points to the crops and trees and beautiful tiered land going down down down.

I leave at this moment, aware that I am the urban visitor who comes to see the farm, revels in the impossible beauty, admires nature, the impeccable hard work of the farmer, and then leaves behind the loneliness.

As I drive away, the word "integrity" comes to me—not in the meaning of morality, but in the sense of integration—the integrity of land and people, expressed in small production of high quality. It is beautiful and fragile. It comes at a high price.

AT THE END of the week, snow falls, accumulating several inches and making the front page of the newspaper. Roads are closed in the mountains. I am advised against travel. But there is one last stop I must make before I go home. My journey here began with ravioli in Giuseppina's kitchen, with her family in the mountains. And so it must also end with ravioli in the mountains. I travel back, one more time, away from the glittery Riviera, up into the hills and woods.

My plane will leave the next morning, but now, a final little bowl of Genoese ravioli in meat sauce sits before me—rectangular ravioli, imperfect in shape because they are hand rolled and hand cut, one and a half inch by one inch. Lovely, simple, very much like Giuseppina's, except instead of being in a mountain home, I'm in a mountain trattoria called La Brinca—a rare place where pasta is still made by hand rather than by machine.

"The amount of meat inside depends on the family," explains Sergio Circella. "It also varies from region to region and family to family. You'll find more meat in the ravioli closer to Genoa."

Sergio runs the restaurant with his brother. Yet another family business. He sits across from me in the elegant and rustic dining room surrounded by exposed beams and brick, bottles of wine. Black-and-white photographs of olive-oil production decorate the walls. If it were light out, I'd be able to see the mountains from this table. But it is cold and dark. The windows are black. Because of the extreme temperatures and snow, all reservations have been canceled. Not a soul comes in all night. And this is my great luck. Sergio has time to sit and talk.

"When we began La Brinca in 1987, it was not popular to eat this traditional food out at night. Why would you go out and pay to eat the food of home? People didn't understand. But now it is fashionable. But fashion does not matter to me. I am glad to bring these foods back."

He opens the menu and shows me a page dedicating La Brinca to the memory of "Nonna." "In Genoa," he notes, "the women are very strong."

The recipes come, more or less, from his mother and grandmother's kitchen. And most of the foods—the fruits and vegetables and meats and cheeses and flour and wine—come from this valley and this town of Ne.

"The first real road didn't arrive until 1960," Sergio tells me. "When they built that road, the people here celebrated with ravioli." He smiles. "Ravioli is the food of the *festa*."

Sergio is about forty years old, and like the others I've met, he speaks slowly and takes his time with me. I'm not used to this remarkable calm. Everyone I know is in a terrible rush, especially me.

As it turns out, Sergio Circella, Sergio Rossi, Guido Porrati, and Franca Damico all know one another, and somehow I have fallen into a network of gentle and conscientious Genoese people—people my father would compliment by calling "soft"—people who do not see themselves merely as business owners, but as caretakers of culture with the mission of being a link between past and future. And this is why they are so willing to talk to me. It's not surprising that they know one another. What is surprising is only that I have traveled so far, needing to find them.

"Ligurian cooking is really a cuisine of the mountains," Sergio confides. He says this more than once so that I will take note and remember. "Fish is not so important—we use mainly small, poor fish, because the big fish went to the market." And then he continues with what others have said. It is a cuisine of vegetables and aromatic herbs, only a little meat—some rabbit, some chicken, some veal, but not much.

"And people still gather herbs?"

"Yes, some old people still go out into the hills and do this. Now is the time, you know, right now after the snow melts. You want to go between Christmas and March, before the herbs begin to flower and turn bitter."

I ask more about the ravioli. I tell him that in my family of Genoese descendants, the meat is raw. "Have you ever heard of such a thing around here?"

"Absolutely not."

"And what about a ravioli press?" I draw him a sketch of Tessie's grid.

He shakes his head. "Never heard of it. My brother makes all the pasta. He uses a checkered pin."

The prospect of such Americanizations (I dare not mention the cream cheese) brings back bad memories for Sergio.

"I think the worst ravioli I ever ate in my life was in Palm Springs." He shakes his head.

"What was so bad about them?"

"I believe they were made with cigarettes," he replies.

We laugh, and as my questions continue, Sergio calls for more dishes from the kitchen to illustrate the different points. When a bowl of chestnut gnocchi made with Franca's flour arrives at the table, the sweet smoky flavor rises up to my face. It is the same smell I sniffed in my own bag of flour. Now it lies beneath a sauce of pesto made just a tad sour by *prescinsêua* to balance the sweetness of the chestnut, Sergio explains.

I tell him I met Franca and saw her smoke room.

"All through these woods, you can find little smokehouses from the old days. It is interesting how our people lived."

Next comes a little bowl of soup—*lettuga ripiena*—a few delicate little green dumplings floating almost ethereally in a golden light meat broth. Inside the lettuce skins are small gems of flavored ground meat; beef, veal, garlic. The effect is a kind of poetry.

"Stuffed lettuce is all over Liguria, but in great variation. In Genoa, they use a little tomato sauce. Some make very big stuffed lettuce. But for us, they must be very small." I barely tear myself away from the bowl to hear him and nod.

I'm full and not interested in dessert. But Sergio mentions *latte dolce*, and before I know it, a plate of small golden cubes is put before me. Fried cream, he explains. "You never had this either?" It is fried in olive oil with just a faint touch of lemon. "Not too much lemon," he cautions.

Details. Specificity. Not too much lemon. Surrounded by these mountains and the people and their foods, I feel suddenly certain that the authentic is possible—at least for these people here who have not left.

Before I leave, Sergio tells me something else interesting.

"Here in Ne, we have a big cemetery."

I raise my eyebrows, and he continues.

"A lot of people emigrated to Argentina or America. So many left and never came back—at least not when they were alive. Many requested that when they died, they wanted to have their bodies sent back here to be buried. This is why we are a very little village, yet a big cemetery."

CHAPTER 15

Esoteric

Y OU'VE GOT TO BE kidding me," mutters Lou. "Oh, Jesus Christ,
Laura, you've got to be kidding me."

We are standing in his kitchen, and he has his nose in the bag of
Franca's chestnut flour, which I have brought directly to his kitchen. It
is ours to share, and we've got a lot of gnocchi to make. I have also
brought him Franca's light golden olive oil, and a bag of dried Genoese
porcini, so big and white they seem almost fresh.

So begin our gnocchi forays. Hot potatoes, riced, then spread out on
a tray to cool.

We try it with egg. We try it without. We try it with hard flour. We try
it with soft flour. We try it with a combination of soft and hard. We want
light dumplings. We try and try again until we get it. We roll out ropes
of dough and argue over size. (Lou makes his bigger. I like them small.)
After we cut them into little pieces, we imprint them so they can catch
sauce. Lou likes his imprinted with the tines of a fork. I like mine with
a thumbprint—as I had at La Brinca.

And we fuss over how much egg. Lou will not give up the egg. But I
see that in my old Genoese cookbooks, there are no eggs. So I hold out,
though this kind of dough is much harder to work.

We share the results with our spouses and kids, who like them all just
fine and give us their votes until they can stand gnocchi no more. Only

when we have the basic recipe down do we try replacing half the flour with Franca's ethereal chestnut. Our favorite, of course. We cover it with pesto that Lou's wife, Susan, made the previous summer and froze for future occasions. Beautiful, all of it.

But there is a serious problem. I have only brought back one ten-ounce bag of flour. This precious stuff won't last forever.

We begin calling specialty shops, but there is no such thing as smoked chestnut flour here in New Jersey or even in New York. We have found unsmoked chestnut flour in a local supermarket, but we don't like this very much at all.

Lou goes up to the ethnic market in nearby Paterson where the neighborhoods are poorer, the streets more dangerous, but the food more full of variety and quirks and life on account of the many immigrants living there. He locates some dried chestnuts in a market and calls me by cell phone, as though on a military mission, to let me know of his success. Back at home, he soaks them until they are tender, cooks them on the stove for about a half hour, then runs them through a meat grinder. They come out something like dry potatoes. (And now it's easy to see how, when the potato came from America to northern Italy, Ligurians quickly and vigorously embraced it. Yes, they were hungry and potato gives a high yield, but also its mealy texture must have reminded them of the chestnut they had lived with forever.)

Lou calls me, very excited. "Laura. I think I'm on to something, something very esoteric." Esoteric is our joke for these obsessions. "You've got to smell this liquid I reserved from the chestnuts." He brings it to my house. It smells a bit like Franca's smokehouse.

It is a great relief to Lou that we can survive once Franca's chestnut flour is gone. But for me, it is an inferior substitution for what came from the hills of Rue de Zerli—that astounding place that does not leave my mind. I don't know how this chestnut of his was smoked. I don't know where it was grown. It lacks the soul and the place.

But I have another, far more serious problem. When I mix my flour and egg and make a nice dough at home, I discover that I cannot replicate what Giuseppina did. I cannot roll it out on a pin, no matter what I do. I go back again and again in my mind trying to see Giuseppina's hands, but the particulars escape me. My dough sticks to the pin. I cannot get it to slap against the board. I cannot get it to grow to a thin transluscent circle. Indeed, it hardly grows at all. My visit with Giuseppina was just too quick, too fleeting. I just didn't get it.

I share my sense of defeat with Lou. "Ah, come on. Why do you worry so much?" he asks. "The pasta machine works great. And when will you get yourself a KitchenAid mixer? Oh, you've got to get one—the professional kind. These things are amazing. I just made a bread this morning and a batch of ravioli. They both came out great."

I do not answer but instead sigh loudly.

Later that day Lou stops by my house and drops off a new tool he's invented. It's a gnocchi imprinter—a small block of maple wood, marked with thin grooves like the tines of a fork. He's made a few and given them to his sons and a couple of friends. "These are for the esoteric few."

CHAPTER 16

Ravioli I Have Known

M Y LIFE WAS NOT BUILT amid the dramatic beauty of mountains cascading down to sea. I have no memory of chestnuts and their sweet starchy taste. But I was raised on another different kind of beauty—this intense green all around. Deep green above us on the midsummer trees, lighter green below us on the lawn, old earthy forest green in the yew bushes and overgrown hemlocks that wrap around our houses. Green plus red. New Jersey's big beefsteak tomatoes sliced on the plate with salt and pepper, the sweet corn on the cob—and the pungent flavor of fresh bluefish, caught in the Atlantic along the Jersey shore by my uncle, and cooked on the gas grill on the porch by my father, wrapped in foil, the skin sticky and sweet, the dark meat full of ocean.

Somewhere in my inner life there is an eternal green summer evening in New Jersey. It is easy to go there again because it never leaves. I am the child in the 1970s, looking out the window of our house. I see my father's oldest brother, Uncle Louie. He's in our driveway again, moving a few pieces of pipe and fittings from his truck to my father's, which is always left unlocked for this purpose. It's the usual clatter of things, and then the loud *thwonk* of the truck door as it's slammed shut. My uncle is here almost every night doing the same thing, year after year.

In my eternal green summer evening, it is always Thursday night, and that means Uncle Louie is going to walk up the cement path and come inside, because Friday is pay day, and we get ours the night before. Sure enough there is the sound of knuckles on the door, the perfunctory knock and turn of the knob. He's standing inside on the landing, calling up the stairs. We leave the backdoor unlocked too.

"Come on in, Lou!" my mother calls from somewhere. She tries to please. She will offer coffee, as it is always on the stove and ready in a percolator pot.

Pay in one hand, thick envelopes filled with cash—and a piece of bluefish in the other, caught at the Jersey shore. My uncle Louie is a fisherman, like his Genoese dad of the same name. One envelope for my dad, who is a foreman in the field. A couple of envelopes for him to give to "the men" on the job the next day—all plumbers from the union hall, all on union wage. After our house, Uncle Louie will probably do the whole thing again—pipes, pay, bluefish—at Uncle Richard's house. He is a foreman too.

At a young age, I figure out that it is a hierarchy all organized—quite obviously—by age. Grandma Schenone is oldest, so she's president. Uncle Louie is the next oldest, so he's the vice president, the son who stepped in after his father died. That means he gets to work inside in Hoboken, alongside Grandma, running things—and also making these Thursday rounds, handing out money to his two brothers. Next in age comes my father and then Uncle Richard. They always work outside in the field on the plumbing jobs, in the fine weather, in the freezing cold weather, in the humid heat, and in the rain. They do the work, with the men. There is a sister too, Aunt Mary. But she's a woman, so she's got a different kind of place in the whole thing but a place for sure—and she's had some hard luck, childhood polio. She's divorced, raising three kids alone in an apartment next to a river that has a tendency to overflow when it rains really hard and floods her apartment ankle deep so she has to pack up the kids and flee—usually to Grandma's house.

My sisters and I—even when we are very young—have our own place in the hierarchy, and we know it well. Our place is to respect them all. It means that whenever Uncle Louie comes, whenever a grandmother or uncle or aunt or second cousin steps into that house, we are to drop whatever we are doing and present ourselves at the door to give a proper welcome. No rough Hoboken manners for us. We are the three girls with good home training and fine manners, the social skills you need in order to move up in life.

No matter that Uncle Louie, or whoever, is there almost every night.

No matter that our house is a center of traffic with people always passing through.

We spend years getting up and going to the door, showing respect.

❧❧

Family is the religion we are raised in, along with Catholicism. We girls go to Catholic school, we sing at mass, we do our confessions and penance and Holy Communion in lines shuffling up to the altar where the priest mumbles "bodyofchristbodyofchristbodyofchrist," saying "Amen" as we've been taught and thanking God for our daily bread, though we also know that it is the family business that puts it there on the table, along with the roof over our head, and the clothes on our backs.

And so on this summer night in the middle of the 1970s, I do what I have been taught and go to greet my uncle respectfully.

Both of my uncles are men of few words, men who frighten me a little. I think my uncles like us girls well enough. And I like them well enough. I kiss Uncle Louie on the cheek, and he smiles at me. My uncle is as friendly as he can be. Yes, he appreciates these greetings.

"Hiya, Babe." He's got a gravelly voice, which is either the Hoboken in his throat or the result of cigarettes.

He turns his attention to my dad, who takes the envelopes, and to my mother, who takes the bluefish, and I slink away when they talk about tomorrow's job.

Only when I'm older do I ask my dad more questions about who's got what. He explains the concept of "shares," how the business is all divided up.

It is only many years later that I will comprehend the design of my grandmother's controlling shares that can never be overthrown, never be overridden.

These shares are the family legacy. Adalgiza passed ravioli and rolling pins, recipes, and cooking tools down the family tree, woman to woman. But we are descended from her son Louie, and the business he left behind. This is our story instead, this is our culture, this clatter of pipe moving from truck to truck night after night.

And so it goes for decades.

IN MY INNER LIFE, there is always Sunday mass—no matter how many decades now I haven't gone—and there is always Sunday afternoon when family is assembled, and grandmothers come to visit.

"What a fancy car! My lans. What did you need such a fancy car for?" Grandma Schenone asks.

The 1974 Pontiac Grandville sits gleaming in the driveway—our first brand-new car, ever. It's silver with a maroon roof and special hubcaps, my father's careful choice. It is a gorgeous car, a stylish luxury car. It's got an enormous V8 engine, and we are all thrilled to take joyrides and be seen in it around town. So smooth, so plush.

Grandma Schenone goes to mass every morning at Our Lady Queen of Peace Church, and on Sunday she goes visiting afterward. She drives her modest little car from house to house, wearing her flouncy skirts, her practical cardigans and gum-soled shoes. She flutters like a butterfly from daughter to son to son. Family is everything to her, she says. She hugs us and giggles, happy to see us and to prove it. But you'd better watch out, because she's got a comment for everything and everyone, especially my mother and father.

"Why bake a cake when you can pick one up?"

"Why percolate the coffee? Just make instant."

"Those muscles are getting too big," Grandma Schenone warns, pointing to my father's biceps. All that running since he turned thirty, all that weight lifting and dieting is starting to show. Now he's got a bulky chest and arms. She points to the bottles of vitamins in the kitchen cabinet, shaking her head. "What a waste of money!"

And when my mother is working and going to school at night, she mentions Uncle Louie's wife. "Oh, Ann is always there for her kids. She's always helping them with homework. It's so beautiful. Six kids," she sings with her trill-filled voice.

Provoking people is a kind of intimacy for her—the way she gets close to you. For Grandma, arguing is fun, a sort of recreation—and not just on Sunday visits but on holidays too, when she gets louder and louder at the table, over silly things, unimportant things, never relenting. The topic doesn't matter really. It can be about politics or the church, or the best brand of bread. It is the provocation that matters most—and the volley back and forth across the table.

"What do you know, you rotten kid!?" she'll blurt out, smiling—and then suddenly not smiling.

Her sons often take the bait. They show love by teasing too, by joking, by trading funny insults, by talking tough.

"Cut it out or I'll show you what's what—right in the mouth."

Then they burst into laughter. It's all a joke, of course. Sort of.

"Bullshit!" A thundering voice. A man's hand bangs the dining-room table, making the coffee cups quiver. And just when you think there's going to be dishes flying or maybe a fist fight, more laughter erupts.

Or maybe not. Once in a while it goes too far and someone stomps out. "Marcia, pack up the kids. We're leaving." And my mother does as told and gathers us up, and we all leave abruptly—until the next Sunday when we gather again.

I am a child, and I love my grandmother even if she is tough and the only person I ever saw make my mother cry (that one time when my mother went storming up to her bedroom and slammed the door saying she wouldn't come out, but then Grandma Schenone came up and apologized). My grandmother, after all, loves to have fun: she's got a big merry laugh. She bangs the pots on the porch at midnight when we stay over on New Year's Eve. She jumps the waves at the beach with the little kids. On the nights she visits, she comes upstairs into our bedrooms and sings old-fashioned songs like "April Showers" or "Me and My Shadow," and rubs our backs with her calloused hands, which still feel quite nice. "Plumber's hands," she says. "Hoboken hands."

Grandma and me at the Jersey Shore.

I HAVE WONDERED many years now about the essence of the problem with family, particularly, my father's family. I suppose you might say it was the death of his father that sent everything wrong. Or you might blame it on my harsh grandmother and her life of poverty. Or perhaps maybe you'd have to look hard at my father and say that the single thing, the single essence of the problem, was that he was different and didn't fit in with them to begin with.

He always has to do things his own way. That's my father. He's got ideas about the way things should be, and who knows where the hell he got them. Muscles and vitamins are one thing. His looks are another. His meticulous dress and style—those fine blazers and silk ties, spit-shined shoes, a gold ring on the pinky finger. There is his way of talking—more soft-spoken than his brothers, more reserved. Then there's the flashy cars, the BMW motorcycle, the jazz music, the scotch on rocks (instead of beer). Even the sauna he puts in our basement, like we're some kind of wealthy people. (And why not? He's a plumber and knows how.) Oh, so many ways he shows it—shows that he is different, that he thinks he's better.

As my father gets older, he becomes more quiet and reserved. He is aloof to them, and this is perhaps the most difficult of all, this aloofness of my father.

Add to it all a wife like my mother. She's different too, different from the rest of them. In her high school yearbook, she was voted Miss Sophistication and stated her career plans as choreographer. Imagine. She doesn't yell or interrogate others. She'd have a hard time saying no to anything anyone wants. Oh, yes, she's soft. But she holds herself tall and says what she wants, with the verbal accuracy of an expert marksman. She's got her opinions, and worse, she's got an immaculate house. She went through so much extreme bother for us girls, it drove Grandma Schenone crazy: the braiding of three heads of hair each morning, the dance lessons, the music lessons, the sports teams, the nice clothes. My mother shares with my father this desire for a more stylish kind of life where there is respect and higher standards.

How my parents will ever go about getting their better life is unclear, because the life they want is better than what Grandma Schenone believes they should have.

Better than what she'll give them.

Down at the shop in Hoboken, it all becomes quite obvious early in the marriage when my mother applies for a Bloomingdale's charge card. Bloomingdale's calls the family shop to confirm my father's employment and income. My mother, long oppressed by her in-laws' judgment, tells the story of how word gets around the family.

Bloomingdale's?

Bloomingdale's!

It was a very high-class store back then, and therefore out of Frances Schenone and her children's league.

"What the heck are you doing getting a charge card from Bloomingdale's?" Uncle Louie and Grandma Schenone ask my father. They can't believe it.

They question everything.

"Why are you taking a week off for a honeymoon? Just take a few days."

"Why are you taking a day off when Marica's having a baby?"

Despite this, my parents never stop believing in this religion of family and raising us in it. And perhaps it is this that's the strangest thing. Sometimes they try to explain to me, "Back then, people didn't have so many choices." But I could tell that it was not entirely safe. Conflicts among us children, our own feuds, betrayals, and alliances, trickled down and rose and fell.

My dad thinks the family will go on forever. Our lives overlap with theirs in many ways, not just business. On the Fourth of July, my grandmother gathers us all in her green yard, where she is in her glory, surrounded by her sons and daughter and fourteen grandchildren. On the side of the house, my cousin Cheryl and I sit under the canopy of a tree and play our guitars, or we hide in the closets of Grandma's house waiting to be found, then shriek and run away giggling, bounding outside past the slam of the screen door.

Out back the adults sit on their lawn chairs in a circle on the grass, mint in their drinks snatched from a bunch growing in the yard. Grandma Schenone laughs loudly, as the long summer day fades. My dad sits on top of the picnic table in the darkening air and takes one of the guitars onto his knee, and Cheryl and he and I sing the standards—"Pennies from Heaven," "Satin Doll," "Blue Moon," and Gershwin's "Summertime," always "Summertime," the standard song of our lives. We belt them out, as we were born with fine voices, it makes us happy. We listen to one another, making harmonies, taking parts. Then the mosquitoes get so bad we all go inside.

It is this faith in family that gives birth to my mother's elaborate Christmas Eve parties. When she first shares her plans, she paints a remarkable vision. She has a certain dreamy tone in her voice and a look in her eyes, as though she's a sculptor seeing the spirit in the stone that no one else can see.

"We'll have wonderful food. We'll have music. We'll have candles lit throughout the house. We'll wear something special. And we'll invite all your cousins and aunts and uncles. The neighbors. Everyone will be welcome."

It sounds great to all of us. We girls believe in my mother's ambitions, her ability to lift us all up above the ordinary, with an enormous labor of domestic grace, cooking, and party making.

The plan does not go over so well with Grandma Schenone, for it conflicts with her own preference for informality and her dominion over her sons.

"Oh, I don't think so," she says. "I don't know if it's a good idea. Louie's got to put together toys on Christmas Eve for all those six kids. They've got wrapping to do." She's got her own tradition of inviting her sons to casually drop by, late on Christmas Eve, while the wives stay home with the kids abed.

My mother won't be deterred. She replies, quite calmly, "Well, maybe everyone can get their wrapping done by the night before."

And that's that. She gets on the phone and starts inviting.

My parents love a party: they are eaters, drinkers, and talkers; they are singers and dancers. They will push aside the furniture and do the cha cha cha. And so they set forth. No detail is spared. No effort is too much, and the food is at the center of it all.

My mother's appetizers feature pure 1970s Americana, with all its confidence in food technology, big brands, and razzle-dazzle form. My sisters and I cut hundreds of slender celery and carrot sticks and artfully arrange them around a bowl of Lipton onion soup sour-cream dip. My mother expertly hollows out a round loaf of pumpernickel bread and fills it with a creamy orange dip made with Kraft Velveeta cheese and beer. She whips a light tuna mouse with Jell-O brand gelatin to create a stately molded form. There's more, too: roasted red pepper puree, warm broccoli and cheese served with nachos. Everything is elegantly displayed.

My father does the drinks—scotch, vodka, wine, liqueurs too. A platter of bottles and glasses, on the buffet. All is ready. He takes the drink orders as aunts and uncles and cousins arrive, then puts another colored log on the fire. We do not have a big house, but everyone squeezes in—many dozens of us—and the cousins run up and down the stairs from room to room or even outside in the dark on the porch for a bit of Christmas Eve air and night sky and stars.

At dinner, the main course is Italian, of course, but not Genoese. We are not that kind of Italian anymore. We are not my grandmother's Irish or German either. We are American, with an Italian bent. No one knows how to make those old Genoese dishes anymore, the salted anchovies or ravioli, the *pandolce*, the roasted chestnuts. No one would want them. True, my mother makes Aunt Tessie's *torta*, that old beloved standby. But the rest of the meal is the Italian food of American technology and industrial production; sausage and peppers, and lasagne made with thick layers of meat and ricotta cheese, a pan of chicken baked in oil, a long loaf of buttered bread sprinkled with garlic powder.

The desserts are the showstoppers. My mother puts out a cheesecake, a red velvet cake, a coffee toffee pie, a pound cake, cookies, brownies, and more. It is abundance and sweetness beyond imagining.

Perhaps she is envisioning something like the great southern Italian feasts—famous in Italian homes all over New Jersey—those Sicilian and Neapolitan families who fry seven kinds of fish for Christmas Eve, a sacred night. Except we do it without the fish. And we do it without being southern Italian. With the exception of the *torta*, the food has no direct connection to us. But this does not matter. We all agree on the meanings—that it is good, that it is right.

And it is a success. Candles are lit. Spirits are high. The cousins run up and down the three floors of the house. Yes, I'd say it is a huge success, though I can't really know for sure because I'm my mother's daughter and quite prejudiced. The event is repeated year after year, and it grows bigger each time. Cousins get older and invite friends and then boyfriends or girlfriends. And for us a fragile happiness with family comes forth each year on this night—the sort of thing you never forget.

Though we girls help, though my father helps, my mother largely carries this event off alone, even though she has a job and punches a time clock. First she starts off as the "intermittent claim taker" at the Hackensack Unemployment Office. Later, she moves her way up, as an administrator in an engineering firm. At night, she's getting a college degree, course by course. But she bakes and cooks weeks in advance for this *festa*, freezing lasagne and cakes. She does this for the sake of family. She does this for us. She does it for herself. And it nearly kills her each year. When the doorbell first rings, she's never ready, a sweaty mess, just jumping into the shower. But a half hour later when she comes down shiny bright in her dressy clothes and made-up face, with her best jewelry on, she is ready to preside as hostess.

After the cousins and aunts and grandmothers and cousins leave at midnight or one in the morning, my mother cleans up and does dishes until 4:00 A.M. Then she finishes wrapping any remaining gifts and sets out the presents from Santa in three piles. Perhaps she lays her head down for an hour or so, before we're all up again, ready for Christmas morning.

IT WAS worth it to her—all these efforts from the kitchen.

When I grew up, men made the real money. Men set the laws. Men were prone to sudden moves and irrational acts of authority.

But in the kitchen, we women had safety—a world that revolved on its own axis. We had our own language there, our own way of telling jokes and stories. Our own way of existing, a form of survival, all hidden within simple acts, like peeling carrots or walking to the oven.

Favors were passed between us. Secrets never to be told. Underground economies of money given and borrowed and paid back. "Shhhhh. Don't tell anyone." At times, the men became almost inconsequential— as long as they were not around, of course. As soon as my father's truck pulled in the driveway or we glimpsed my uncle walking up the path, we jumped. We scurried. We made like we'd been dusting or doing homework. Our kitchen life became invisible once again. Not a trace.

There always comes a moment when mothers go their own way and daughters walk alone, scattering toward the future in whatever direction they must, like seeds blown off the flowers of a tree. For me, that moment took place along the cement path to the garage when I was sixteen years old. I had told my mother, in these coming-of-age years, that her relationship with my father was unjust. Why was he the boss? Why did he get to go out and have fun with his friends on a Friday night, while she always stayed home taking care of us, working until late? Why couldn't she go out with her friends? I was a question asker even then.

She listened carefully but did not answer me. Then one day, she simply said, "Your father is out in the garage. He wants to talk to you."

And so there I was walking along that cement path in a perfect straight line, next to the weedless grass. I left the world of the kitchen, the sound of running water and clanging pots and endless talking. I went out to the garage, which was my father's place—well organized with the tools hung in place, his ropes neatly looped, paint cans neatly stacked, motorcycle up on its kickstand, a weight-lifting bench. In my father's world, there were never enough words for me, never enough signals of reassurance, never enough explanations, and so I was always nervous.

"Mom says you wanted to see me?"

"Yep," he replied, and made me stand there a good long time while he polished the wheels on his motorcycle.

"Laura," he finally began. "I hear you've had some complaints about my relationship with your mother." His voice was calm and sure. Another lengthy silence. The wheel came shiny bright.

"Well, I wanted to tell you that it isn't really for you to say." He paused again. "You know, Laura. You never really know what goes on between two people," he added. And in the finality of his tone, I know that this was all there would be, and that I was free to leave.

Later, when trying to give my father the benefit of the doubt, I'd reflect on the truth of his statement. No, you never did know what went on between two people. No, it wasn't for me to say. But humiliation burned in my teenage breast for years. I felt ambushed and betrayed by them both. On the walk back up the cement path to the house, I knew with certainty that I would have my own life, that I would leave home and walk another way.

※

WHEN IT all ends, our parents never tell us the details. They never tell us what happens. The mean things that are said. The way things are divided up. How they all say good-bye.

All we are told is that it all started—and it all ended—because my father asked for change.

What kind of change? He wants more say. He has a vision: lucrative private jobs, not just public work in schools and hospitals and munici-pal buildings. A more ambitious business. Maybe some projects in all those condominiums going up on Hoboken's waterfront, because by now it's the end of the 1980s. My dad is in his forties. He thinks this is time, finally, to come forth, to ask for what he wants. He has waited this long.

We know there are meetings, first around Grandma Schenone's kitchen table. But it doesn't get better. They are mad he's making these demands, and they are mad that he's never happy with what he's got. Always different. Always better.

Then come the lawyers and mediators. But still, the situation doesn't improve.

Grandma Schenone is at a precipitous moment—seventy-eight years old, holding on all these years. But now, when it is time to make deci-sions, she begins to fade. What is she to do?

All is in turmoil. The business and two sons allied in one camp. One son—my father—alone in another.

Somewhere in those rooms, wherever it is they meet, my sisters and I know a disaster is happening. We are young women now, living our own lives. *This isn't just about business*, we say to one another knowingly, with head-shaking comments about repression and the need for ther-apy. The truth is we know nothing, except that it is all coming loose.

And then there is another meeting, and this is the last one. My father is out of the family business after thirty years. And out of the family too.

And when my father runs into his brothers or nephews on the street, they turn their backs and walk the other way.

———

NOW MY PARENTS spend Christmas Eve by themselves, while we girls spend it elsewhere with whomever we want.

On Christmas Day we gather round the table, and my mother serves enormous meals as though extra people are about to walk in the door. These are the years that the Christmas dinner falls into confusion and store-bought ravioli.

AFTER THE BREAKUP, Grandma Schenone regrets what happened. Her two sons continue the business, but my father is alone. He is starting his own business, but it is tough going. He goes back to school and takes some courses for contractors, then begins bidding jobs.

Her sons do not speak. She realizes her sons will never speak again in her lifetime. And then she begins to lose her mind. It happens slowly at first, the way dementias often do. But then it comes more quickly. She repeats herself. She cannot retain her memories. She cannot hold on. She gets confused. The present and the past blur together and then fly away through a hole in her mind. You tell her something, and she asks about it again. My uncle decides she cannot drive anymore and removes the battery from her car. Soon after, she's in a nursing home.

Her dementia is not a peaceful fading away. It is angry and panicked. She calls 911. She gets into fights. She has to be restrained by the nurses. She gets moved from one home to the next because she is too hard to handle.

One time, my father and I go to visit her after some of these awful events. We sit on the couches in the nursing home parlor. She's clutching a cardigan tightly around her arms. "Mom, have you been causing trouble again?" my dad teases. "Going out late, getting out of control?"

Grandma Schenone is now eighty-six years old. I have a two-year-old son.

"Oh, yeah, yeah," she answers and shakes her head. She looks worried, and her eyes dart from side to side as though looking for something she has forgotten, something she wanted. We talk for an hour or so, going over the same things as she repeats and repeats. When it's time for us to go, she walks us to the elevator to say good-bye. A nurse comes over, putting her big square body in front of my grandmother, telling her, "You can't go any further."

And then it gets horrible.

"I'm just trying to walk my son and granddaughter to the car!" my grandmother insists.

The nurse gives a nod to the front desk. Two additional nurses appear.

"It's just my son."

We tell her not to worry, to please go inside. We'll see her again soon. But she won't listen. She's intent on following us. They pull her back. She tries to fight them.

"I want to walk them to the car!"

"It's okay," we reassure her. "We'll see you soon." But it's not okay. Another nurse is advancing quickly to help pull her back. We must leave.

It is on the way out into the sunshine that I see my dad is crying with me. He's dressed this day in an olive sweater and olive wool slacks. It is a bright and beautiful October day. The leaves are blazing gold and the sun shines hard on the asphalt parking lot.

He says nothing, just pulls his keys out of his pocket. We are silent. Just before he opens the car door, we hear a sound above us, an imperative knocking on glass. We look up, and there's Grandma Schenone in the full-length window, waving and smiling in her flowered skirt, held at the elbow by a nurse who was kind enough to figure out a way for Grandma to see us off. We wave back and smile and blow kisses, then get into the car.

There will be no peaceful ending to her life. My father puts the key in the ignition and we drive away.

CHAPTER 17

All the World's a Dumpling

T O MAKE TEN SERVINGS: take half a libra of aged cheese, and a little fatty cheese, and a libra of fatty pork belly or veal teat, and boil until it
comes apart easily . . . take some well-chopped herbs, and pepper, cloves,
and ginger . . . make a thin sheet pasta and encase the mixture . . . these
ravioli should not be larger than half a chestnut; cook them in capon
broth, or good meat broth that you have made yellow with saffron . . ."

I look up from my cubby in the New York Public Library and realize
that the sky has turned from day to night while I have been trekking my
way back through the centuries via ravioli recipes. I'd begun the day with
"authentic" Genoese recipes for fillings made of lean meats mixed
together with borage, cheese, eggs, and offal—udders and brain. Now I'd
made it all the way back to the fifteenth century. I put my head back down
to the page at hand in *The Art of Cooking*, by a Renaissance man named
Maestro Martino.

"Let the ravioli simmer for the time it takes to say two Lord's
Prayers."

Two Lord's prayers?

With one eye on the clock above the door, I whisper the "Our Father"
two times.

In English it takes only fifty seconds. But then again, these are half-
a-chestnut-size ravioli—quite small—and they would cook up very

quickly. Yes? No? Maybe. Fifty seconds seems awfully short. With old recipes, it's hard to know.

Maestro Martino (what a wonderful name) was the so-called first celebrity chef. He was not only a good cook but a good writer too, with a flare for lovely recipe titles like "heavenly summertime sauce," "melon pottage," and "elderflower fritters." I could go on and on. Garnished turnips, golden sops, hemp-seed milk soup, a tart made with squab or pullet, snails, eel *torte*, and July custard. This combination of Renaissance beauty and strange meats makes him exotic and exciting, but I try to shake myself free of his seduction. A stack of cookbooks beckons me, and it is a long journey yet.

My question is this: How far back can I go?

How far back can I trace our family recipe from Adalgiza to antiquity? When did ravioli begin?

Earlier that day, I sat in the cool hush of the rare books room, awaiting a 1610 copy of *Opera dell'arte del cucinare* by Bartolomeo Scappi, personal chef to two popes. When the enormous old book finally arrived, it was hard not to be overwhelmed by its sheer girth—some one thousand recipes on brittle pages with woodcut images of cooking tools and iron pots suspended by chains over a flaming hearth. I turned the pages with light fingertips, so they wouldn't crack. Despite my struggle to read the archaic Italian, I could discern many ravioli-type dishes in Scappi, most by a name of tortellini. There was *torteloni* made with capon, tortellini made with pork belly, tortellini of herbs, *tortelletti* of fresh peas or beans. Stuffed pastas all of them. And many *torte* too. (Of course, it is no coincidence that the names are nearly the same: tortellini and *torta* come from the same family, indicating that perhaps ravioli descends from pie. It is a good theory. The fillings are often quite the same.)

I pushed on backward to the Italian Middle Ages, *Libro del cocino* (from a fourteenth-century anonymous Tuscan), then *Libro per cuoco* (by an anonymous Venetian, about the same time). Again, many ravioli. But a funny thing is happening for sure along this backward journey. The meaning of the word *ravioli* is changing, slip sliding out of control. True, some ravioli are boiled and look just like the ones I make today. But some are fried. Some are entirely different, made of nothing but *ripieno*, wearing no pasta wrapper at all—sent straight into lard like a fritter, or dropped "nude" directly into boiling water or broth. It is a confusing mess. I had believed all along that ravioli belonged to the family of pasta or perhaps pie. But now, I'm wondering what to make of ravioli that is obviously a fritter or a dumpling. From where do *these* ravioli descend?

What a mystery this all is.

One more book awaits me on my desk: *Dal liber de coquina,* an aristocratic cookbook, from much farther south in Italy than the others I've read, probably from the Court of Angevin in Naples, probably the thirteenth century.

I crack open *Dal liber,* written in Latin and translated into Italian, and I begin to search. But before I get beyond the first page, I am interrupted by the dreaded sound of the security guard opening the door to the study space where I work. All the other writers and readers have gone home. I am the only one left, and he is, most annoyingly, flickering the light switch.

"Closing, five minutes," he calls gruffly.

Naturally, I ignore him and continue.

After this *Dal liber de coquina,* my backward trek through the cookbooks of Italy will hit a wall—the eight-hundred-year silence of the so-called Dark Ages. The next recipe collection from the Italian peninsula will come from the ancient Romans, a collection named after a gourmand named Apicus, compiled sometime in the late fourth or early fifth century. I already know that there are no ravioli recipes in there—unless you count a pig baked in pastry as a ravioli.

Sure enough, in *Dal liber de coquina,* I find "Dei raviolis." It begins "To make ravioli, you take the pig belly and its liver. . . ."

I do not get a chance to read it, as now the security guard has returned and is advancing toward me.

"Closing," he repeats, and walks up to my cubby to stand there at my side, ensuring I will move.

I have no choice but to jump up and begin unplugging my laptop and closing my books—not just the Italian cookbooks but the ones about Chinese, Uzbek, and Turkish cuisine too. Dumplings and ravioli are in those books, yes all of them. He looks at me queerly and asks, "What you study so hard?"

I do not want to answer or talk. I do not want anything to break the spell. But I must.

"Pasta," I reply.

He raises one large and bushy eyebrow, amused.

"Pasta?" He pauses. "Why you study this?"

I have no idea how to answer his question. He is an older man with gray hair and a generous paunch—from Russia, perhaps, by the tone of his accent. Like many immigrants in New York, he looks as though he has endured many extremes and hardships, has lived many lives before this one. How would I explain myself? Since I can't, I reply with a question of my own.

"Do you know *pel'meni*?"

He pauses and looks at me, confused, as though he has not heard correctly. "*Pel'meni*?" he asks.

"Yes, *pel'meni*," I repeat.

His face brightens with recognition. "*Pel'meni!*"

"Do you know how to make it?"

"Of course!" He begins to make imaginary rolling motions in the air, then filling and cutting. Yes, he knows exactly—*pel'meni*, the ravioli of Siberia that ultimately became a famous Russian dish.

"Do you make the filling with raw meat or cooked?" I ask.

"Raw," he replies, without having to think. "The meat cooks in the water." Then he adds, "You should open up a *pel'meni* restaurant here in New York. You'll get very rich! We have them in Russia. *Pel'meni* restaurants are full."

I put my many cookbooks back on the shelf and zip my bag shut before I head for the door.

On my way out, he repeats, "Open a *pel'meni* restaurant," and again he gives the promise of great riches.

WHENEVER I TELL PEOPLE of my ravioli adventures, my interest in stuffed pastas and dumplings, I nearly always receive a happy response. There is something about the topic that fills people with enthusiasm. I wonder why. They want to tell me about all their homemade pasta loves—of a Sicilian grandmother who made ravioli with cinnamon, a Lebanese aunt and her *shushbarak,* the Hong Kong relatives who work all night to make *jiaozi* for New Years, or the Polish in-laws who ritually make pierogi each Christmas Eve.

Every culture has a dumpling—so people say. Also true: everybody loves dumplings. Indeed, I become something of a collector of dumplings and stuffed pastas and take joy in building a growing list. I chart the world trail of dumplings from east to west and around the world again. Germans have meat dumplings called *Klopse* and a Swabian ravioli called *Maultaschen.* Go farther east to Poland, and you enter pierogi land—with dozens of variations for fillings of meat and fruit. In the Ukraine, you find *vushka,* which are triangular pierogi stuffed with mushrooms, served in borscht at Christmas Eve dinner. In the Jewish world, there is *kreplach.* Down in the Balkans, dumplings stuffed with plums. In India, there is the fried category of *samosas.* In Japan, you find *gyoza.* And then of course there is China; oh, how to begin in China with all those wontons and potstickers, steamed, boiled, and fried, filled with pork or shrimp or taro root or cabbage and scallion. I need an entirely separate file for China.

And so, while I am traveling backward in imaginary time through the Italian cookbooks, I am also, for many years, traveling across the imaginary globe searching. As time goes on, the number and variety of stuffed pastas exceed my dreams, and I discover in these infinitely varied creations boundless goodwill of humanity toward the various shapes and forms. It is this sense of happiness about dumplings and ravioli in all shapes and forms that utterly astounds me. And in this way, I find myself loving Adalgiza's ravioli all the more.

True, on some strange days I'm out of control, seeing ravioli everywhere. Is a blintz a ravioli? What about a French crepe filled with ham and cheese, or a tortilla wrapped around meat? Welsh pasties, apple pies, and cream puffs—are they ravioli too? Surely a grilled-cheese sandwich is a form of ravioli, is it not?

THE STORY of pasta is a complex one, and it is a fool's mission to wander down this road strewn with controversy. The only minor consensus of the story is that pasta could not begin until the emergence of cultivated wheat, in about 10,000 B.C., in the Fertile Crescent, a strip of land that stretches from the Mediterranean coast to the Persian-Arab Gulf. Wheat was different from all other grains known to humans because of its elastic, glutenous nature, which would eventually make leavened bread and pasta possible. However, from ears of wheat to the development of milling stones and a ready supply of flour, to waterproof boiling vessels and kneaded dough, well, that involved many steps. Pasta did not happen quickly. Its transformation probably took many thousands years more.

And this is the end of the scholarly and global majority consensus regarding wheat and the Mediterranean world.

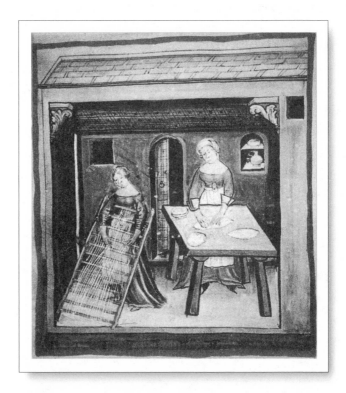

Women making pasta.
From Tacuinum Sanitatis, *a late-fourteenth-century manuscript.*

After this comes an array of overlapping and conflicting theories and uncertain evidence. Mix with this people's ethnic pride—apparently many countries in the world secretly, or not so secretly, want to claim responsibility for inventing pasta. Add on the conflicts of scholars, and the limits of what languages are read by those doing research on a truly global food, and you've got an enormous entangled mess. To get to the bottom of it, you'd have to read all the world's languages—not just in their current forms but in what they were two thousand years ago. Then you'd also have to account for the cultures that didn't write about cooking or food, and left no records of what they did. All this becomes even more complex when the theories are framed by disagreements over what the heck pasta actually is. Must it be made of wheat? Must it be a certain shape? Must it be hard wheat that can be dried? And must it be boiled? For example, is a strip of ancient Roman *laganum* a forerunner of lasagna even if it's baked?

Honestly, I'd really prefer not to get involved. First of all, I suspect that ravioli may well have a different lineage than pasta. And second of all, if I get into the whole messy story, I might have to explore my reservations about whether or not Italy independently invented pasta, as many people believe. No thanks, I'd rather not. So let me finesse the whole matter with this: If a gun were put it to my head, I'd say that the ancient Persians, the Arabs, the people of India, the Chinese, and the Italians all have histories of pasta that are very ancient and impressive, and each unique in its own way. When did it all begin, you ask? I don't think anyone knows for sure. To be on the extremely safe side, I'll give the whole thing a wide berth and say that documentation for wheat pasta collectively emerges in these various parts of the worlds between 500 B.C. and A.D. 1200—give or take a few years (and no, I'm not counting those strands of millet dug up in China and dated four thousand years old). Of course, this is all based on the written records that endured. Maybe pasta was in use even earlier, and maybe tomorrow some archaeologist will dig up something new. I'm going to leave it there.

But anyway, ravioli is not the same thing as pasta. Pasta is a food of ordinary life and ordinary people—a kneaded, boiled dough. Ravioli, on the other hand, is much more elaborate. It is a form of sculpture and design. It takes a lot of work and time and some skill to make ravioli, and therefore it is historically a food for the wealthy or a celebratory food for ordinary people who, on special days, devote extensive energy and resources to preparing something unusual.

I am certain that this association with celebration is why ravioli—whether it's *mandu* or *kreplach*—brings such an overwhelmingly positive response from people. Historically, ravioli is for a special occasion. It is the food of happy times all over the world.

WHERE RAVIOLI began or how it migrated is uncertain, but a handful of words raise intriguing possibilities. Ravioli in Turkey is called *manti* (pronounced "manteu"), and it has a raw meat filling that cooks in boiling water. Ravioli appears under a similar alias across the globe from Turkey all the way to China. *Manti* in Uzbekistan, Azerbaijan, and northern Afghanistan—usually served in a sauce made of yogurt. In Tibet, it turns up as *momo*, made with meat. In Korea, it is *mandu*. And in China, we find a steamed bun called *mantou*.

Similarly, the Arab stuffed pasta named *shushbarak* is related to the word *joshparah*, which, according to food historian Charles Perry, comes from the ancient Persian, *joshparag*, a dumpling he dates back to at least the tenth century. From *joshparag* comes a list of mangled but similar names across Central Asia, again, straight to China—*dushbera* in Azerbaijan, *tushbera* in Tajikistan, *chuchvara* in Uzbekistan, and *chochura* in China's Xinjiang Province.

But again, there is no clear proof of whether this movement was east to west or west to east, or perhaps from Central Asia outward. Probably dumplings made their journey along the trade routes called the Silk Road, hundreds, or perhaps thousands, of years ago.

I RETURN another day to the New York Public Library. My security-guard friend is nowhere to be found, but my collection of cookbooks sits waiting on the shelf of the Allen Room, where I work. It is early in the day, and the children are in school. I pull down *Dal liber de coquina* again, and this time, there is no rush. I go slowly, translating bit by bit. I believe it is the first published recipe for ravioli from the Italian world. It comes out something like this in English.

DEI RAVIOLIS

To make ravioli, you take the pig belly and its liver, or the innards of a kid or other animal that you want or other meats; beat strongly on a board with a knife. Then take sweet fragrant herbs, spices, and saffron and grind in a mortar. Add beaten egg and mix all of these things together with the other ingredients so that you have a dense paste. Then take the skin that was around the guts of the pig and make little cloths, wrapping in the skin the mixed ingredients about the size of an egg or a little more. If you want, in place of the skin, you can use pasta instead. Then fry them in a frying pan with oil or with another fat and take out of the pan, then if you want, dip them in honey.

How interesting that the meat goes into the ravioli uncooked. But by far the most notable thing here is that the ravioli wrapper is made from the film or skin of the pig's stomach. This I find rather shocking. Pasta is suggested merely as a substitute, an option. It is clearly not the essential nature of the dish.

A new door opens.

Might ravioli find some of its ancestors, then, in the old recipes for stuffed stomachs and blood puddings, such as haggis, known to the Romans in the first century? All over the world, people have used the organ sacks of animals as containers for cooking and preserving meats for perhaps as long as they have been butchering animals. Might sausage be a forerunner of ravioli too?

But perhaps it is not the animal sack that is so important, but the gesture of wrapping and stuffing itself. From there it's a short trip to many other similar ancient culinary motifs of wrapping. I think of prehistoric people using banana, bamboo, lotus, fig, and other leaves to wrap around rice and meats to be cooked in outdoor pits. Might the beginnings—the concept—of ravioli go back this far?

Perhaps the funny thing about history is that you can get so caught up with thinking about what happened, and the small things, that you lose sight of what is important.

I'd say with wrapped dishes what is most important is that, at some point, they eventually changed and became something artistic and creative—an elaborated food. Pasta—whenever or wherever it finally came around—offered a perfect contribution to an old theme of wrapping one thing inside another. Here was a material that would offer an ideal texture and malleability for an infinity of shapes and sizes. It would offer new potential for the expression of mysteries. Pasta provided a wonderful addition to the story and the art.

In this spirit, I turn to a wonderful book called *Pasta: The Story of a Universal Food* by Silvano Serventi and Françoise Sabban, where I find a poem titled "Ode to Bing," written by a scholar named Shu Xi around the year 300. *Bing* is a Chinese word for "pasta." Here is an excerpt where Shu Xi sings forth about *laowan*, a stuffed and savory dumpling.

Flour sifted twice,
Flying snow of white powder,
In a stretchy, sticky dough
Kneaded with water or broth, it becomes shiny.
For the stuffing, pork ribs or shoulder of mutton,
Fat and meat in proper proportion,
Cut into small bits,
Like gravel or the pearls of a necklace.
Ginger root and onion bulb
Are cut into fine julienne,
Sprinkled with wild ginger and cinnamon ground fine,
Boneset and Szechuan pepper,
All mixed with salt and seasonings,
Blended into a single ball.

CHAPTER 18

Bella Cosa

Y HUSBAND IS AN EARLY RISER, a lover of mornings, and an optimist as those people often are. He is saying something to me, but I am not awake enough to hear, still lying in bed. He pushes open the green shutters. The outside comes in—air and light. I slowly open my eyes to take it all in: the tall ceiling, the mahogany armoir, swallows flitting about in loops outside the window. Am I really in Italy?

Is he really here too, finally, with me in Italy?

This guy who called me for a date when I was twenty-four—this editor of books, this lover of trout streams, this Protestant man with modest manners from the scrapple heartlands of German farm country in Pennsylvania. Long ago, when our first days turned into months, I thought to myself, *Could it be possible that my life would take such a lucky turn? That a happy life would be mine?*

Now, eighteen years later, as I wake up in Liguria, he leans over me saying, "You've got to wake up. It's the most beautiful morning ever."

Long gone is the smooth-faced lanky guy in a ripped-up denim jacket. Long gone, too, the lightness of youth. He is a man well into midlife, his face showing the roads of time—creases around the mouth, the routines of daily responsibility imprinted permanently in the brow. I witnessed these changes one by one in him, and in myself, over the years, along with the transformation of our relationship into a partnership, marked by endurance raising children, moving in search of better jobs, pursuing two careers and the endless choices that modern life has given us. Continually stretching ourselves, reaching. At this moment, I see all this, but also my optimist—his eyes open wide, his head shaking with disbelief, as he points out of the window. "No. I'm serious, Laura. The most beautiful morning *in . . . my . . . entire . . . life.*"

Yes, he is here with me. I get up from the bed and look out to the intense blue sky, the green hills, and beyond them, the deeper blue of the Ligurian Sea. It's true: the most beautiful morning ever. We stare, blinking together, as though seeing a mirage.

A month earlier . . . a week earlier, even, say, three days earlier . . . he was rolling his eyes at the prospect of taking two young kids with all our messy family life across the Atlantic to Italy.

"Are we really doing this? Are we really taking a four- and nine-year-old overseas?"

You'd think it would be easy to come to this joyous decision. But it was not. We are in the exhausted phase of life—unable to fathom the energy it would take. The expense. The obstacles. The luggage. The jet lag. The long flight with children who would surely cause disturbances on the seven-hour plane ride. The potential panic attacks (on the part of the parents). But most of all, the demon work. There is really no such thing as a vacation if you've got a desk job in New York. You just have to do it all before you leave or after you come back.

When we are not worrying about work, there are always the children to worry about. Number one son is inward, averse to new places and strangers, preferring to stay at home and read or watch television. How will he react? Number two son is still young and unpredictable, like a little wild animal, not to mention loud—prone to long fits of crying over even the smallest mishaps. What if he has one of his two-hour crying jags on the plane? Will we survive?

"Better not to leave the house," my husband insists. He has never been to Italy. Why bother now? Truth be told, he'd prefer to go to northern places, like Scotland or Ireland, perhaps Alaska if he had the chance, places with white-capped mountains and cold water that make for good fly-fishing.

He says something then, but I can't hear it over the sound of the little one—who just bumped his elbow—howling in the background as though he is being tortured with sharp knives.

"I said," he gives a loud passive-aggressive sigh strong enough to knock me over, then repeats loudly, "can't you just go by yourself?"

"No. I can't. I need more than a week, and I've got two kids. I can't leave them again. I need you all to come. I want you all to come. It's important to me."

And with this, I convinced him to empty the bank account and buy four plane tickets to Italy. We have never done such a thing, never undertaken such an expense. We probably could not find a financial advisor who would think it advisable.

And so we went forward. And somehow just yesterday with unfathomable amounts of luggage, we stepped into the taxi cab and sped to the airport. Number one son, beautiful and bright eyed, clutched his stack of dragon and mystery books, all ready for the night flight. Number two son rhapsodized about the clouds he would see from up in the sky, then put his head down and passed out for the entire seven-hour journey.

Finally, seventeen hours later, we arrived at the three-bedroom apartment with terrazzo floors, high ceilings, and a terrace with a view of the big blue sky and sea. It's located in a town we endearingly call "Little Village," a beautiful seaside family town, very near Recco. And the apartment is all ours for three weeks.

And so it is here that I wake now with my husband. We are fools in midlife, perhaps. But he is right. It is the most beautiful morning ever and I wrap my arms around him and pull him down toward me and hold this part of him tight, this brightness in him that I have missed.

※

ALAS, I must rush off. Time is short. Time is precious. I have an appointment at 10:00 A.M. Jet-lagged but armed with video camera and notebook, I hop into our Smart Car, navigating up into the hills, stopping not once but twice for focaccia and cappuccino—relishing the crunch and salt of the bread dunked into the bubbly foam. My destination: back to the village of Ne, to La Brinca, the restaurant where I'd spent a snowy evening six months before. Today all is reborn and green— the fields with grapes, the olive trees, and next to each house, vegetable gardens in the leafy splendor of late June. At La Brinca, the Circella brothers promised that if I returned, they'd show me how they make ravioli. Today is the appointed day.

"*Ciao*," says Sergio Circella, smiling warmly at the door. "Nice to see you again. Come in." This visit, Sergio, the dining-room brother, leads me through the restaurant into the kitchen where he passes me off to the behind-the-scenes brother, Roberto. At 10:00 A.M., the kitchen is quiet, and immaculate. The pots hang peacefully on their hooks. The stainless-steel counters are wiped down, gleaming and empty.

Roberto is dressed in chef whites standing at the pasta board near an open window that looks out to the hills. He's evidently waiting for me.

Roberto Circella rolling pasta.

"*Piacere*," he offers, with a diffident smile. Roberto has intense blue eyes and a handsome face, mellowing into his forties. He does not speak English, but with six months more Italian under my belt, I understand nearly all he says. Not that this is really about words anyway. Roberto is a master pasta maker, and he has spent too many years bending over the pasta board for speeches. La Brinca is one of the rare restaurants that makes all pasta by hand anymore, so he's a busy guy with a lot to do. He's eager to get the demonstration under way. Already he's opening a plastic bin to reveal several round loaves of pasta dough lined up—already kneaded, stretched, and rested, already supple and smooth as baby cheeks, ready for rolling.

I am disappointed to see the pasta dough is already made. How much water and egg did he use? How much moisture? How much kneading? And what did it feel like? After years of trying it myself, I know that with so few ingredients—flour, egg, water, and salt—the secret of pasta is in the proportions you use and how you handle it. Now all this work has already been done. Alas. There is no time for regrets. Before I know it Roberto is tossing a hunk of round dough onto the board and rolling his pin rapidly back and forth.

"Wait! Wait!" I cry. My video camera isn't fully set up. "Please." He indulges me and pauses while I adjust the equipment. I am a hunter this visit, determined to bag the footage.

Roberto resumes his energetic pace. The pin makes a *thwonk* as it falls on the dough, then Roberto's arms move expertly, rolling it back and forth. His speed astounds me. Back and forth, back and forth, with force and determination. Lots of pasta to make. Every few minutes he snatches a handful of flour and showers it down abundantly over his dough to keep it from sticking.

"How often do you make pasta?" I inquire.

"Often enough." He barely looks up, then adds, "Every two or three days: gnocchi, lasagne, *tagliarini*, tagliatelle, ravioli . . . " He rattles off more names. His arms keep moving.

I pray my camera is working properly. It's all happening so quickly. In just a few minutes, Roberto's circle of dough is now doubled, perhaps tripled, in size—about fifteen inches in diameter. He's ready for the next part. He lifts up the edge and begins wrapping it around his pin, showering down more flour all over the pasta. Now, here it comes— the pulling, the stretching, the *shoosh shoosh shoosh slap* of dough hitting the board. Each time he unrolls, he rotates the circle so as to stretch each side evenly. It is two feet wide. Then three feet. And now it is transformed into a large fluttering white sheet, a sail in the wind. It gets air before it hits the board. The *slap* grows louder, and the dough grows so big it exceeds the length of the rolling pin—hanging and draping and folding over the edges. I'd panic for sure. But for Roberto, no worries here. It never sticks or gets jammed up. He tosses out another handful of flour and just proceeds, calm and cool. Only when he's got it, only when it's all done, does he pause and look at me with a small half smile of satisfaction.

"*Elastica*," he offers, holding the dough between his fingers for me to inspect the texture. "*Molto delicata . . . sottile.*"

If I were younger, if I were older, if I were without husband and children, I'd throw myself at his feet this very moment and beg him for a job. I'd offer to slave in this kitchen. Yes—elastic. Yes, delicate. Yes, thin.

The smile fades, and Roberto briskly picks up his sheet of dough and carries it to another work-top area, laid out with floured wax paper, and proceeds exactly as Giuseppina did when I'd seen her six months earlier in Lumarzo. This is the way *nonnas* do it. And so Roberto explains that it was his *nonna* who taught him how to make pasta, and that all the recipes of La Brinca come from home.

"How much water do you use in your flour?"

He laughs. "It depends on the day. It depends on the heat. It depends on the hands." And he holds out his hand for me to see. "Each person has different hands. Different heat."

Pasta circle ready. Next, the little glass bowl with foil on top. The foil is lifted to reveal a bright green fragrant mush—*ripieno* all prepared this morning—all secrets folded in, and buried in smooth green mystery.

"Meat?" I ask.

"No." Roberto looks up, and shakes his head and smiles slyly. "No meat." He wags a finger no.

"*Prescinsêua?*" I press on.

"No." Again a shake of the head. A smile. "*Non prescinsêua.*"

Okay. I get the game. He will not give the recipe outright. But I can guess.

"Cheese?"

"*Si,*" he nods, conceding. "*Parmigiano.*"

Chard?

Si.

Egg?

Si.

In this way, I deduce that this filling is made of minced borrage and the chard called *bietole*. It is mixed with egg, and parmigiano. But the secret is really in the herbs.

"Wild herbs of the countryside," Roberto adds, waving his hands in the air, one of those Italian hand gestures, to show the mysterious unspecificity of it all—just "wild."

"And a little marjoram—not too much!" he is quick to add, but I believe this precision is theatric decoy. Any fool knows not to add too much of this perfumey herb. I also know that back at home in New Jersey, I will hunt high and low and grow my own borrage and *bietole* and search for wild and cultivated herbs. I will use leaves of purslane from the farmer's market, parsely, dandelion lines, spinach, and yes, marjoram. And it will never be like this. Never. Yes, I see it all before me.

"Herbs are the difference in Liguria." He offers the same old theme I've heard before. "In Piedmont, they make ravioli. But they don't have our herbs."

He picks up a spatula and begins rapidly spreading *ripieno* in a smooth layer over his half moon of dough. The other sheet of dough gets sealed on top, and then comes the checkered rolling pin—just like Giuseppina did it. I tell Roberto I've seen all this in Lumarzo, "where all persons are Schenone."

He nods, pleased. Yes, there are still families in these mountains that make pasta by hand, for Sundays or special occasions. His eyes light up. "*Bella cosa.*"

Yes, I agree. It's a beautiful thing.

Now, Sergio returns to the kitchen, and I look at the two brothers together and think of my own father and his siblings and the struggle that defines family from the moment of birth. Most of the restaurants and food shops and farms I encounter here are based on family businesses with unending hours of work. Here at La Brinca, there can only be one brother in the front of the business. The others have to be in the kitchen or trenches. How to decide? How to keep the delicate balance of power so that each brother can succeed and be content, and so that the parts can add up to a whole?

In Italy, more than eighty percent of all businesses are family owned. And sure enough, every single food enterprise I visit here is a family enterprise. How do they succeed this way? I cannot help but wonder, coming from the experience I witnessed.

"We work all the time," Sergio explains. "We each have a house across the street. We are here until one in the morning many nights. I don't see my kids as much as I should. But I hope they will understand."

Roberto doesn't comment. He continues to demonstrate, showing me next how to make gnocchi, and then thin strands of wheat *tagliarini*. All the while, my camera is on. When he is done he goes back to the ravioli, still sitting on the board, imprinted with squares. Now it's time to cut, and when Roberto does so, I see that a couple of ravioli break in the process.

"Made by hand," he shrugs. "They're not supposed to be perfect."

Do I detect a little irony? The customers need to see some broken ones, some irregular shapes as proof that they are handmade? Nearly everything in our lives is mass produced now and uniform, never touched by human hands. Even people's faces are starting to look the same with plastic surgery. Of course customers yearn for the handmade. Roberto knows it well.

THE BROTHERS give me a tray of the ravioli to take home. With only a miniscule amount of arm twisting, I gladly accept. That night, we boil the water and make a simple marinara sauce and sit at the Formica kitchen table, ladling out the ravioli into four bowls.

Roberto's ravioli.

My husband takes a couple of bites and then begins shaking his head. "I'm sorry, Honey. But you and Lou have never even come close to this."

It's true. This pasta is lighter and so much softer than we've ever achieved. What is the secret of this lightness? Perhaps it's the special fine grade of Italian 00 flour Roberto uses? Perhaps it is the drop of olive oil he told me he mixed into the dough? Or maybe it's his hands. Or perhaps it was that part of the pasta making I missed—the ratio of liquid to flour to make a very soft dough but then having the skill to handle it so well without tearing. The filling is rich with cheese and egg, but subtle notes of bitter and sweet greens. Each rectangle is a gem, not only delicate but small. No doubt, these are the best ravioli I've tasted then or now.

And yet, as good as they are, I know that what is far more important than the fleeting beauty in my mouth is the video footage I've snagged of Roberto. No, I cannot leave behind my children to work in the kitchens of Liguria. Thank god for modern technology. I've got the tape hidden away in my bag for safe passage back home. I can watch again and again. Little does Roberto know, but he will be my tutor on the video screen in my kitchen at home.

THE APARTMENT we've rented is on a slightly shabby property with a big patch of weeds in the backyard and a picnic table infested with bugs no one will go near. Yet roses and flowering cactus surround the back door, and all around there are olive trees, fig trees, and lemon and peach trees filled with fruit.

On our way up the long stone driveway, a statue of Mary greets us from a cove inside the garden wall, and holy pictures hang in most of the rooms. A church lies just below us, a few steps down the hill, lit up festively with string lights each night. At first, we are shocked, almost frightened, by the bells, which are so close and loud they startle us through the day with thunderous spiritual ringing each fifteen minutes, counting the hours. We cannot speak until they are done. It is a reminder every quarter hour that we are in Catholic country. Long ago, I was raised in that country myself—surrounded by Jesus and Mary, organs and candles, nuns and priests—and the familiar feeling of mind and body pressed into prayer. Standing on the steps by the church, my skin vibrating, it occurs to me that Adalgiza's ravioli is a Catholic dish, and my ravioli are merely secular humanist. And I consider for the very first time that perhaps this is the most egregious adaptation of all—even more infidel than that soft cheese in the silver foil. Which, after all, is the greater betrayal to the culture of Christmas ravioli, a four-ounce package of Philadelphia or the loss of spiritual faith?

To get to the beach we walk down hundreds of steps to the water. It takes ten minutes to get there but a half hour back up. I imagine Salvatore, trudging up and down, seeking shade from the relentless glare of the sun—Adalgiza, religiously closing the shutters each summer morning to keep out the heat.

"We love Italy," my sons declare as they bound down the twisting paths of stone steps toward the water, chasing lizards that run across the stone walls, examining the green figs that grow wild. We are particularly impressed by the large gardens in front of nearly each house—immaculately tended rows of beans and tomatoes and zucchini plants with giant orange flowers. Fruit trees are everywhere.

We can see our neighbors here, close by on their terraces, watering plants or hanging out their laundry. We hear them call one another and clatter dinner dishes. We hear their televisions, barking dogs, and yowling cats. In the church square below us, the men and women stand and talk in the evening, and the boys kick soccer balls until ten or eleven at night. It reminds me a little bit of Hoboken and the neighborhoods nearby from which my parents rescued us—the kind of place to which I am always longing to return—a place where things are out in the open, and I can hear voices of people rather than the constant rush of cars.

We watch, also, the neighbor below us religiously tend his vegetable garden each morning, watering and weeding between 7:00 or 8:00 A.M. He's got perfect rows of beans and tomatoes, basil and zucchini, peppers, eggplant, and potatoes, and he's got a mysterious smokehouse too—what goes on in there we don't know, but smoke comes out, and one morning my husband wakes early in a panic. "Fire!" he cries, bolting upright from a dead sleep. "Fire!" No, it's just the smokehouse. "What the hell are they doing in there?" It remains an unsolved mystery.

This same neighbor also frames his vegetable garden with fruit trees, and his apricots look so exquisite that one evening, in the dark, I lose control and reach out and touch one, just out of curiosity. I have no intentions of stealing. But it falls inside my hand. What am I to do? When the coast is clear, I hide it inside my palm and head straight into the blue-tiled kitchen where I place it on a cutting board and take a knife and slice through its glorious pale orange skin, making small wedges, which I eat in slow bites, one at a time. It is sweet as candy, scented with an ethereal perfume I never find again. All throughout our trip I am looking for apricots, buying them at fruit stands and markets wherever I go, but I never will find one so amazing as the one I stole from this tree. I search for the same smell, but I can't re-create it in my mind. Smell is our most ancient sense, closest to the memory part of our brains. Yet it is the most fleeting, almost impossible to call up again, like images and voices we can still strain to hear. I think of Adalgiza—when Salvatore was gone to America—waiting and waiting for him. Months and years gone, as he almost slipped away from her. Did she try to imagine his face, his skin, his voice, singing? Did she yearn for his smell?

LITTLE VILLAGE has a lovely seaside promenade where modern life hums along brightly with galleries, cafés, and crowds of people on cell phones. In our first days, my husband and I marvel while we sit on the pebbled beach watching our children swim. To our left, Portofino Mountain cuts a jagged line from sea to sky and several stands of cypress and cedars grow up insistently from small ledges. To our right is the harbor of Little Village where fishermen still set off in the early morning in small boats. A few steps beyond them, a ferry boat that whizzes across the water to a seven-hundred-year-old monastery set in a cove where you can sunbathe, swim, and have a beer at the bar, beneath the ancient bell tower. Yes, it amazes us the way nature and civilization intertwine here. We are envious of such a place—aware of the void we Americans have with our lack of history and traditions. And yet, we know that too much tradition brings suffocation, and burdens. An Italian friend who admires the American freedom to reinvent ourselves no matter how old we are tells me that "in Italy, people don't violence themselves in midlife with great changes if not necessary." Which way is the better way? One culture with not enough memory, another with perhaps too much? I do not know.

Focaccia in Recco, plain and with onions.

"Ten more minutes," the children beg from the water. They jump the waves and float and splash and never want to get out. When they finally emerge, glimmering and wet, we all walk up to see the theatrics of the focaccia man at noon pulling out big pans of bread from the oven, finishing them with a stream of oil on top. People line up in big clusters, peering through the glass eagerly. Focaccia is the popular lunch here, and we grow accustomed to the ritual, standing in line and carrying forth lengthy debates as to whether this time it will be focaccia with onions, or focaccia with cheese.

For my boys, Italy is a place of holiday—gelato and pizza and pasta. It is a place of boat rides and hikes, cartoonishly tiny cars, and the excitement of motorcycles. Italy is swimming and sunlight, medieval castles, and the stingrays in Genoa's marvelous aquarium. It is a trashy pop song they hear all the time on Italian MTV. They are happy, of course. What's not to like? But they are happy, too, because their parents are happy—which is what I imagine all children secretly wish for.

Of course, we have our difficulties. As the sun climbs to its peak in midday, burning our eyes and skin, the Italians disappear for their rest time, and we don't know what to do with ourselves. "We hate Italy," littlest pronounces when we arrive at a shop at 1:35 and discover the steel gates shut until 4:00. The next day we miss lunch—all the restaurants and food shops are closed, and our refrigerator is bare. Everything is closed. We just can't seem to get the schedule right. These are the hours when we bicker and grumble with the same struggles we have at home.

I would like to go to the beach. Husband wants to go driving about the mountains for many hours. Number one son wants to return to the apartment and stay there all day. Number two son begins howling because his shoes don't feel right.

"What kind of a country is this?" Number one shakes his head with confusion over the long siesta.

"Maybe this is the way life should be," I reply.

And my husband gives a passive-aggressive sigh. "Oh, please stop," he says, because I sound like one of those Americans in stupid love with Italy.

IT MUST be annoying to Italians the way we Americans romanticize them. We use their country for our fantasies and fill our kitchens with Tuscan-inspired tablecloths and earthenware. We cook "Italian" dishes that never existed east of Brooklyn. We swoon for movies and books that deliver baroque architecture, silver olive groves, dazzling mountains and sea—and always the transformative flavors where culinary lives can be born.

An old postcard of Recco, date unknown.

I wonder if Italians understand that we really have no choice. We Americans desperately need Italy and our dream of *la dolce vita*. I wonder if we could do without it. Living in the fastest economy in the history of civilization, migrating continuously in search of a better life, living in our way without safety nets of village, family, or national health care—we need to believe there is a more humane country out there where art and beauty prevail, where monuments of civilization endure, where the Vatican and its shrines are kept safe, and where the people resist McDonald's (at least more than others). We love the concept of Italy—a country of warm climate and warm people, who insist on taking a rest in the afternoon, a place where the cars are small instead of big, and where yesterday is not so easily paved over by strip malls and chain discount stores.

Perhaps most of all, we want to dream of a country where the food is good and families are strong. Be all this true, somewhat true, or grossly exaggerated, is secondary really. We need beauty and relief. Italy, the concept of Italy, gives us this.

Even our youngest son seems to sense that Italy is a welcoming place for things past, a place where even ghosts might find sanctuary. We learn this one evening, at the end of our first week, when he calls us with great urgency to the yard.

"Come quick!" he cries. "I've got some big news." He stands by the back door, hair turned gold from the sun, one hand holding a shovel he has transformed into a magical tool by wrapping it around and around with masking tape.

"What is it, Honey?"

"Reenie and Peenie are here!"

"You're kidding. Here in Italy?"

"Yes, it's true," gray eyes wide.

For the last six months, he has repeated the story a number of times about Reenie and Peenie, his parents from a previous life, and how he came to this world in a taxi wearing water shoes. Sometimes he embellishes the story—adding, for example, that they're from the Middle Ages or that they rode horses. They have become fixtures in our family, like mascots, except of course that we never see them because they are long dead.

"Come meet them. They're in the yard," he whispers with excitement and a bit of dramatic awe.

He begins to lead us there, then halfway he stops short and commands us to be quiet because "they're very shy, standing right there by the tree—right there. Can you see them?"

"Reenie and Peenie," he announces, preparing his introductions in a formal but respectful voice, as one might use with the spirit world. "This is my family. Family, this is Reenie and Peenie."

We act appropriately, of course, and say our greetings to the empty area behind the trees. We inquire about their well-being.

When our little one is satisfied, we gingerly back away on tiptoe and return inside.

Some months later back in New Jersey, back in our routines, and under duress from his older brother who is sick of the whole affair, youngest son will renounce Reenie and Peenie. He will claim that the whole thing was made up and false. My husband and I will be sad, urging him to believe what he wishes, no matter what his big brother thinks. But he insists.

"They were imagination, I tell you. Imagination! It's over. It's over once and for all."

※

FOR ME, this interest in ghosts is not so easily brushed away.

It is 9:00 A.M., and I'm at the municipal building in Recco, looking for the office of the registry of birth, marriage, and death—the *anagrafe*. I'm in line with dozens of Italians anxiously clasping their various documents, ready for arduous battle over one problem or other. Before the gates open, they are already shaking their heads with frustration, as though to prepare. They look at me curiously. Perhaps my holiday demeanor is obvious; I am not here for the usual problems. When, finally, the office doors open, revealing civil servants at their desks, I steer myself to the correct place, before a middle-aged woman who acknowledges my presence with a frown and a nod. "*Si?*"

I make two cautious steps through the door of her office and explain in my most polite, stuttering Italian that I'm looking for birth certificates from the late 1860s and early 1870s for Adalgiza Amianto and Salvatore Schenone. I'm also looking for their wedding certificate. And, if it's not too terribly much trouble, I'd appreciate the birth certificates for my grandfather Luigi, and his various siblings too.

Ms. Anagrafe starts shaking her head. I can't just walk in with such a request, she explains. I'll need to put it in writing with all the exact dates. "Recco was bombed in World War Two, you know. Most of the records were destroyed."

"Yes, I know. But is it possible to look?"

She begins speaking very rapidly, and though I don't understand all the words, the general essence is clear—it's unlikely that she'll find a scrap for me. To make matters worse, no I don't have exact dates. She throws up her hands. "You'll have to put all this in writing," she repeats.

Yet, just as I am about to leave, she takes out a loose leaf of paper and pushes it toward me.

"Write down the years of your great-grandparents marriage," she concedes. Yes, she can check this one right now. Then, she rises from her chair and disappears, shaking her head with doubt once more as she heads, I suppose, to the archives. I pull out my Italian grammar book to pass the time, and conjugate verbs in the conditional tense: *sarei saresti sarebbe saremmo sareste sarebbero* . . .

Ten minutes later, she reappears carrying a huge brown leather-bound book, so imposing and heavy that it appears to have come from God's library—perhaps the same one St. Peter would use at heaven's gate.

"I found it," mutters Ms. Anagrafe. She begins to smile, pleased with herself, but stops, then sits down and opens to a specific page, from which she begins to copy some data onto a preprinted form. My heart jumps.

"You found it?" I am incredulous.

"Yes," she nods. But when I try to peek at the actual page—the actual 1890s entry for the marriage of Salvatore and Adalgiza, entered with big curling letters of old Italian script, she pulls it close to her body in a state of alarm, and wraps her arms around it like she's guarding a baby. "No, you can't look! It's a matter of privacy." Only when I back off does she relax and resume transcribing the information. I sit quietly while she affixes the stickers to the pages—making them official documents—and asks me for the equivalent of half a dollar, the *anagrafe* fee.

My heart is beating fast. I don't know why, but it is. "Salvatore was born in Recco," she explains. "But she was born in Genoa. You can go there to find her birth certificate. But your grandfather Luigi, no, he's not here. Maybe they immigrated before he was born. Maybe he wasn't born here." I nod, still studying the pages.

"Can I find out where they lived? Can I find out what church they went to? Can I find out anything else?"

She looks at me as though I have a mental problem. "How?" She repeats once again about the *bombardamento*. "We have nothing else."

"Doesn't it name the church on their original marriage information?" I persist, nodding to her sacred brown book.

"No. No church. They got married in a civil ceremony," she replies. "That can't be true."

She points to the paper. "They did not get married in a church," she insists, pointing at the facts, right there in black and white. A civil ceremony. No church.

I thank her profusely and depart.

Out in the bright sunshine, I look at the page once again. Married on the twenty-fifth of July in 1895 in Recco. Salvatore was twenty-seven. Adalgiza was twenty-one. Other than this, there are few details. Standing in the center of bustling Recco, with its shoppers and traffic, I look up at the 1950s buildings. Where was the place where he once sang to her beneath her window? I wonder. And why did they not marry in a church?

It makes no sense.

Walking to the car deep in thought, I pass the local fish cooperative run by the fishermen of Little Village. My skin is tingling from the encounter with these family documents, and I don't know why but I nervously jump inside. The strong fish smell makes my head spin, but I walk around perusing the bins. Salmon from Norway. Shrimp, probably from Southeast Asia. Finally, local fish—the poor small fish that Adalgiza knew—typically Genoese, a crate of shiny silvery anchovies.

I ask the women behind the counter how to prepare them *al limone*, an old technique still popular here. "Snap off the head, and pull out the backbone" they advise, and when I show some uncertainty, they demonstrate with gestures how to snap off the head and debone the fish, how to add salt and lemon juice and let it sit overnight.

"In the morning, pour off the liquid, then you dress with whatever you like . . . olive oil, oregano, herbs. . . ."

With a bunch of anchovies wrapped in paper and a copy of my great-grandparents marriage certificate, I drive from Recco to Little Village, wondering why in the world they didn't marry in a church. Of course they were Catholic. They raised their children Catholic and went to St. Joseph's Church in Hoboken. I am looking at the sea, and the rocks, when suddenly I hear my cousin Catherine's voice.

Oh, was her father mad when he found out about Salvatore. He chased her around the table.

I stop the car. It wasn't just talk. Perhaps he was mad for a reason. What? *Did they elope?* Did he chase her around the table when she announced she'd gotten married? Was such a thing possible? Could you even go to the town hall and do it without your parents? She was old enough, but would they even let you in a small town in 1895?

I look out at the sea and think some more. Then I pull onto the road again and continue home.

Back in my kitchen in Little Village, I immediately go to work, snapping the heads off the fish and stripping away their backbones. While I am squeezing lemon juice into a bowl, another scenario comes to mind.

Perhaps Adalgiza told her father she refused to marry the soldier. Perhaps she told him she had broken the engagement and was going to marry Salvatore instead—no matter what her father said or did. *No matter what you say or do!* She was feisty that Adalgiza, and strong. And he was furious, and chased her around the table.

Then don't expect your mother and I to come your wedding. You can get married alone!

Yes, maybe this is what happened. Maybe that's why Adalgiza and Salvatore just went to the municipal hall and did it themselves.

Of course, this is just fantasy. I will never know. . . .

One by one, I place the anchovies in a bowl and toss them with lemon juice using my bare hands, making sure they are all coated with citrus. Into the refrigerator they go, covered with clear plastic wrap to sit overnight.

The next morning, I am eager to see them. Exactly as I was told, I pour off the liquid, and to my delight the anchovies are perfectly "cooked" by the acids of the lemon, exactly like a ceviche, which I have made before. I add oil, a little extra lemon, and herbs and a little salt. Their flesh is white now, delectable and sweet—contrasting with the sour lemon—melting in the mouth. My sons love them and scoop large amounts on their plates, eating one after the next with a hunk of focaccia. I am both proud and shocked.

CHAPTER 19

Brother Chestnut

THE CONFERENCE ROOM is quiet. He is seated at one side of the table, I at the other. "Is it possible for me to cook authentic Genoese food when I return to the U.S.?" I ask, tentatively.

"Yes. So long as you learn here," replies Giovanni Rebora. "Then you can do it."

I feel as if I've come before an oracle.

"What about with cookbooks? Can't I learn with Genoese cookbooks?"

"Impossible," Rebora insists, and he waves away the offending idea with a hand. "We don't use cookbooks so much here—except, of course, the young people who like to read about some ridiculous dish of curry."

Rebora has a worn and creviced face, which he wears to advantage. He's got a deep, gravelly voice and speaks slowly and surely—just as an oracle should.

I ignore the curry remark and press forward. "And pesto? Can I make true Genoese pesto with basil grown in U.S. soil?"

"Yes. Use the Genoese seeds, and fertilize the soil like we do here, and get the pH correct."

I exhale a long breath of gratitude, as though I've been blessed.

"But," he continues, "never use leaves pulled off the plants."

"Excuse me?"

Does he see the past? Me in the overgrown New Jersey yard, heading to my big bushy basil, colander and scissors in hand, ready to commit another act of ignorance, snipping stems repeatedly from one or two poor plants all summer long to make pesto.

"For pesto, you must harvest the whole plant from the root, while it's young and tender, otherwise it's bitter."

I pledge silently to do it this way forever more.

Giovanni Rebora probably has the entire recorded history of Genoa in his head, but I wonder if it is woven into his skin as well. He was for many decades a celebrated professor of economic history at the University of Genoa, and head of a department there, though recently retired from these posts. Rebora is admired internationally for his work in Italian food history, but he's also something of a local hero, who writes witty columns in Genoa's newspaper and acts as a judge in the annual local cooking competition here.

One by one, he suffers politely through my scattershot questions. He describes the port of Genoa in the Middle Ages, and the trade of olive oil. He tells me about Recco in the era of Salvatore and Adalgiza. He describes an economy once built on mule trails, and of lively trattorias where people used to learn about food and share recipes by tacking them up on a wall. "Long ago," he recounts, "priests used to read recipes aloud to the illiterate. But, no, that's not how you learn to cook. This was just for the pleasure of listening. People liked to hear recipes."

When I make mention of women and men not having time to cook anymore, he becomes visibly irritated.

"This is because we modern people make so much time to do so many *stupid* things," Rebora booms. "People don't have time to read a book. They don't have time to cook. . . . I don't understand how they don't have thirty minutes a day to care about how they eat." A pause. "I don't know why young people don't have skills."

"Everyone is in a rush," I explain.

"Why are people in a rush? It's stupid to rush," he says with the same tone one might ask the question "Why do people become heroin addicts?" To send it home, he repeats, "Why rush?"

When I change the subject and tell him that ravioli lasted in my family a hundred years, he smiles a little wearily and softens a bit, perhaps with a bit of embarrassment for me and my obvious grasping. "I'm not surprised that this is the dish that would last so long."

In addition to his university post, Rebora is also the president of the Genoa chapter of the Conservatoria delle Cucine Mediterranee, which was introduced to me by Sergio Rossi.

"Who is going to save your local Mediterranean cuisine?" I ask. "If not the home cook, then who?"

"The trattoria, the farmer, the baker," he replies with certainty. "These small businesses hold the responsibility. These people do the best work."

"The best work saving traditions?" I ask.

"No. We don't worry so much about saving traditions. Traditions change all of the time."

"What then?"

"We want to save the *culture* of food here."

"The culture?"

"Yes, the culture of food."

A COUPLE OF DAYS later, driving north out of Genoa, I am asking myself, What is the culture of food? What is important? What is the rock beneath the surface that endures?

I'm in the car with Sergio Rossi. He and I have picked up the conversation from six months earlier, with him reminding me of the levels of depth and the question "How deep will go you?" I have been looking forward to this day for months. We are driving north to a small village called Montoggio where we will see his mother, Enrichetta Trucco, a keeper of the culture and a master cook of the Genoese way. Today Enrichetta will show me how to make a *torta di bietole*, and perhaps some other Genoese things. I am eager, and a little nervous too.

On our way out of Genoa, we cross the Bisagno River, *Besagnu* in

Genoese. Sergio tells me that hundreds of years ago, small farmers grew fruits and vegetables on these banks and sold them in the markets of Genoa. Though these farmers are long gone, people here who go grocery shopping might still say in Genoese, "*Vadu da-u besagnin*" or in Italian, "*Vado dal besagnino*," evoking the river, evoking the grocers who were called *besagnini*. To Italians from other regions, the phrase would be meaningless.

For those of us living computer-screen lives, bombarded by national brands, the physical world is fading away. But in Liguria, the terrain is so full of extremes that one cannot help but confront it: mountain after mountain, hemmed in to the south by the sea. It's easy to recall that geography once gave rise to culture, that mountains would breed hundreds of isolated, remote, and tiny villages—each a universe of particulars, each with its own variation of weather, language, and food, each contributing to a whole.

Modern democracy and industry came late to Italy, in part because of its geography, its intense history of fragmentation by mountains, its disunity. Supermarkets came here late as well, and commercial television did too. As a result, despite being the seventh largest economy in the world, Italy still stands heavily on small- to medium-sized family-owned businesses, most handed down through generations, with a shockingly small number of large, publicly held corporations on the stock market. It is this economic model that allows for the unique trattorias and bakeries, and the small food shops and farmers, all of whom defend the local culture of food, the specific heritage of place.

The Genoese will tell you how much change has come in the last twenty years. That the corporate supermarkets and chain stores are growing in force, that the lira is replaced by the euro, and that Ikea is now furnishing Genoa apartments. The U.S. government is encouraging Italy to create an economy more like ours, to loosen its laws to allow more venture capital and large corporations. Driving over the Bisagno River, I wonder, is it possible that a big-box chain store might stand here someday on the banks of this river, selling clothes and auto parts under the same roof, along with low-cost organic basil and pine nuts imported from somewhere far away where the labor is cheap?

✤

ENRICHETTA wears a blue-and-white striped housedress, sandals, and an apron. She has white hair and a straightforward, friendly manner. We follow her into her well-organized and serious kitchen. Yes, this seventy-six-year-old Italian woman has the view of terrace and flowers and of the mountains beyond. She's got the pretty painted plates on the walls, copper pots, and the all-important table in the middle of the room, with a pasta board atop. But Enrichetta has also got an unmistakable technological bent. I quickly note the impressive five-burner stove, a microwave, and an entire counter crowded with professional equipment: a stand-up mixer, a meat slicer, a grinder, a restaurant-grade scale, and a blender. (My friend Lou would like her.) I'm sure all this equipment came from Trucco, the family food shop that she and her husband, Giorgio, started in 1960 in Genoa. For more than three decades they worked together, until Giorgio died in 1982. After this, Enrichetta's children, Gabriella and Sergio, dropped what they were doing to go and help, and Sergio's wife, Etta, eventually joined the family business too. They kept Trucco thriving another eighteen years until Enrichetta decided to retire, and they closed the shop doors for good, five years ago.

"Would you like to make the pesto in a blender or mortar?" Enrichetta asks me. And for a moment, I wonder if it's a trick question or a test. The term *pesto* comes from the word *pestare* which means "to pound," and in Genoa this ideally means with a wooden pestle, a deep marble mortar, and lots of bicep power. The question of machine versus pestle is a heavily loaded political issue around here.

"Whatever you wish," I defer.

Enrichetta nods and goes straight to her blender. She places a handful of pine nuts then the basil inside. The leaves are small, still tender-looking, shaped in a delicate concave. She has plucked them from a plant that was only six or eight inches tall. She adds salt, then garlic with the green germ cut away, then oil. Then Sergio fills a small cup with a little water at the sink.

"For a restaurant family, cooking secrets are carefully kept," he explains in his slow, calm voice. "This is livelihood, learned from generation to generation. You don't just give your secrets away."

He hands the water to his mother. "Here is one of these secrets," he says, as Enrichetta pours a few drops of water into her blender, and the basil leaves are free to turn in a bright green whir.

"This makes the sauce creamy," he explains. "Some restaurants use a blender then leave little pieces of chopped-up basil in their pesto, like this is proof that it was hand pounded in a mortar. No. Not true. Genovese pesto must be like cream, whether you make it in a mortar or a blender." Next come many generous handfuls of *Parmigiano-Reggiano*. Enrichetta operates the blender like a musical instrument, pulsing and stopping to wipe down the edges with a spatula, getting to the texture she wants.

Pesto purists would balk at the blender. I have some sympathy for the overzealous and the orthodox. Those who have no traditions sometimes can become so religious about recovering "authentic" old foods that they do not know how to distinguish what is important and what is not. I fall prey to this fault often enough. But Enrichetta and Sergio do not suffer such rigidity. They have been handed the real thing and are confident in what they know. Yes, the mortar is best, but if you are good—really good like Enrichetta—well then you can make excellent Genoese pesto in a blender, and if you have a shop where you're selling large quantities every day, you must use the blender. "Better to make good pesto in a blender than bad pesto in a mortar," says Sergio. And, as in busy modern life, perhaps it's better that you should make your own pesto in a blender than not at all.

Even the most flexible people, however, would find Enrichetta's next move to be a bit of a shocker. She goes to the refrigerator, gets a container of heavy cream, adds a dash—then another, perhaps two or three tablespoons in all—to her pesto.

"The people from the Slow Food movement would call us vampires," Sergio laughs. "But look around here. Do you see olive trees living this high up in the mountains? No, it's too cold. Sure, some wealthy people could afford olive oil, or maybe the trattoria. Even a few workers might have been paid in olive oil. But most farmers here made butter and cream at home. So it was common to eat pasta sauced with nothing but cream." The local story, yet again.

When the pesto is done, Enrichetta makes chestnut *troffie*. She shows me the old recipe, containing no luxuries of egg or potato—just half chestnut flour, half wheat flour, and water, that's all. After she kneads and forms her ropes of dough, she begins to cut it into gnocchi. They fling off her thumb in rapid fire, accumulating into a pile in no time.

But really, the showstopper, the drop-dead amazing thing is Enrichetta's *torta di bietole*. And this is really why I am here. Enrichetta is a master artist of Genoese *torta*.

Enrichetta stretches dough for her torta.

To watch her is an opera in itself, an unfolding drama, act upon act, as each step moves forward. It begins simply enough—first in making the pie dough with flour and oil, kneaded and set to rest. Then the filling—*bietole* greens with delicate stems, which Enrichetta washes and swaths in towels to dry, then expertly chops into ribbons on her wooden board.

Next, she adds flour and an exotic spice blend of cinnamon, coriander, clove, nutmeg, and ginger, straight into the greens.

"If you were Genovese, she'd never show you this," interjects Sergio.

But it is not just the ingredients, the secrets, but the process of building the pie that is so dazzling. Enrichetta rolls out several layers of dough and stretches them with her fists in the air until they are round and thin and silky. Two layers on the bottom of her round *torta* pan, which she raises up on a small bowl so the extra dough can hang down. She adds the green filling and spoons generous amounts of *prescinsêua* on top. Then the final act, several more layers of silky dough on top—drizzled in olive oil. When she is finally done, she pulls the top layer of dough tightly so that it traps air and forms a translucent bubble on top. I've never seen such a thing. Her fingers fly around the edge of the pan, weaving the excess dough into a twisted-edge border.

Stupefied, I capture all this on videotape. But what is extraordinary to me is nothing special to Enrichetta, just life itself. She does not perform; she just carries forth as though making *torta* is as simple as breathing or walking down the street.

Weeks later, back home, I bring this videotape to Lou's house to show him and his wife. We pull up chairs close to the television video player, enthralled, hanging on Enrichetta's every action. And they gasp too, with each addition, each new drizzle of oil, and finally the bubble at the end. "No. No! You've got to be kidding! Get out of here!" Susan cries with disbelief. "You could never *never* write this in a recipe. Never. It's impossible. You'd have to see it to believe it."

And, of course, she's right.

LATER, in the car, the landscape enlarges, becoming enormous beyond my imagining, the mountains higher, the ravines plunging further, all filled with vast green lushness.

"I find Liguria so beautiful," I remark dreamily. "I wonder if my great-grandparents saw it that way. I wonder how people could leave such a beautiful place."

Sergio does not answer. But coming to the village of Péntema, he tells of a legend about how there were two brothers who came here to this difficult wilderness long ago. They each chose the different end of a steep precipice: one chose to live at the top of the mountain, the other at the bottom. After a while, the two brothers met, and the one at the bottom asked the brother at the top if it was good up there. He replied that it wasn't; he regretted his choice, but was it any better below? "No," replied the other brother. "It would have been better to be lost." There are many variations of the story, but all center on the idea of regret, for which the Italian verb is *pentirsi,* and this is why the village is named Péntema.

After we park the car, Sergio asks around for the keys to a strange little museum that the people of this nearly abandoned place have put together to tell the story of their existence. He speaks in Genoese ("You really must learn to speak Genovese," he tells me), and the locals reply with friendliness, unlocking doors so that we may enter several dim and dusty rooms to glimpse a bit of the chestnut people portrayed by eerie mannequins, dressed in handmade clothes, inhabiting small rooms with dirt floors and few windows, partitioned by dark walls and beams of chestnut. In the entry to the kitchen, a few cups and plates hang on a shelf along the wall, along with decorations made of newspaper. In the other rooms, mannequin villagers buy necessities at a little store. They work. They play music. There is community. But the scenes are also staged to show an undeniably harsh poverty.

"*This* is why people left and went to America," offers Sergio.

Outside, walking along the road, is the breathtaking view of poverty set upon beauty. The buildings are made of worn stone, covered in red Celtic tile. Houses—once built for children and grandchildren—extend down from the original homes so that as they grew, families literally built themselves into this mountain, named after the story of two brothers.

"It was all very different then. The mountains looked very different than what you see now," Sergio continues. "Many were logged out and bare." And he explains that if we went in the woods and forests we might find remnants of furnaces that made lime and coal, shacks for preserving ice to sell in the city, flour mills built on the river, stone fences for separating pastures, and terraces for farming.

"Come look." Sergio walks to a small ledge built with rock, hauled up and carefully placed to extend a shelf of earth by a meager few inches. "Imagine that land is so precious that a few extra inches matter this much."

The great historian Fernand Braudel describes the difficulty of the mountains surrounding the Mediterranean since prehistory—a place of hindrance where only primitive life could exist. The people on the low-lying plains aimed for civilization and progress. They had more varied diets, sophisticated cities, and a more elite existence, while the people of the mountains sought survival. And yet, there were certain advantages to mountain life. A certain protection from being high up, away from floodwaters, a certain superiority in independence and freedom.

LATER, while we are driving back, I wonder aloud about the chestnut trees surrounding us and how the mountain people might have felt about them.

"Chestnut was like a brother," Sergio answers, without hesitating. "It's a good brother because it's yours. But like many brothers, you didn't choose it. Like a brother, it might not be the best brother but the one you have. You have to preserve it and take care of it."

A chill comes over me as I look out at the trees, their roots visibly anchored to the ground, and I feel some emptiness as big as one of these mountains, buried deep inside myself.

"As the years go on," Sergio continues, "I know these things more clearly, at a place deeper inside myself. That place is like home."

We are driving along switchbacks going back down toward civilization.

"This is what I don't have," I answer. "This is why I am here."

We are silent for some miles. As we move ahead on the highway, the buildings become denser.

"So many people are looking for tradition," Sergio sighs with frustration. "But tradition is what people just did. Once you are trying to re-create it and say 'okay, let's bring back tradition,' well then it is not the same. Once you are performing, it is gone."

❧❧

THE TRAIN pulls into Little Village with a screech. Down on the street below, we hear the automatic doors open with a sigh.

"They're here!" my littlest exclaims and does a little dance. "They're here!"

"Stop. You're embarrassing me," snaps oldest son who's got the video camera in hand, pointed at the station exit so he can capture their imminent arrival. Occasionally, he pans from left to right, mumbling into the recorder, documenting the scene.

Finally, our two smiling travelers emerge from the station.

"*Ciao bello!*" my husband's sister cries out nearly in song, as she saunters toward my husband and gives him a hug. Colleen and her husband, Filippo, have arrived from England, where they live and work as professors. They seem youthful and bright, in their shorts and T-shirts, carrying suitcases with ease after a mere hop across Europe.

Back at our apartment, we are chatting happily. The children are gleaming—tanned and talkative, filling in their aunt and uncle on the best places to swim and to walk, and the best kinds of focaccia too. "Will you come with us to the Genoa aquarium?" little one pleads.

There's no doubt that when relatives are around, our boys are happier and seem to blossom. I can't help but note how different their twenty-first-century concept of family is from the one I grew up with as a child. Unlike my family, in which my parents and grandparents and aunts and uncles shaped their lives from the struggles of immigrants, our generation has shaped itself around the pursuit of self-betterment and endless personal choices. The result for my children is a small network of warm and loving relatives, most of whom are far flung and extremely busy in a twenty-first-century way. Our sons have a handful of cousins whom they see on special occasions, usually after lengthy journeys by car or train, and they've got a wildly diverse and quirky bunch of aunts and uncles scattered from New Jersey to Massachusetts to Florida to Liverpool. Everyone has married someone very different, with spouses coming from Istanbul, Lagos, and Rome. Our religions range from atheism to Christianity to Judaism to Islam (and not a single one among us practices the faith to which we were born). Certainly no one took on the mantle of family business. Everyone chose a career based on personal passion or mission.

Colleen and Filippo win the prize for the most interesting careers of all, as they are scientists who have chosen not to have children but rather devote themselves to the study of primates. Our kids often see them on their pit stops on the way to the jungle where they sleep in hammocks, trek through snake-ridden bush, and pursue spider monkeys. They give our children a stream of attention and kindness, plus many fascinating stories about monkeys, scorpions, and crocodiles. We bring them all our science questions, ranging from whether gerbils need baths to the metaphysics of life.

"Aunt Colleen, will you tell me all about lemurs?" asks youngest son.

"What kind of dog should we get?" queries the oldest, holding forth his dog encyclopedia.

"Come on," provokes my husband, as he always does. "Not even the slightest possibility of God?"

One night after the dinner dishes are clear and the children are in bed, we four adults are sitting beside the window, wide open to the darkening evening sky. I ask them a science question of my own.

"Is it possible certain foods can become programmed inside us?"

They look at me curiously.

"I mean, if a people live intimately with a food for millennia, might they become biologically wired to love those foods, to feel connected to them?"

I explain about my visits to the chestnut hills. I tell them about chestnut pasta and chestnut bread and chestnut porridges, chestnut furniture and chestnut walls and floors. I tell them about chestnut brother.

"We know a little about this," Colleen starts.

Filippo adds, "At our field site in the Yucatan, we see the same thing with corn—brother corn. Corn in the morning, noon, and night. The Mayans do not believe they've really even eaten a meal if there was no corn tortilla."

"Chestnuts have probably been here at least two thousand years, keeping people alive for much of it," I add, as though this length of time is forever. But even as I say it, I know that for evolutionary biologists this is a mere flicker of an eyelash.

"I don't think it's possible for two thousand years of experience with a food to lead to hardwiring," Colleen says confidently. "In the history of the human species, this is just too short a time for natural selection." She looks to Filippo, who agrees and expands. "There is no 'chestnut gene.'" They remind me that for a long-lived species like us, evolutionary time frames work not in the thousands of years but the hundreds of thousands.

"But perhaps," he offers, "this deep attachment to chestnuts has what we call a *proximate* explanation. From living so close with chestnuts from birth to death, the reverence for these trees and their fruits becomes so deeply internalized that it is nearly unconscious. But there is no chest-nut gene," he repeats.

"What about place?" I ask. "Can a person feel connected to a place he or she has never been to before? Is it possible that we have origins inside us? How do I explain that I feel comfortable here, that in some way I belong? I've got ancestors from northern Europe too. I don't feel pulled there."

"The law of probability is that you draw on more of your family genes than those of others," answers Filippo. "And you may have more genes from here than from other places, so perhaps you're more adapted to the Mediterranean, and this is why you feel more at home here."

We pour out the last of the wine. Outside, nearly all the light is gone, and cool air moves through the unshuttered window.

"But it is interesting," he continues. "As the world changes so quickly now, and more and more places look the same, you might never find where your people came from. You go back to the place, but it doesn't exist anymore."

Colleen and Filippo do not have a need for God. For them the process of evolution gives answers for nearly everything, and in this way, I suppose, it is ultimately a form of the divine. While other people may stare at the sky in search of God, Colleen and Filippo will see the same sky and notice how the birds fly, how they find their food, how the codes in their brains tell them it is time to migrate.

With evolution, they can explain why primates, including humans, love. Why they fight. Why they have memory. Why they stick together with their tribes. Why they reconcile and foster long-term relationships. Even why they have a deep need for forgiveness. It's all about surviving. And most of these qualities evolved during ancient times when humans and prehuman ancestors were hunters and gatherers—situations impossibly different from our present way of life.

We continue to chat late into the night.

Before going off to bed, Filippo has one more thought. "Remember," he says. "You're talking about nature and humans. But just because something is natural doesn't mean we do it. Human beings go against their nature all the time."

⚕

BEFORE WE LEAVE Liguria, I visit some of my old friends: the Guigonis of Genoa, my very first ravioli mentors, who have closed their shop and are retired, enjoying their time together. Maria Carla is as kind as ever. She tells me that if I want to return, I can stay at their home, and she'll give me another cooking lesson.

Marialuisa Schenone comes to Little Village and has a glass of wine with me on the terrace of our apartment. She tells me that Giuseppina is well, though slowing down a little. She invites us all to Lumarzo to spend a Sunday in the country, but a few days later my son gets a terrible fever and we cannot go. Giuseppina is almost ninety now, and I wonder how many more occasions I'll have to see her.

Before we leave, there is one place I must go again. We pack the children in the car and set off one evening. Unfortunately, I cannot remember the way, and we take one wrong turn after the next, as the hour grows later and later. My husband and children are annoyed. "Let's turn back," they say.

"Please," I implore. "We'll find it."

"I hate Italy," cries the little one from the backseat, getting tossed from side to side on the switchbacks. "I want to go home to New Jersey."

My husband is grumpy and aggravated. Adrenaline is high in the little Smart Car, but finally we emerge on top of the correct hill and make our way to Franca's Rue de Zerli. When we turn our car past the yellow steepled church and the pink farmhouse and terraced hillside come into sight, sloping down the hill, I hear my husband say quietly beneath his breath, "Oh my gosh."

It is almost dusk, and the air has that magic in it when the sun has set but light remains in the sky. We park the car, and find Franca outside in shorts and flip-flops with some earth in her feet and hands, her hair tied back. She's clearly been working in the field, along her rows of plants. Again, I'm stunned by the sight of this still-young, earnest-looking woman doing everything from hard labor in the fields to writing brochures for her products.

I introduce my husband and children. They look at Franca's herbs and many rows of vegetables, her olive trees, and her grapes for wine. They play with her dog, then she takes them to the barn and shows them her cow. We spend a few more minutes there and I buy as much chestnut flour and oil as I can carry back. While she is giving it to me, I ask her a question that's been on my mind.

"Did you have other things you could have done with your life? Did you have other choices?"

"Yes, there were other choices," she responds. "Sometimes I grieve for these. But it gives me satisfaction to make these things that would have been abandoned. Over the years we've built a small market of people who want to know these foods and the way of life in these mountains."

The sky is darkening, and it is time to leave and get the children back to Little Village and to bed. We say our good-byes to Franca and drive away.

In the car, on the way back, my husband says quietly, "There's something in you that is a little like her, you know."

I do not answer, because I fear what he is going to say.

"There's a part of you that's always alone, always trying to pursue something beautiful. Way up high, alone at the top of your mountain." His voice is a little sad.

I am unsure of what to say, so I reply, "Thanks for coming with me." And I mean it. I know that over the years, if I ever want to say to someone "Remember Franca's farm?" he will understand completely. We are like that, he and I. So I repeat. "Thanks for coming with me. It makes me less alone."

A FEW DAYS LATER, my husband leaves for the States to return to his job, a week before the boys and I. On the morning of his departure he says "It's breaking my heart to leave you all, to leave this place." Then he kisses us all good-bye. I am tearful as he gets on the train to the airport. I don't know why. I'll see him in only one week. As soon as he's gone, the children are edgy and unsettled. They start talking about going home.

"Don't worry," I tell them. "Soon we will all be together, and this will all seem like a dream."

About twenty hours later, my husband calls from the States to say he arrived safely. He goes on, "I think that journey changed my life. We live with too much stress."

"Yes, yes, I know."

Then he pulls a surprise on me. "Honey, I think we should get rid of this big house on the busy street."

CHAPTER 20

Alchemies

THE CHEESE MAKERS HERE at Caseificio Val d'Aveto have no shortages of what to do with *prescinsêua*.

They all chime in with suggestions. "You can put it in *pansotti* and stuffed vegetables. You can add it to pesto or *torta*. You can mix it with olives and serve it over pasta."

"It's good for desert too," Claudio adds. "You mix it with cocoa and sugar, or with marmalade or whole fruit."

Claudio is the master cheese maker here, a young man who's been at the factory since it began in 1991. That was when a group of idealistic people who'd left this valley for education and jobs got the idea that they wanted to start a cheese business. Their goal was to keep alive the very particular local cheese of this place, the Val d'Aveto, where they'd grown up. Since they were businesspeople, not cheese makers, they looked for a local expert who could do it, and they found Claudio Bassi, who came highly recommended from a farming family with a long history of making cheese.

The flagship item of this *caseificio* is a wonderful cheese called San Sté, made from nonpasteurized milk from the *bruna alpina* or *cabanina* cows that graze in this valley.

"We find that if we make cheese from the same kinds of cows who graze outside this area, the cheese comes out wrong," explains Violeta Bach-varova, an assistant who is giving me a tour.

This is a small factory, and though there are machines for pasteuriz-ing and heating, much of the rest of the work is done by humans and nature. After the milk is heated and slowly develops its curd, the cheese makers lift it out of the big vat, then use their hands, their legs, and all their strength to repeatedly press out the whey. After this, the cheese goes into molds, where it must drain further and eventually go to the aging room where it takes its time evolving and intensifying in flavor. The *caseificio* offers San Sté in three stages: sixty days, four months, or eight months, which range in taste from fresh and creamy to something quite sharp and complex. Violeta lets me go downstairs into the over-whelming fragrance and see the large round cheeses, covered with nat-ural rinds made golden with a simple wash of olive oil, row upon row.

I have come here to learn how to make *prescinsêua*, which is a little ridiculous, I suppose. It is the complexity of hard and semihard cheeses like San Sté that warrant attention. These take the measure of a cheese maker's ability—his mastery of the art and science of acids and cultures and bacteria and curds. A soft unmolded cheese like *prescinsêua*, however, is nothing special at all, just a fresh cheese of home production, some-thing that probably came into being in the kitchens of housewives who—in the days before refrigerators—needed to do something with their milk so it wouldn't go bad. Perhaps the milk would sit out on the counter and accidentally sour and form curds. Then they'd add some rennet and push the process along so that curd and whey would sepa-rate. The next day, they'd drain it and there it would be—fresh cheese. Kay told me that this is what Adalgiza did on her kitchen counter in Hoboken. She or Salvatore wouldn't dream of throwing away perfectly healthful whey, so they drank it. When you get down to basics, fresh cheese can be many things—variations of farmer's cheese, or cream cheese, or cottage cheese, or Liguria's *prescinsêua*.

In fact, *prescinsêua* is not distinctly from this valley high up in the moun-tains. Claudio learned to make it from a woman in Little Village. He explains that it was in the towns along the coast where families would have a single cow at the back door for family use, and in the hotter weather down there, the milk soured easily. *Prescinsêua* was a way of saving it.

Violeta hands me a little paper hat to wear on my head and a mask I must put over my mouth, as everyone in the factory must wear according to health regulations. The floors are wet, and the cheese makers wear boots. The factory has a capacity of only three giant pots that can hold a thousand liters of milk each. It is a loud place where the sound of machines—milk steamers and pasturizers—creates a continuous *whooshing* sound so that we must shout to hear one another.

To make *prescinsêua,* Claudio explains, you begin by heating milk. However, because pasteurization has removed most of the natural and healthy bacteria, he adds these back, using "cultures" much like yogurt. Then he adds rennet. And finally, there is simply the ingredient of time—twenty-four hours to get the small cottage cheese–like curd and tangy taste. After draining, that's about it, he says.

I express my gratitude and head back to my boys, who are being watched by a friend who has come to visit. I bring them some cheese, which I've purchased at the little store here, and some honey too, from local bees. I head back, feeling on top of the world. I have conquered *prescinsêua.* I will make it at home. A song fills my heart as I head back down to Little Village along the switchback roads, eager to see my sons and go swimming with them in the afternoon.

※

"YES, IT'S TRUE. A man might sing under a window. But are you happy now? Are you satisfied?"

We are listening to light and bright mandolin strings, plucking a steady simple rhythm, with vibrato, and a man's voice pledging adoring love.

Might this be the song Salvatore sang to Adalgiza beneath her window? Perhaps not the exact one—but something like it?

"It's a little bit silly for me," laughs Mauro Balma. And it's true; it's a silly love song—pop music from the nineteenth century, a little ditty that traveled up the peninsula from Naples. "Heritage music," Mauro calls it. "Yes, it's true, men would sing under the window. Yes, it's true. Are you satisfied, now?"

Mauro Balma is an ethnomusicologist and a teacher at Paganini Conservatory of Music in Genoa, a scholar and serious man who has spent decades traveling into all corners of Liguria, recording the songs of old and fading vocal traditions. His passion is choral music—the bare a cappella voices of churches, public squares, the streets, and halls. We are in his office now, where he plays this silly love song for me.

"And traditional Ligurian music?"

"Traditional Ligurian music is very distinct," he explains. "There were no love songs like this from here. There were no work songs. There were not even fishing songs."

"No?"

"No. The fishermen didn't want to scare away the fish."

"Well, then, what's left?"

"*Trallaleri*," he replies with a satisfied smile. He is speaking of Genoa's legendary choral music that was born in taverns and took root in the streets around the ports. Facing one another in a circle, men would sing in five-part harmonies—few words, and many sounds. It is something like the street doo-wop my father sang when he was young, but far more layered and complex. One voice takes the falsetto, another the tenor, another the baritone, and then there's the power of the bass that holds the line while the fifth voice, most astonishingly, takes the part of a vocal guitar—producing the sound of strings. The freedom of sounds, vibrating in chantlike rhythms, flying away with speed. In many parts of Liguria, singers formed teams called *squadre*, which competed with one another. Immigrants in America begged their relatives to send them the records. Later, I will learn that Salvatore's father was a singer in the Recco band and often got into trouble with his wife for disappearing to go off and sing.

Mauro goes to his impressive equipment to play for me a recording of the famous *trallalero* song "La Partenza." It is a devastating piece. But who is departing? What does it mean? All that emotion, all that force. It is like opera, like liturgy. He waves his hand, saying he could never explain it to me. He's spent thirty years writing articles and books about it. Look at them all. He points to his bookcase.

"Can I go and hear *trallaleri*?" I ask.

Mauro explains that men still gather informally in Piazzetta Luccoli each week in Genoa and sing, but I'll have to come back because they take a break in summer.

"Do women ever sing it?" I ask.

"Rarely." Mauro smiles, shaking his head. And when he sees my disappointment, he tells me that women have their songs too. "In western Liguria, there is a tradition called *canti narrativi*. These are songs that tell stories, and they are sung by women. Less complex musically," he explains. "They are often melodramatic tales that recount catastrophes. You could pay them and they'd sing, or they'd do it out of their own desire."

With his help, I find recordings of these songs in a local store. And on the way back to Little Village, in my car, I listen to the bare unaccompanied voices of women, singing tales of life's loves and misfortunes, songs of forced marriages, soldiers gone to war, shepherdesses in fields, and many love songs.

True, these are not the complex harmonies of *trallaleri*. Often the singer is alone—and the voice is crying out with a need to tell. A voice, at times, almost unbearably naked and droning. They are women driven to tell the things that happen, the beauty of the world around them, the love of family, ther losses, their desires.

DRIVING along the Ligurian Sea, I realize that I am one of them.

I am one of these old women singing, driven by some force I can't understand to tell the stories of everything that has happened. Cooking and singing and storytelling—perhaps all these are variations of the same human desire to communicate over time and space, to make the invisible real. This is what I do, whether I like it or not.

CHAPTER 21

Rolling the Dough III

Wᴇɴ I ʀᴇᴛᴜʀɴ to New Jersey, one of the first things I do is find a cheese-making supply company that will sell me rennet. When it arrives, I heat two quarts of milk to ninety degrees, add a little plain yogurt, and then a couple of drops of rennet, as Claudio advised.

I set the pot on my kitchen table and wait for the magic to occur, checking hourly for signs of change. Sure enough, nature does its job, and slowly the milk divides itself—liquid moving to the top and solid mass forming below. This drama continues for more than twenty-four hours until, yes, by god, I've made cheese. I pour the whey into the sink (apologizing to Adalgiza that I'm not drinking it), and then hang the curd in cheesecloth so it can drain over the sink for several hours.

When it is done, I am quite pleased indeed. This fresh cheese of mine is smooth, rich, and pleasantly tangy. It spreads beautifully over bread. But it simply is not *prescinsêua*. I take another bite. "Hmmm. What exactly have I done?" It takes a while, but eventually I realize that I have made cream cheese.

Aᴛ Lᴏᴜ's house, when we come to the footage of Roberto rolling pasta with his pin, Lou leans forward in his chair, eyes widening. "Look at *that*," he says, in obvious awe of how Roberto uses his arms and of the magic in the transforming dough. He is under the spell of the pin. Visions of his mother and the old ladies in his childhood neighborhood arise like ghosts before him. He is spellbound and murmurs in a reverent tone, "I'm going to make pasta with a pin."

I smile smugly. "It was worth going to Italy just to hear you say those words."

A week later, I walk into Lou's house and he has his Atlas electric pasta maker out on the granite countertop island, cranking out the last batch of a hundred delicate cheese ravioli.

"Look, I began a little over an hour ago!"

I can't help but admire the dough, which is silky and thin, and the ravioli, which are all perfectly shaped. Ever production oriented, Lou has refined his system considerably. His preferred method now is the silver ravioli form, which is something like an ice-cube tray. He sprinkles it with fine semolina to prevent sticking. Then, once his pasta dough emerges from the machine, he lays it down. Next, he spoons *ripieno* into each slot. Then the top piece of dough is laid down on top.

"Now watch carefully, Laura. Don't drift off on me. This next bit is important. I figured out the best way to do this."

Out comes a special wooden board he has cut to the exact dimensions of the ravioli form. He presses this gently on top of the ravioli to press them shut. The final coup: a two-inch-wide wallpaper roller. Indeed, it works fabulously to seal the entire perimeter of the form. A flip of the form, and the ravioli are falling out, ready to be cut.

"Beautiful. But Lou, when are you going to try the pin?"

He shakes his head.

"Huh? What happened?"

"No," he replies. "It's not for me. I love the machine."

WHEN FALL comes and the children are back in school, I lug my big pasta board and pin to the kitchen table and pledge to roll pasta each day until I finally get it right. I set up my camera on the counter and open the two-by-two-inch screen. There is Roberto again, my virtual teacher. Perhaps not the flesh-and-blood *nonna* I wish for, but then again, you can't use the rewind button on real-life *nonnas*. With my videotape I go back and forth watching his movements as often as I wish. I also follow Roberto's advice on flour, but perhaps the most groundbreaking lesson of all is when I begin adding a small amount—"*poco poco*"—of olive oil to my dough at the very beginning, just as he suggests, and I discover a dough that is far softer and more obedient in my hands.

But still, the whole endeavor is a huge inconvenience. Each day there is flour on the floor, and we are tripping over pasta boards and my assortment of dowels and rolling pins. My oldest son goes into the pantry and takes out a bag of dried pasta, which he holds up to my face. "Hello. Have you heard of this marvelous new invention?"

In my freezer, a pile of plastic-wrapped, hand-rolled noodles begins to grow. They form a record of my progress. Each day's experience builds on the previous one, so that I am coming along, slowly, learning to slap, pull, and stretch. I work in small batches, able to control only small amounts of dough at once. Finally, my pasta is becoming thinner and more supple. I'm still an amateur with years to go. But there is no doubt that after two or three weeks of near daily practice, I am getting closer.

AROUND this time, a whirlwind of relatives descends once again from far away. This time, it is my sister Lisa and her husband, Kayhan. They are newly married and live in Florida, where they relocated only a few months earlier. I have missed Lisa terribly, and when I open the front door I nearly cry when I find her there with her bright blue eyes, full of joy for her new life, and carrying big bags of enormous juicy oranges and lemons from the trees in their yard. After our hellos, Kayhan shows us photos of their new house, which my husband and I call the "Florida Love Pad," because two trees have naturally grown together in the front yard forming a circle, or perhaps even—how could it be—a heart. They show us photos of their garden bursting with vegetables and herbs. My sister is happy, and after forty years of having her very close by, I let her go freely, despite knowing she may never live near me again. Even now, they are only passing through.

To celebrate their brief visit, I decide that today, when I get out my pasta board for my daily roll, I will go all the way and make ravioli. Lisa and Kayhan stand close and watch each step. In Lisa, I find the eager sister who wants to learn and share.

"Can I try?" she asks.

"First watch Roberto," I reply, snapping on the video for her tutorial while the dough rests. When it is time to begin again, I start the process of rolling, get it halfway there, and then hand over the pin to Lisa. Though she is a little clumsy and giggling during the process, she quickly gets the idea and starts stretching and flipping.

"I want to show this to my mother and aunt in Istanbul," says Kayhan. "They make *manti*. And they will like to see it."

In the end the ravioli come out fabulously, and we gather the family that night and eat with gusto. The children chatter away with their aunt and uncle. A feeling of goodwill comes over the table.

THREE weeks later, Lisa and Kayhan pass through our home once again, this time on their return trip from Istanbul to Florida. They arrive again with gifts, but this time instead of oranges and lemons, they've got the Turkish red pepper I love, little bowls of brightly painted pottery, a handblown glass pitcher, and Turkish candy bars for the children. They show us photos of Istanbul and of their many adventures.

"But wait," says Kayhan. "Here's a surprise for you." He plugs his video camera into our television.

"I showed my mother and aunt that video of you making pasta. They send this back in return."

With this introduction, the image of a Turkish woman fills the screen. It is his aunt, kneading dough. Instead of working at a big wooden board in the Italian manner, she is on her knees, working at a three-legged table placed on an immaculate tile floor. This table is specially designed for this job, as it allows a woman to kneel and put the full strength of her elbows into the kneading. Next, my sister gets on her knees to try. They put a peasant's babushka on her head, a good-natured joke. I marvel at the sight of my sister in her new life, the wife of a Turkish man, in an Istanbul kitchen with views of the Bosphorus, cooking with these women—her new family—making *manti* in a language we don't understand. Once the dough is made (with milk!) and kneaded and finally rolled out, the women sit at the kitchen table and put bits of raw chopped meat, onions, and garlic in the center of small pieces of dough, which they wrap into little packets. After they are boiled and put steaming onto the plate, the *manti* are served with a sauce of thick Turkish yogurt, raw chopped garlic, and a small bit of cooked tomato drizzled on top.

My brother-in-law extends an invitation. "They want me to tell you that you are welcome to come and make *manti* any time."

DURING THE MONTHS that follow our visit to Italy, my husband suggests again that we sell our house. He wants a place that is smaller, less expensive, and on a quiet road. We go house hunting. I visit kitchens that are cramped. Kitchens that are big. Kitchens that have large islands with granite countertops. Kitchens that are perfect and sterile with maple cabinets and terra-cotta tile. Kitchens that would best be torn apart.

"Less stress," my husband repeats. "Less stress."

Each time I look at a place, I check first to see if it's right for the boys. Then I try to see myself inside the kitchen, rolling pasta, with all my family around me at Christmas. When I can see this, I'll know I've found the right one.

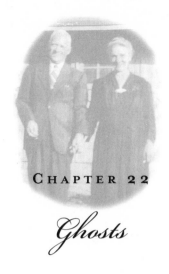

CHAPTER 22

Ghosts

THE HOLY CROSS CEMETERY in North Arlington, New Jersey, is surrounded by busy streets, auto parts shops, and florists selling their wares for the grave. Paved roads wind through rolling green grass. In New Jersey fashion it is a crowded place, with people buried on top of one another and the names on the headstones evoking countries from all over the world.

Cousin Catherine had promised me years earlier that one day she'd take me here so I would know where Salvatore and Adalgiza lie. Finally I called her to ask if we could plan the outing. "Invite your mother, and I'll bring my daughter Valerie. We'll have lunch at the golf club afterwards," she said brightly.

And so we set out one Indian summer day. Mothers in the front, daughters in the backseat. Along the way, Valerie, who is also a great-granddaughter of Adalgiza, tells me that she remembers holding Adalgiza's hand and can still see her image in her mind's eye. *Nonna,* she calls her. On the half-hour drive, Valerie and I are chatty and familiar. She is a pretty woman in her fifties, with blond curls and blue eyes, one of those "soft" Schenones.

My mother turns past the cemetery gates with its sign: "We remember. We believe."

"A lot of memories here, huh, Catherine?"

"Yeah, a lot. And many not so good," she laughs. "The best memories are now. I tell you, this man I married is wonderful." Then Catherine directs my mother to the right part of the cemetery, past mausoleums with big crucifixes.

"Over here," she says. "No. Over there." She is frustrated at first, but after some moments we find the way and park the car. Catherine knows the place well and is in charge.

"This way," she points. "All the Schenones are over here." She leans on Valerie for support, walking on the grass in her heels, and leads the way toward a cluster of gray headstones in the open sunlight.

"Laura, take your mother's arm," she calls over her shoulder. "Marcia, don't be so darned independent. Let her help you." And she is right, because the grass is uneven and my mother walks unsteadily.

And so we walk arm in arm through the grass and trees, and suddenly all is quiet and peaceful, the sound of traffic distant. The leaves are beginning to turn from green to red, so that we see with our eyes that fall is here, though the air still breathes of summer. Finally, we arrive.

The headstone is simple. The name SCHENONE in large letters, and beneath: "Salvatore 1868–1944" and "Adalgiza 1874–1955." We pause a moment. And I imagine Adalgiza here in 1944, weeping for her husband, surrounded by her five children.

"Catherine, were they happy together at the end of their lives?"

"Who?"

"Salvatore and Adalgiza."

"Well, what do you mean?"

"They were so in love when they were young. How did it turn out?"

"Well, they weren't like couples you see today," she replies, stumbling a little at this crazy question. "I mean, they didn't show open signs of affection. I didn't see them kiss all the time. It was different then. He was a sweet, quiet man. She was a strong woman, who told you when she was angry."

She pauses. "They talked together. They laughed. They were . . . " She searches for the right word. "They were together," she replies. "I can't say they were *un*happy."

Then I ask Catherine what I've never asked her, which is how they died.

Salvatore and Adalgiza, together in old age.

All she says is that Salvatore had some kind of tumor growing in his once-beautiful face, some kind of horrible cancer. He was sick for a long time, and Adalgiza took care of him to the end.

"The morning of his funeral, she got up and made minestrone because the people would come back to the house. That's how they did it then, you know. They didn't go out to restaurants like today."

And Adalgiza?

"She was fine. She was healthy. And she used to tell me that one day she'd just fall on the floor and that would be the end. Well, that's exactly what happened. They called me one morning to come. And when I got there, I didn't want to believe it. I took it very hard. She raised me. No, I didn't want to believe it." But she soon lifts her voice and resumes the tour of the Schenones.

"Now, of course, Tessie's not here. She died on the West Coast. There's my mother. And there's Lena," she points. "And down over there, your grandfather Louis, and here is Al, and his daughter—so sad, in her thirties."

Tessie and Adalgiza.

In the sober light of death, Catherine remains upbeat. "You know, it's not morbid to be here. It's not sad."

"No, I don't think it's morbid," I reply far too quickly, embarrassing myself. What do I know of death? I have my parents, my sisters, my husband, my children all alive.

Catherine smiles and continues. "It used to be hard. But now, some-times it's good to come back and check in once in a while. Come on, Valerie. Let's go see Dad." They walk off up a hilly patch of grass to her first husband's grave.

My mother's right arm is shaking. Whenever she is upset or emo-tional, her Parkinson's flares. We look each other in the eyes, mother and daughter, inextricably linked. When I was a girl, she always told me that I would go to places she never would. That I would go far beyond her. Whenever this has come true, I have never been able to be purely happy because of my sadness in leaving her behind. But in this glance, we understand everything, she and I.

We take a breath and look on the single headstone before us, shared by my grandparents under the word SCHENONE: Louis 1905–1957. Frances Patterson 1911–1999.

WHEN GRANDMA SCHENONE died, it was not from a broken heart, not from anger, not from Alzheimer's disease, but rather from cancer in her stomach—and this seemed a terrible indignity, somehow, to die of something so purely physical and organic. My father got a call from his sister about the funeral date, and of course the Catholic wake when her body would be laid out for respects at the funeral home in her town.

"Wakes are for the living, not the dead," my father said, to explain why he would not be going. He could not grieve with his siblings.

As an alternative, my mother phoned his friends, put out food and drink, and held a gathering at their home. In this way my father, red-eyed and a bit bewildered, received condolences. His Italian friends came, some neighbors too. My sisters and I were all there. My father's old friend Michael brought a bottle of wine that his father had made in the basement. It tasted brutal and strong. We all drank a fair amount that night, knowing that the next day was the funeral. We were sad, but we were a bit nervous too. How could we not be? What should we expect after ten years?

THE NEXT morning we arrived at Queen of Peace Church with plenty of time. We took a seat in a pew near the front—my parents, we three girls, and two husbands. We sat there contemplating the images of Christ on the cross, Joseph the carpenter father, holding the beautiful baby boy, and Mary the virgin mother with her bare foot crushing the serpent's head. I took in the old familiar setting, memorized deep within me: the peacefulness, the wood pews, the flowers on the altar, the shape of the pulpit, lifted up high, and the stained-glass images of the stations of the cross, which offer comfort because even Christ endured humiliation in his human form.

This is the church where Grandma Schenone went each morning for mass, where my father was an altar boy, and where my cousins took their sacraments and got married. We were sitting there quietly in our good clothes, knowing we were carrying out something that had been decided long ago, waiting, wondering why the pews were not filled with my father's estranged family. The minutes passed. Why so empty? Where were they? I stole a glance at my parents, who looked like two people standing on a windswept mountain alone. Their faces, flustered, their bodies not quite rooted to the ground. My sisters and I moved in toward them, tightening the circle.

The sound of wheels from the back of the church took us by surprise.

Startled, we turned to look at the back. There they all were. Dozens of them. The priest, dressed in white robes, led the way, swinging incense that dangled from a chain. Behind him, my grandmother's casket on wheels, and all around her, my uncles, aunts, their children, and grandchildren—faces drawn and sad—ushering her up to the altar with a slow and solemn walk.

It was a shock. Some cousins had transformed from teenagers to adults. Others had moved from youth to midlife, their faces thin and fallen. My aunts and uncles had become gray and old. Just like that. And they were greater in number too, having expanded over the years with marriages and births, so that now there were dozens of them—beautiful young children whom we'd never met. We had the space of their stately walk up the aisle to take in the vision in its entirety. The rhythm of the incense swinging, side to side, click click, from the chain. The mysterious and confusing whoosh of time, blowing in our faces, to leave us all soon in the dust.

When the casket arrived at its place before the altar and the holy incense had been fully given, the priest went to his place and all of my father's siblings and their children and children's children took seats in the pews in front of us. Instantly, the church seemed full.

"The Father, the Son, and the Holy Spirit," the priest began. And as we were programmed from birth, we blessed ourselves with the sign of the cross and replied in unison "Amen," grateful to know exactly what to do.

"We are gathered here to bid farewell to Frances, a child of God. . . ."

And so the funeral mass began. From the beginning of the mass, I was anticipating the moment when it would come.

Give us this day our daily bread and forgive us our trespasses as we forgive those who trespass against us . . .

I was wondering what would happen. Would they be able to say that most essential prayer? Or would they fall silent? Amazingly they recited each word. My cousins, my uncles, my aunt, and my father said the prayer loudly in unison—perhaps that part even a bit louder than the rest.

And so the mass proceeded and the priest opened his arms and called out "Peace be with you," and we replied "And also with you." And now we arrived at the kiss of peace, that point before sharing the body of Christ when all good Catholics turn to the person next to them, whether family, friend, or stranger, and extend love and peace. In front of us, they were all shaking hands with one another and hugging. Then an extraordinary thing happened. My cousin Michael, now a man of forty, stepped out of his pew and walked straight to my parents and put his arms around them. "Peace be with you, Uncle Pete. Peace be with you, Aunt Marcia." My parents, stunned, hugged him back. "Peace be with you," they whispered.

And after this many more cousins came toward us, shaking our hands, hugging us, and wishing us peace. It went on so long that it seemed the priest would never resume, but finally he did, and we began the last prayers for Grandma Schenone.

AT THE cemetery, we emerged from our cars into the mellowed October light. It was an odd day, warm but with roiling purple and silver clouds in the sky, moving lower each moment. As the priest recited prayers at the graveside, the wind blew wildly. Yellow leaves swirled about us as Grandma's casket was lowered into the ground.

The funeral director gave us roses. One at a time, each person walked up to the edge of that hole in the earth to toss in a flower. When my mother's turn came, I watched her step up to the grave of the woman who had dominated her life. Her body shook so violently I wanted to wrap her in my arms tight enough to hold her still.

When it was all done and everyone was dispersing, a group of cousins approached and invited us to come to the reception at a little restaurant where arrangements had been made. My sisters and I agreed to go for a drink, and most amazingly, my father—still in an otherworldly state from seeing his mother's casket lowered into the ground—shrugged his shoulders and muttered, "Okay."

An hour later, we were all sitting at the bar, my Uncle Louie buying my sister Lisa and me drinks, catching up and laughing as though nothing had ever happened. Some relatives kept politely distant, saying hello but nothing more. Others hugged us and suggested we all stay in touch again, inviting us to their homes, and offering phone numbers. It was too much. It was all just too much. So when the lunch trays finally came, and everyone moved to sit at the table, we gave our thanks, got our coats, and left.

In the car, a few blocks away, I asked my father if he thought he could repair the damage with his brothers, if he believed there was hope.

He did not hesitate and shook his head no. "What happened in there didn't mean anything," he replied with brutal calm, while my mother looked out the car window in silence.

"Really?"

"Really," he replied with certainty.

For years to come, I'd think of this day and my father's words, at times angry and bitter, at times knowing this was the most honest response of all.

THAT DAY of my grandmother's funeral had been the last time my mother and I stood on this spot. Now Kay and Valerie return from their rounds, and my mother and I are glad to leave. I walk back to Salvatore and Adalgiza's grave for one last parting glance.

After a merry lunch at the golf club, the four of us disperse. My mother and Catherine return to their apartments across the street from each other, while I agree to give Valerie a ride home. When we pull up to her house, she invites me in, and I follow her down the side path to the back door and into the kitchen. Inside, Valerie promptly takes off her heels and climbs up, onto her kitchen counter, reaching to a shelf high above the cupboard. "Got it," she says, climbing back down with two rolling pins in her hand. One is a massive round dowel, the other a checkered ravioli pin.

"These were Nonna's." She holds them toward me.

A chill glides down my spine as I take the large pin from her into my hands. I am astonished. It is a huge thing, far bigger and thicker than I've ever seen, at least three feet long and perhaps three inches in diameter, dark wood, worn with age and experience.

"Oh my god," I whisper. It is so solid and heavy in my hands. "And look at this one!" I take hold of the checkered pin.

"If you like, you can borrow them for a while. I'm not using them."

"Are you sure?" I ask, almost afraid of the responsibility.

"Yes, take them," she replies with certainty.

Adalgiza's checkered rolling pin.

❧

THE NEXT DAY, I wake up agitated. I can't work. I can't think. So instead, I go to Lou's and show him the rolling pin.

"Wow. Look at that beauty," he exclaims, and I hand it over for him to examine.

"Maple." He says, looking closely. He finds a little notch in the wood that seems intentional—perhaps slashed with a knife—and he wonders if perhaps Adalgiza had put it there as a marker of some kind. "Well, we'll never know, will we?"

All day long, I carry the pin with me throughout the house. I've got it in the office while I'm working. I've got it out on the counter at night while I do the dinner dishes. I pick it up frequently and touch it.

Finally, a few days after I've received it, I get up my nerve. I go to my pasta board and put several handfuls of flour on the board, crack the eggs, and begin making *sfolgia*. A half hour after the dough is rested, I take a deep nervous breath and say, "Okay, come on. Let's go."

And of course, it is with this pin that something changes. Whether it's the sheer weight of it, or the spirit of Adalgiza, or just all my cumulative efforts of practice, I cannot say, but from the first time I press Adalgiza's pin down on my dough, I become more confident and sure. I'm finally doing it—rolling out dough so that it is smooth and thin.

For a brief while, I come to believe that my ancestors are sending me messages. No, it's not that they are ghosts in the sky or shadows whispering to me. It's that all human beings leave messages for the future. It's that my ancestors lived their lives in a certain way and they left behind these things for me—the ravioli press, the tools, the people who would keep the scraps that could be pieced together. It was all there. I just had to try hard enough.

I even come to believe that Adalgiza brought her ravioli here from Genoa partly for me and my children. She didn't know it, of course. She didn't know who I would be. But she taught her daughters and they taught theirs so that it would be there for those who wanted—or needed—to find it someday.

————

SHORTLY after this, real voices do come back from the dead. A package arrives in the mail. It is from my father's cousin Rosemary. I open it up and find a CD, which I immediately put in my player. There is static and scratchiness and then a voice.

"Good evening, everyone."

It is Adalgiza's youngest son, Al, who got a new tape recorder one Christmas in the 1950s. Amazed with his new technology, Uncle Al went about interviewing all family members.

"I'm here with my mother, and I'm going to ask her a few questions," he says. Then comes Adalgiza's voice, the voice of an old Italian lady, still a little fiesty. In Genoese, she gives her age and states how long she has been in this country. She says she's a Democrat and became an American citizen a few years earlier.

"*Quante figli ai?*" asks Al.

"*Cinque,*" she replies, five children. At this point she breaks into exuberant English.

"I got thirteen grandchildren! And seven great-grandchildren!"

"Mom. Do you speak English?" he asks her.

"A lily bit," she replies.

LATER in the tape, Al goes around at a merry holiday gathering and asks everyone to sing. Everyone is a hambone. Everyone has got a song. Whether it's "Ma Vie en Rose" or "Ain't Misbehavin'," or an Italian number because the room is full of people from Naples, Sicily, and Genoa, the unification of Italy, right here in New Jersey.

When Al brings his microphone to Grandma Schenone, she giggles and begins her old favorite, "When Irish Eyes Are Smiling." She starts off a little unsure, but soon she finds her way, her soprano grows stronger with vibrato, making the most of each note. It is beautiful, and she gets huge cheers. She always was a wonderful singer. I smile while I listen, sixty years later, proud of her.

After this, Al brings the microphone to my grandfather.

"Now we're going to talk to my brother Louie. You working hard, Louie?" And my grandfather replies, yes, yes. And though I've never heard his voice, it is familiar to me, because he gave some of it to my father and uncles. Like his wife, he chooses an Irish ballad. Without hesitation, he begins, as though he's been perfectly ready for this moment.

There's a spot in my heart,
Which no colleen may own.
There's a depth in my soul,
Never sounded or known . . .

There's a place in my mem'ry
My life, that you fill,
No other can take it,
No one ever will.

Like a candle that's set
In the window at night,
Your fond love has cheered me
And guided me right

Sure, I love the dear silver
That shines in your hair,
And the brow that's all furrowed,
And wrinkled with care.
I kiss the dear fingers,
So toil-worn for me,
Oh, God bless you and keep you,
Mother Machree

He reaches for the high long note at the end and belts it out with gusto.

CHAPTER 23

See the Good in Me

W E'RE ALL SET," says my dad with enthusiasm on the phone. "You know how to roll the dough. You've got my grandmother's pin."

Ravioli day. This year, I finally will not be doing the job alone. My parents have offered to hold the event at their home, and to help too. My father is especially enthused.

"And now we've got the authentic recipe," he says.

"Really?" I ask. "Which authentic recipe do you mean?"

"The one with the cream cheese of *course*. Come on Laur," he teases in New Jerseyese so it sounds like *Law*. "That's the one! That's the authentic one."

"I don't know, Dad," I hedge. "I don't know what's authentic."

"Oh, come on," he teases. "Don't go and get all difficult on me!"

My parents make a day of it. Of course, Lisa is too far away, and Andrea never really says whether she'll come or not. But a few of my father's Italian friends will be there, and Catherine and Valerie too. When my mother hears this, she puts her foot down. "Now, Laura." And this is her I-mean-business-tone. "I'm sorry, but you must do the Schenone recipe," she insists. "Catherine is coming. Let's show some respect, please."

She's got a point. I purchase raw chopped meat and the cheese in the silver foil, pack my car with pasta boards, rolling pins, ravioli cutters, and dough scraper, and head to my parents' house for the big day. They are in a festive state with the tree decorated and lit and the table spread with a simple lunch of sandwiches, salad, and of course a spinach *torta*.

The work begins at the pasta board. Catherine stands close while I pull the *sfoglia* together. When I make a fuss over my wonderful imported oo flour, she responds good-naturedly, "Well, Nonna didn't have *that*. She only had Pillsbury Gold Medal."

While I make the *ripieno,* she is at my side. "Start with your cream cheese," she instructs. "Do you have a handheld mixer? Use it then." She peers into the bowl and says decisively, "Add another cream cheese," then talks me through the rest of the ingredients: the egg, spinach, meat, and cheese. Quickly, the *ripieno* is ready.

When the moment comes to take Adalgiza's big pin in hand and begin rolling, Catherine again is there. "Oh, no, keep the pin closer to your body. There you go. No need to lean out so far." She is surprised at the small size of my dough—a mere three feet in circumference. "I used to make it so big, it hung off the side of the table!" she laughs.

I am happy for her corrections. With Adalgiza's pin in my hands and

her granddaughter at my side mentoring me, this moment is the final link in the chain.

Meanwhile, everyone in the kitchen watches with awe, eager for a chance to hold Adalgiza's magical pin and give it a try. One by one they step up for a turn. First my father. Then Valerie. Then my parents' friends Michael and Susan and their teenage son. Then my mother. Each person steps up to stretch and flip the dough, while Catherine oversees and encourages. And as each batch is transformed to a smooth sheet, we fill and fold and cut and move and then lift the ravioli to a tray on the counter where they can dry. With extra hands, this work goes more easily than ever.

Of course I can't resist certain things. After the first 350 ravioli are done, I quietly bring forth a secret Tupperware bowl filled with a *ripieno* I made a day earlier—the *ripieno* I learned to make in Italy, fragrant and braised in wine and spices, then put through the meat grinder with borage grown in my garden. My father and Kay look at me confused. "Huh?" They crinkle their noses. "What's that?" But they allow me to use it, shrugging their shoulders.

We make seven hundred ravioli that day. Half are Hoboken. Half are Genoa. Though this distinction annoys my father. "Wasn't my grandmother from Genoa?" he asks. "Maybe you just didn't figure it out. Maybe there were people there who made them this way."

And he may be right.

We make a box for Kay and Valerie and a box for my father's friends. We put aside the rest for Christmas. Once Kay and Valerie are gone, we put a small pot of water on the stove and boil up a couple to taste and compare.

My father's friends prefer the foreign ones. My father prefers his family recipe. It couldn't be otherwise. I sense a slight irritation with me for confusing the issue, and this is understandable.

For me, there is no resolution. Of course not. There never will be. I had originally hoped that I'd someday be able to say that once, I went on a quest for something. I traveled through time and place and searched for a single beautiful dish that I could revive and pass on. And I found it.

Now I know that this was naïve.

As Sergio told me, there is no one recipe. I have many teachers and many recipes now. Yes, I found what I was looking for. But not a single dish. There is simply no choosing between Lou's machine and Giuseppina's hands. Between Maria Carla's slow-braised meats and Millie and Susan's recipe with cream cheese, between the herbs and cheese at La Brinca and the organ meats in the recipes of Niccolò Paganini.

But all this was decided long ago, the day Salvatore got on that boat and left home; the day Adalgiza set off to find him, with whatever desperation, ambition, and love that set her course. And in this modern world we inherited, there are so many more paths to take, so many more choices, that we must somehow learn to live with a fair amount of conflict. When it comes to tradition, there will never be any single recipe for me. I have a heritage handed down to me, and I have one that I had the means to discover. A family I inherited. And a very different one that I created. There is no resolution for the woman who loves her children and the one who flies to Italy for a personal quest. The woman who loves her husband, and the one who disappears into obsessions.

To survive, we create whatever intimacies we can bear. We make ravioli. We make songs. We tell stories. I have tried my best to cast off what was wrong. But after this, I must carry what I need to hold the parts of my life together.

THIS IS THE PART when any good storyteller or singer of a *canto narrativo* would return to the chorus and close the circle. I'd like to tell the story of how I finally enter the kitchen with my two sisters. But I can't write this one yet.

When the ravioli are all in my mother's freezer, when the huge wooden board is hauled onto the counter and scrubbed, my sister Andrea drops by with her son. My nephew is intrigued by all the equipment. He too wants to try to roll pasta. But Andrea just peeks in the ravioli boxes and takes a look. "Hmmmm," she nods.

Later that night, I come home and sit on the couch with my husband. I lay my head on his chest and tell him about the day and my sister's lack of interest.

"Why doesn't she care?" I ask him, not really expecting an answer, but he gives one anyway that I don't want to hear.

"Because you don't care about what interests her."

"What—like I'm supposed to go join her church or something and become an evangelical Christian?"

"Well, no, not exactly," he replies. "But there is this thing in you," he begins. "Listen. You're a wonderful person"—and that's how I know I'm going to get it—"but you act like you know everything. That's why your sister won't talk to you."

A few weeks later, we are at Andrea's house for Christmas dinner. Standing in her kitchen, I watch as she nervously boils the ravioli, expecting me to find fault. She manages just fine and brings them to the table. But when I see her quiet, awkward way, I think about my husband's words and know they are true.

LOU AND I stand shoulder to shoulder with strangers on the elevator going to the Institute of Culinary Education in New York. It is packed. Friday night, and the recreational cooks come out in force. Mothers and daughters. Husbands and wives. Partners and singles of every kind.

Classes in pastry and pasta. Classes in Chinese cooking. French culinary arts. Knife skills.

"Hmmm. Guess people really want to learn to cook," notes Lou.

Searching for our classroom, Lou and I walk the halls as though we are undercover spies. No one needs to know that we've been making pasta for nearly three years now. We want to see what we do and do not know. We'd like to learn some new tricks. Being home cooks, we can't help but be excited by the scale of things here: the enormous shining prep tables, the giant ovens, the fleets of stand-up professional-grade mixers.

"We will use the pasta machine here for rolling," announces our teacher, Gerri Sarnataro, an Italian-American from Brooklyn. "And we will get very good results."

Gerri explains that she has been teaching pasta for years and has traveled all over Italy, finding older women to teach her. "And that's how I know I could *never* teach you with a rolling pin in a single night."

Our class of twelve breaks into teams to make lasagne, manicotti, and tagliatelle. Lou and I try our hands at some new shapes—long threads of pasta cut by the strings of a *chitarra* and thumb-imprinted *orecchiette*, which look like little ears. We learn some sauces, a braise of rabbit, a ragu with lamb.

Gerri shows us how to make pasta dough two ways: first by hand and then with a stand-up mixer. When I ask which method she prefers, she responds, "The KitchenAid is a great tool that will let you have pasta as part of your daily life." Then she adds, "Listen, there is a point where technology allows you to do certain things better. And then there is a point where technology wrecks food. You've got to figure out the difference." And perhaps more than anything that evening, I take these words with me. I tell Lou that okay, maybe, I'll get a KitchenAid.

The next day, he invites me and my boys to stop by his house. He's all excited to show us something. We follow him out to his garage, where he keeps table saws and sheets of wood for various carpentry projects. He has some of the kitchen in here as well. A handmade smoker for meat and fish, plus barrels of wood chips soaking in water. Lou points above my boys' heads and they look up and *soppresatta* is hanging from the rafters. Lou explains to my sons how he mixed pork with spices and put it into large casings, which he pressed in a vice for four days.

"Those up there have been hanging here six or seven weeks. And now they're done."

He pulls one down and we follow him into the kitchen. He gives us thin spicy slices on bread he's baked.

Lou Palma in his garage with his cured meat.

"Mom," says number one son with clear amazement. "Why can't we do all these things?"

I say, "Don't worry, Honey. We will."

The *soppresatta* reminds them of Italy. They talk often about wanting to return there.

"Why?" I ask, when they bring it up.

"Because it was *beautiful*," says number one son. "Because of the mountains and the sea. Because of the swimming and the food."

Whenever the little one, now almost six years old and full of drama, sees some photos from our trip, he puts a hand dramatically over his eyes. "Oh, don't show me those pictures of Italy. I'll just want to go back even more."

&ca;

THE CONVERSATION I had in the garage with my father when I was sixteen wasn't quite the end of it. Part two came nearly twenty years later. By then, we were all grown up, my father and I, with little left to struggle over. We'd gotten on well for a very long time by then.

But then I had my first child, and trouble began. My father was kind to my children. He was generous. He came to birthday parties and played with them at holidays. And yes, my outlaw oldest son found him to be very cool with his gray ponytail and tattoos.

But at the very outset of his relationship with my sons, my father let it be known that he did not wish to play grandfather. He asked that our children not call him "Grandpa," but rather use his first name. He also pronounced, to my mother's dismay, that the two of them were not available as backup. "We don't babysit," is how he put it. "We just don't do it. I don't believe in it."

I tried to ignore this. But then there was a moment when the earth shifted. My husband and I were living five hours away with our two-year-old boy, and we needed to travel back to New Jersey to attend a wedding. My mother agreed to care for our son, and so we came over with his bundles of diapers and toys and big smiling cheeks and happy dances. Then off we went.

Later that night when we crept into my parents' house, my sixth sense warned me that something was wrong, but it was late and all the lights were out and there was nothing to do but go to bed.

The next morning at the breakfast table my mother was sullen and gray-faced, barely able to speak. "What's wrong?" I kept asking, but received no reply. My father wrapped himself tight, just clearing his throat while reading the newspaper, turning page after page. It was obvious they'd had a fight. And we knew perfectly well over what.

We packed up the baby and drove back home.

It was then that I experienced the mysterious changes in my body. First while on the road, then in the days that followed. My heart began to beat more quickly. My skin was continually prickled. There was a clamoring and changing of colors behind the lids of my eyes. A heavy knot of ropes twisted and slowly unraveled about in my chest. Finally, three days after returning home, with eyes on my brown-eyed beautiful baby, I dialed my father's number to finish the conversation we'd had in the garage two decades earlier.

Unlike the first conversation in which there were few words, this time there were many words. This time all of them came out of my mouth. So many, I can't remember what they all were. Mostly, I recall that while I was screaming, the room was moving upside down and spinning so quickly that I nearly blacked out. Only this stays with me now and the words: *You never wanted me, and you don't want my son. I never felt welcome.*

After I slammed down the phone, I shook violently. I clutched myself. I took deep breaths. I drank hot tea. But for a long while I could not stop shaking, and perhaps it was this deep-down, indefinable fear that disturbed me most of all, because I know now it is always there.

⁂

A DAY OR TWO after this, my father called me wanting to resolve things. I was grateful for the two-hundred-mile distance. His voice not quite steady, he spoke in a conciliatory tone.

"I know I am not always the most welcoming."

I listened and said nothing.

"I would like to do better."

I did not speak.

"I just ask," and he paused a moment, "that you try to see the good in me. And I'll try to see the good in you."

We left it at this point. At times, I go back to that moment, those words, when I must, often contemplating what they mean between father and daughter, husband and wife, mother and son. Perhaps this is really the only way that love can endure, the only way to prevent betrayal, the only way to be true. How else? Could my father ever really explain to me his reasons for not wanting to be called "Grandpa"? Could I ever possibly understand? Perhaps at the deepest level words really aren't possible. We are stuck instead with the unfurling knots in our chest, the smell of skin we can't recall, drunk father coming home, the color green, the rhythms of language and of song when all the words fly off and away. I accepted my father's request and have tried to hold on to it all these years since.

CHAPTER 24

Grace

M Y PARENTS DO NOT EAT much anymore. They are thin and watching their weight. My father and mother and I are at a New Jersey diner together, that kind of place where you can get coffee at three in the morning, or a hamburger or a piece of spanakopita. They order broiled fish and vegetables. My father takes a vodka martini. Though he is still a youthful man for his age, still in excellent condition, there is always a weariness in his face, and tonight I see it more, the wrinkles and fatigue, the redness in the eyes.

"I think maybe we should move to Florida near Lisa," he announces, smiling. "Get away from all this mess. We need to go somewhere easier, where there is less traffic, less stress, start something new. Maybe open a business. I'm tired of New Jersey," he says.

My mother sucks her cheeks in silence. She wouldn't want to leave her two daughters or grandchildren. And we wouldn't want her to go.

Of course I understand. I understand the need to leave New Jersey, as I had to do it too. I had my chance and took it. Yet he has never left.

I change the subject. There's a question I must ask, finally.

"Would you tell me what happened with your brothers and sister? You never really explained to us."

My father takes a sip of his vodka. He is quiet. He takes a deep breath and begins, but he doesn't get very far. He begins to say the words "They denied me." Only the first part comes out when his voice cracks. He begins again. "They denied me," he says. Then he covers his face. The rope in my chest begins to unfurl again, but it is different this time because it is not his anger I fear but his sadness. We are all surprised at his reaction. Perhaps most of all him. "I'm sorry," my father says several times, apologizing because he is not the kind of man to show tears in public. "It is like a death. It never goes away."

My mother puts a hand gently on his arm.

"You know," he says, "sometimes I look back and I wonder. Was there never anything there at all? But I just don't know." He takes another drink. He has trouble collecting himself.

"Much of the good in you girls was because of your mother," he says. "The harshness of these people was in me when we were raising you."

"It is in me too," I offer. "I can be too harsh, too remote. I go into my own mind."

"I don't doubt it," he replies. "I'm sure you got some of that too."

Later, I try to talk some more with him but he becomes fiercely angry. And I see clearly. I know I am done asking questions for a long time. I have the recipes. I have this: My father has explained himself to me. I have what I need to know, finally.

My sister Andrea knows it is coming. Knows it for months and months because the pains are growing. She'll have to sit an hour, very still, waiting for it to pass. Then she gets up. Talks to her husband. Plays a game with her son. She lives her life, pretending it's not there because what else can she do. There have been many specialists. No one has anything good to say.

But then it comes. It always does.

She hits the ground one Friday night and can't get up. Can't stand still. Can't walk. Five years have passed since the last operation. Again her stomach has completely shut down.

At the hospital they heavily sedate her. But it doesn't matter. If they touch her stomach, she screams to the moon. Days go by and she is still

doubled over in pain. They decide that they must take her into the oper-
ating room and do what they have done before. They will open up her
middle and peel apart her intestines, scraping away the scar tissue.

The doctor says it's like moss growing in the dark damp shade. This
scar tissue that cannot be stopped. It wraps around her organs and makes
everything stick together and finally shut down. It is a mystery. No one
knows why it grows—why her body does this. But there is no cure. All they
can do is scrape the thick tissue away, clear the blockages, and hope that
after they put her back together and sew her shut, her system will rise up
and work again.

I visit her in the hospital late at night, stay for an hour or two. The
hospital is quiet and her room dark.

"Hi," I whisper quietly, and kiss her on the forehead. She looks at me
with big saucer eyes, a tube running from nose down to stomach. Instead
of speaking, she shakes her head slowly, then begins to gag and heave, as
she has for day after day.

I don't know what to do. It goes on and on. One night, I need to leave
the room so I don't cry in front of her. But most of the time, I just try
to sit with her and help her pass a few more minutes. I tell her some funny
stories about what my little one did. I make jokes. I give her husband a
break and take the job of getting her tissues or calling the nurse.

When the doctors take the tube out, she just glares out of those eyes,
unwilling to speak. She is too angry and refuses words. She is forty now
and has been through this since she was sixteen.

When they finally say she is ready to eat again, they are wrong. Her
system refuses to come back for many more days. Her intestines remain
shut down in rebellion. And she gags and heaves for many more days
after that.

PERHAPS IN FAMILIES there is always one person with worse luck than
the rest. I think I have been worried about my sister since the day she was
born. I was four years old, waiting for the call. Waiting. Waiting. Finally
they handed the receiver to me and I took a deep breath—dying to hear.

"It's a girl," my mother said. "It's a girl. And I think we'll call her Andrea."

And then we were complete. The three girls.

Andrea long ago.

Andrea was always more beautiful, more angry, more vulnerable than the rest of us. She was the one who had the crooked legs put into casts when she was a baby. She was the one who had her nose broken by softballs time and again. The one who lost people from the time she was very young—a kindergarten teacher who had a heart attack, an eight-year-old playmate who dropped dead of an aneurism. Andrea was the one who got into car crashes, like the time that girl's mother took her to tennis practice and my mother could hear the loud crash and went running down the street in her nightgown to find Andrea unconscious and stuck in the backseat. Andrea was the one who got in with the wrong group of people in the wrong places. When I was young, I wanted to help but I never knew how. I worried. Then I left home and left her behind. And she found her way without me.

Now, looking at her legs beneath the blanket, the rise and fall of her breath, her eyes closed, I think how little our differences matter, so much time already gone.

After two weeks of not eating, she finally begins to get better. "I'm glad you're here," she says in a quiet, calm voice one night.

"I'm glad to be here," I reply. "In fact, I'd like to be more useful in my life. Look at these nurses and doctors. Look at how they help and all they do. Real actions. Not just words."

"I feel like I'm so useful now," she says, her voice so low and weak it is nearly a whisper. "I love teaching Sunday school. Bringing kids away from the world, closer to God. I am so happy."

AFTER MY SISTER gets home from the hospital, I try to go over to her house so she is not alone during the day. She is so weak these first weeks, so vulnerable, with her hair hanging and no makeup on. She slowly shuffles from chair to bed.

I take the opportunity to cook—plain things that won't upset her traumatized stomach. Baked apples. Rice with cheese. Broiled chicken. But she can't eat much. All food causes her pain. I cook some things for her family too. Fresh noodles and even some gnocchi, which her son and husband like but which make Andrea sick. She must go slowly.

She thanks me often.

"I'm glad to do it," I say. "Anyway. You're too weak to be mad at me for anything. It's sort of nice."

One day during this time, when she can still hardly walk, I ask, "What is the worst thing I ever did to you?"

Without hesitating she replies, "You left."

At the end of another two weeks, she is a little better, though it will take at least two full weeks more. I look at her. "Our parents might be leaving."

She nods. "How can it be that we have no one here but each other? Who will our kids have?"

"Well, Andrea, looks like it's going to be just you and me. Your worst nightmare."

And she laughs.

AT THE Bible Baptist Church, the people are jubilant when they sing. Who could blame them? The music is lively and full of joy. They hold their palms in the air. Everyone joins in. There is no cross in the church, no altar, no set prayers. My sister arrives like the rest of them with a Bible zipped up in a special black case and takes notes during the service, while the pastor talks. They believe the Bible contains everything—the truth, the meaning, the joy, the way.

At the beginning of the service, the pastor asks the congregation where they would like to wind up at the end of their lives. He talks about the failure of money to bring happiness. The joy of Christ. All good things, for sure.

"There is one real choice," he calls out, and the congregation nods and murmurs with recognition. "One true choice."

It is a choice I cannot make. I cannot be saved. I simply cannot. Then again, I am not here for this. I am here because I want to understand my sister better.

After the service, people greet Andrea with warmth and kindness. She obviously has many friends. Everyone knows her. She is at home.

Walking out to the car, she laughs. "I've got to give you credit, Law. Don't know if I would have done it myself."

I tell her I enjoyed it, which is mainly true, but I also admit that I cannot believe there is only one path, one way, one book. I must be honest with her.

"Read your Bible first. Then choose," she says.

Well, yes, this is good advice.

Maybe I will. But in the meantime, I'm settled for now. I know that if I ever find religion again, I'd like it to be a place where there is some kind of confession and absolution, whether face to face or in a little anonymous black box.

"Bless me Father for I have sinned." Those words go deep inside of me.

When I was twelve, I made my first face-to-face confession, and the penance lasted my whole life.

It was a few days before Easter and I still hadn't done this necessary spiritual task. The black boxes were closed. Only the face-to-face option was open that night, and my mother was willing to give me a ride.

What was it I needed so urgently to confess? What in the world would a twelve-year-old do that was so wrong? I cannot remember anymore. All my life, even as a child, I was burdened by some unspeakable weight, some sadness. I wonder now if I was carrying the sadness of my parents and ancestors, of things I witnessed and didn't understand but had absorbed through my skin. I was always seeking forgiveness, and I relished the opportunity to walk out of that dark little box with a clean soul.

Face-to-face confession was held in the rectory. And it made me nervous to walk into that mysterious building, with its dark woodwork and oriental carpets, its heavy imposing furniture in the glow of yellow lamps. I sat down in a big chair. Luckily, the priest on duty was Father José, an earnest young man with a kind face.

Perhaps I confessed that I had lied or cheated or fought with my sisters. Or that I'd disobeyed my parents. Perhaps I was hating someone or didn't study. Perhaps I'd just been all around bad. Father José looked at me with sincerity and kindness, grounded in faith.

With an incantation in Latin, he closed his eyes and blessed me.

"Now, for your penance, go outside tonight and look up at the sky and the stars and thank God that you are here. Thank God for allowing you to be a small part of his enormous and beautiful universe."

Following the father's orders, I did not say any prayers but went outside in the chilly night and looked up at that black sky lit up with millions of stars. I remember breathing cold air into my lungs. And for the first time in my life, I glimpsed the vastness of it all, the eons of stars and planets and time. I saw that I was nothing at all and realized the odd consolation of my own beauty as one tiny speck of no consequence but part of some larger whole. Just a girl. A small girl. Breathing air into small lungs that would someday die. I put down my burdens, and for that moment I felt gloriously free and joyful.

For a long time, even after I lost nearly every scrap of faith, I carried around this moment, this prayer, like a special treasure code I would take out and utter as needed. "Thank you, God, for allowing me to be a small part of your enormous and beautiful universe."

But then I forgot it for perhaps a decade. Now, I take it out again. Some things take a lot of time. We get better with practice. And when it comes to religion, this will have to do.

When the fall comes once again, I write to Sergio Rossi and tell him I am thinking of coming to visit Genoa, but I'm not sure when. He writes back and says that I would love it in October when the chestnuts are in harvest, and the smells and colors of the mountains are alive. I also hear from my friend Marialuisa Schenone. She is happy to know that I am still making ravioli. She writes that her mother, Giuseppina, will soon turn ninety-one and awaits my next visit to Lumarzo. Of course I will return. Of course.

I discover that I can even become an Italian citizen someday. One of the ironies of my heritage is that I wanted ravioli recipes that descended down the mother line. But I have now learned that a paternal heritage comes with its gifts as well. Because Salvatore never naturalized as an American, the nation of Italy still considers him and all his offspring to be Italian. And in theory, that means me too. If I want to reestablish this heritage with mountains of paperwork, then I can do so and become a dual citizen. I can pass it on to my children as well. Strange but true.

With Christmas approaching, my sister Andrea tells me she'd like to make the ravioli with me this year and learn everything from the beginning, all the steps. I study my new kitchen and look for the best place for the operation. My husband and I have moved to a lovely smaller place on a quiet street, and we are quite satisfied. It is a small kitchen, with a good amount of light from two windows. But I am arranging things to create space for the pasta board. This will be our first holiday here.

I turn to my oldest son who is growing up, now eleven years old, a boy with big brown eyes, ever known for honesty. "Was all this stupid?" I ask him. "What do you think? All these years learning to make ravioli on a rolling pin, and I've still got a lot to learn. All the effort studying the language. All the hours to make these little things you and your brother inhale in five minutes. Is it worth it?"

I expect him to roll those eyes of his and tell me about the perfectly good ravioli at the store. But he surprises me.

"Of course it is!" he blurts out with unexpected passion. "We need to have tradition. We need to have history. I'll make the ravioli some day and pass them on to my kids too!"

Later, when we are alone, my husband remarks, "We may not be able to give them everything, but we're giving them a pretty warm and loving family life, wouldn't you say?"

I pause. Since I had my first child more than ten years ago, I've been holding my breath, trying so hard. But now, I look back on all the days and nights of those years—all that my husband and I have done.

"Yes, I'd have to agree," I reply, and this, more than anything else, makes me feel finally content.

Most of us want to pass on something of ourselves. After we are invisible and gone from this world, we hope to leave behind something that is not full of mirrors—something real and enduring, something true. It may be a recipe for ravioli, the dish of happy times. It may be a song, or a voice that might be heard in the future.

And so I send forth this story of my family, as best I can, this story of how Salvatore, a mason, came down from the mountain with his mandolin to find Adalgiza, the story of how my mother first saw my father stand on that stage and sing that love song, and this story of the moment, that one single moment, when I stood on all their shoulders and saw my husband's face stand out amidst a crowd in New York City and thought, *Could it be possible?*

Lost and Found
Recipes

CONTENTS

I T IS TRICKY BUSINESS to set forth recipes at the end of this book. The Genoese cooks who taught me the old dishes did not themselves use written formulas, but rather learned from family members—usually their parents and grandparents—and in ways that were particular to their families. It is impossible to translate the context of such experience on the page.

I prefer this old way of learning—directly from another human being. Cooking is physical work, and one hour at the side of an expert is worth thousands of words. I suggest that anyone who wants to make pasta should find a mentor—even if for only an hour. If you don't have a relative, borrow one from a friend. Or perhaps sign up for a pasta-making class. If, by your lucky stars, you hear of someone who still uses a rolling pin, go quickly. Time is short for these old ways.

I also suggest a trip to Liguria—its markets and mountains and trattorias. It is an irresistible place, and even a short visit will help you make ravioli.

But when such options are simply not possible, we have no choice but to bravely set forth with written recipes, despite their flaws. It remains an honorable endeavor.

As a writer, I am fascinated by recipes, which can be so many things, ranging from propaganda to art. Most times, they tell us what life should be, rather than what it is. Perhaps this is why so many recipes lie—or, I should say, omit the ugly and difficult parts. Just another example of how cooking can be treacherous and not for the faint of heart—somewhat like family life. People are always assuming you understand things you don't. To survive, you need to learn some skills.

Some of the recipes I've written are a bit long. Please don't be intimidated. They are long because they are written for the novice and assume nothing. Yes, I know that when you're busy, you want a list of three or four ingredients you can put together in two steps. If this is you, go straight to the recipes for pesto, walnut sauce, and spinach *torta*. But for those who have a little more time or are seeking adventure, I provide a detailed description of pasta-making techniques as I learned them. I include photos to help you understand the process. In time, I will post video clips on my web site as well, so that visitors can see hands in action.

Those who have read this story know that any successes in these recipes, I owe to the people who taught me, and that any flaws are mine and mine alone. I wish you courage, good luck, and pleasure along the way.

I also offer you the following suggestions:

• Read each recipe from start to finish slowly, and imagine yourself doing each step. Yes, you've heard this before. You may even think you do it. But perhaps you do not. Slow down and envision before you start doing.

• Get out all the ingredients you need to make a recipe before you begin. Make space for your work. Put it all in front of you.

• When you make pasta, flour will get on the floor in your kitchen. Take off your shoes before leaving the kitchen, otherwise you will track it through the house.

SPECIAL TOOLS FOR MAKING PASTA

Pasta machine

You can get a manual pasta machine for a very modest sum, or an electric variety for a little more. Mine is a Marcato Atlas machine with an electric motor. It is an amazing invention. If you already have a high-quality stand-up mixer such as a KitchenAid, you can purchase a pasta attachment to do the job.

Pasta machine, checkered rolling pin, rotella, and dough scraper.

Pasta rolling pins

I still believe that pasta expertly rolled out on a pin is a better product than machine-made pasta. If you undertake this journey, you'll want a rolling pin that is suited to the job—not the American pin with its three-inch handles. A pasta rolling pin has a longer surface and is simply a straight cylinder. Roberto and Giuseppina both used pins that were about two feet long with small knobbed handles. Some are much longer and heavier. Adalgiza's is three feet and made of heavy maple. See "Resources" (page 319), or go to the hardware store and buy a long dowel.

Checkered ravioli rolling pin

Highly recommended. They are inexpensive and readily available.

Ravioli press

Our press (see photo) was probably made by Tessie's son. In the old cookbooks there are references to ravioli presses, but I've never seen one sold commercially.

Aunt Tessie's ravioli press.

Pasta board

You can make pasta dough on any smooth, cool surface, whether granite, wood, steel, or even Formica. But when cutting it, you will leave track marks with your knife or *rotella*. I work directly on a large butcher-block counter, unworried about the nicks and grooves I leave behind. But most people will want to protect their counters. For small batches of pasta, a large cutting board will do. If you plan to roll and cut three hundred ravioli, get something larger. Pine is adequate but soft. You may wish to have someone make a board for you of a stronger wood, such as maple, glued together in sections to prevent warping, with a lip that anchors to the edge of your counter so it won't slide. It will last a long time. Whatever you use, rub it with mineral oil regularly to keep it in good condition.

Meat grinder

You can make a simple ricotta cheese ravioli, and some others too, without a grinder. But to prepare fillings made with cooked meats, you will need a meat grinder. (Long ago, Italian cooks used to chop their fillings and grind them in a mortar.) I use a grinder even for mushroom ravioli. Electric ones are great, but a modestly priced hand-cranked one will serve just fine. Lou will be glad to hear another plug for the stand-up mixer, as you can buy a meat grinder attachment that will work well.

Rotella

You'll want one of these as it is a lovely object. It is called a ravioli or pastry cutter in English. But the word *rotella* is much better, so I only call it by its Italian name.

Sharp, nonserrated knife

If you are cutting ribbons of pasta such as tagliatelle, you absolutely must have a sharp nonserrated knife. Even if you don't plan to do so, you deserve a good knife. See "Resources" (page 319).

Dough scraper

Essential for pasta, but it also has a million other uses—from scraping up spilled coffee grinds to easily lifting a bunch of onions from cutting board to pan.

Mezzaluna

You can use a mezzaluna (which means "half moon") knife to rock back and forth over your vegetables, cutting them into very small pieces. But a good chef's knife can do the same.

Large slotted scoop or long-handled strainer

It's nice to lift ravioli out of the water rather than pour them into a colander, as they can get roughed up and broken in the process.

Stand-up mixer

These expensive devices have been mentioned numerous times in this book, in particular the KitchenAid brand. I think I will not add any further comment here.

Genoese Ingredients

Herbs

Basil, marjoram, rosemary, and oregano are common in Liguria. Use fresh herbs whenever possible and avoid dried basil entirely.

On the topic of basil: I've found it nearly impossible to get good Genoese basil in the United States. Most farmers grow large-leaf varieties that grow far too big and mangy with sprouting flowers. Basil should be harvested young and tender. Know that it is quite perishable when cut. Wrap it in damp paper towels before putting it in the fridge. Even better: find someone who sells it in a root ball that you can keep in a little cup of water on your counter until you need it.

Greens

Ligurians use a lot of leafy vegetables, and two of the most common ones—*borragine* and *bietole*—are nearly impossible to find in a U.S. supermarket. *Borragine* is borage, often grown in American gardens, not for the sweet leaf but for the edible purple star flowers. *Bietole*—also called *bieta*—is a smooth-leaf, thin-stemmed green chard that has a sweet flavor. Until *bietole* and *borragine* become popular, I substitute various combinations of spinach, escarole, chard, and sweet delicate greens I find. I also grow my own with seeds from Italy. See "Resources" (page 320).

Oil

Genoese extra-virgin olive oil is light and golden and very delicate in flavor. However, Liguria is a small territory, and so this oil is scarce in the United States. Try to obtain some from one of my sources (see pages 319–20), especially for pesto or focaccia. If you cannot find Ligurian oil, seek out some other mild golden extra-virgin olive oil, though of course Ligurians will tell you that it will never compare.

Wheat flour

For fresh pasta, all-purpose flour will work fine. However, I prefer to use a portion of imported 00 flour in my pasta, as was recommended to me in Liguria. The 00 refers to the sifting process that leaves the flour as fine as talcum powder and makes a manageable silky dough. You can seek out 00 flour at an Italian specialty shop or ask your food store to carry it.

Chestnut flour

No, you won't find small-production hand-harvested and smoked chestnut flour—such as that produced by Franca's Rue de Zerli—at your local grocery store. But it's worth whatever you have to go through to get it. Try Buon Italia in New York, which ships nationwide. Corti Brothers in California also sells this item. Be cautious of any flour not imported from Italy, as it may not be smoked and therefore will have little flavor; you will be disappointed. See "Resources" (pages 319–20).

Prescinsêua

This cheese does not exist in the United States, so you'll either have to make it yourself or use the substitute I describe (see page 308). But of course there are a couple of Adalgiza and Tessie recipes here for which you will need the authentic Hoboken article: cream cheese.

Pignoli

Pignoli or pine nuts in English, *pinoli* in Italian, are abundantly available in the United States, mostly imported from China.

Porcini

In Liguria, some people still gather mushrooms in the wild, and porcini are especially treasured. When recipes call for dried porcini, seek out plump whiter mushrooms with less dust in the packaging. Rinse well, then soak in hot water for a half hour. Strain and reserve the liquid for flavoring various sauces and soups.

Techniques for Making, Rolling, and Filling Pasta Dough

There are many methods for making dough and forming ravioli, some quite personal. Here are a few techniques that have worked well for me and should work well for you too. We begin with a dough recipe in a very small, easy-to-manage quantity and travel through several options for rolling, stretching, filling, cutting, drying, and freezing ravioli. Double (and triple) the recipe as you become more skilled.

A Basic Pasta Dough for Ravioli

Sfoglia per i ravioli/Sfogie per i ravieu

Yield: 1 pound pasta

1 cup 00 flour (if not available, use all-purpose)
1 cup all-purpose flour, plus extra for dusting work surface
½ teaspoon sea salt
1 teaspoon olive oil
1 egg
tepid water, beginning with 4 to 6 tablespoons, adding a little at a
    time; you may need more depending on your flour

Following are two methods for making your dough: one by hand, the other by machine. After this, you'll find three different ways for rolling and filling your ravioli. Choose whichever is right for you.

Making dough by hand

I. Pour the flours into a hill on your work surface and mix them together. Sprinkle the salt on top. Make a hole in the center so it looks like a volcano. Be sure to leave some flour at the bottom of the hole.

2. Add the oil into the hole. Next, crack the egg into the hole. Use a fork to lightly scramble the egg and then gradually pull in flour from the inside walls of this volcano. As you do this, cup your hand around the exterior walls to keep the sides from collapsing and the egg from running all over the pasta board. (If this happens, however, don't panic; just use some flour to quickly pull the egg back into the flour as best you can.)

3. Continue to scramble the egg and pull in flour a little at a time. As the egg absorbs the flour, begin to add the water, gradually. At some point soon, you will no longer have a volcano but a mass of sticky dough. Don't be shy. Abandon the fork and use your hands with confidence to gather the dough up into a ball, adding enough water as necessary, little by little, so that the dough is workable and elastic but not too sticky, as you continue to pull in the loose bits of flour on the board. If you must err with your liquid, better to be too wet than dry. You can add a little more flour later, while kneading. It's much harder to add more water.

4. As your dough comes together, it will be sticking to your fingers. (Did I say to remove your rings?) Scrape your fingers with your dough scraper. When you have a dough that you can knead, wash your hands and scrape the pasta board clear of crusty bits and gumminess so that it is smooth.

5. Knead the dough for about 8 minutes (longer for a larger batch). Generously sprinkle flour on your board as needed so that your dough is strong and absolutely not sticky. I suggest using the heels of your hands to push, then fold the dough in half, then rotate your lump a

quarter turn and do it again. Everyone has a different kneading style. Get yourself into a nice rhythm. Push, fold, turn, push, fold, turn, etc.

6. When your dough is satiny, soft, and elastic, cover it with plastic wrap and let it rest for at least 20 minutes if you plan to use the pasta machine, but at least half an hour if you plan to roll on a pin. You can let it sit longer, too, as much as 2 hours. It will continue to develop flavor as it rests, and the glutens will relax so you can roll the dough without having it snap back at you.

Making dough with a heavy-duty stand-up mixer

1. Add the flours and salt to the bowl of your mixer, which you have fitted with a dough hook.

2. Turn on the motor, using a low speed. Add the olive oil and egg and a little water to create a ball. Gradually increase the speed and work the dough. Sprinkle in water (Lou suggests a spray bottle) to add the amount necessary.

3. When the dough becomes soft and elastic, take it out of the mixer and knead it a few more minutes until it is satiny. Cover it with plastic wrap and let it rest for at least half an hour or an hour before you roll it out.

Rolling and filling: The rolling pin method

1. If this is your first time, cut your dough in half with your dough scraper. (This is a very small quantity of dough. As you become competent, you will easily roll the whole thing at once.) Cover one half with plastic to keep it from drying out. Turn the other half out on your work surface and sprinkle it with an ample amount of flour.

2. Swiftly roll your dough into a flat circle from various angles. Turn it over and roll on the other side. Sprinkle abundantly and frequently with flour to prevent sticking, and try hard to keep a circle shape. You must work quickly so the dough does not dry out. When you've got a circle at least 12 inches in diameter, you're ready for the next step.

3. Roll the dough around the pin. (Sprinkle with flour to prevent sticking.) With the pin on the work surface in front of you, place your hands down and gently smooth the dough out along the pin, stretching it hor-izontally, so it extends to either end of the pin a little farther.

4. Now pull the rolling pin *toward you* with a little drag action against the board. You should hear an interesting *sh sh sh* sound. Then, with a strong decisive flip of the wrist, push the rolling pin the other direction, *away from you*, with a strong motion so that the top bit of your dough flies free and slaps down on the board (and hence grows a bit). Repeat this two times. Unfold the dough off the pin so it lies flat on your work surface.

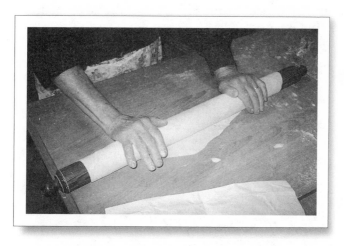

Giuseppina demonstrates steps 3 and 4.

5. Rotate the dough about a sixth of a turn clockwise. Reroll the dough up again on the pin, as you see Giuseppina doing in the photo. Repeat the process until you have stretched the dough in every direction and it is no more than $\frac{1}{16}$ inch thick. Ideally, it will also be a large perfect cir-cle. If yours looks more like the state of California, don't fret. It will work out.

6. Fold the dough gently in half for the sole purpose of marking a crease in the middle, so you'll know which half will be the bottom and which the top. Or do as Giuseppina does and fold it underneath, using a piece of wax paper to keep the pieces from sticking.

7. Put some spoonfuls of *ripieno* on the dough and spread it evenly with a butter knife or some other trowel-like tool—about ⅛ inch thick. It must all be level. Leave a ½-inch empty border at the edges. When you are done, take the clean half of the dough and fold it on top. If it is not meeting all the edges exactly as you would like, gently stretch it just a little. (If at any point you tear the dough, repair it with moistened fingers.)

Giuseppina demonstrates steps 6 and 7.

8. Sprinkle the dough generously with flour and then take your checkered rolling pin and firmly roll across it, imprinting a pattern of squares. Or use your ravioli press (if you have one) to do the same. Or do as my cousins do and use the edge of a ruler to imprint a grid of squares.

Giuseppina rolls with her checkered pin.

9. Using your *rotella*, press firmly along the grooves, cutting the ravioli. Lift them with your dough scraper and transfer to a cookie sheet dusted with cornmeal, semolina, or wheat flour. Do not let the ravioli touch one another.

Giuseppina cutting with the rotella.

10. Repeat the process with the other half of the dough.

II. Let the ravioli dry at least a half hour before cooking. If they seem very wet, gently turn them over to dry both sides. Do not make my mistake of placing the cookie sheet next to a boiling pot of water. The humidity will make the ravioli sticky.

12. Alternatively, put the cookie sheet in the freezer. Once the ravioli have frozen, scrape them from the sheet and put them back in the freezer in an airtight plastic bag. You may like to put them in the freezer even if you will cook them that night, as it makes them easier to handle. If you have a side-by-side refrigerator and cookie sheets do not fit, use the Millie-and-Susan-shirt-box method. Place the ravioli in a shirt box lined with wax paper sprinkled with cornmeal or flour. Cover them with wax paper. Put down another layer of cornmeal and then ravioli. Continue to layer until the box is tightly filled. Put a layer of wax paper on top, cover the box, and freeze it.

A note on freezing ravioli: When properly packed in airtight bags, ravioli can last months in a non-self-defrosting freezer. But in most freezers, temperatures fluctuate and quality is best if you cook the ravioli sooner rather than later. Giuseppina says she prefers them fresh, and so do I, though it is usually not possible and I often make them ahead. Also note that should you freeze them, cooking time will depend on your stove and the force of your burner. Frozen ravioli immediately chill down your water. If you have a weak burner, it takes a long time for boiling to resume. Put a lid on your pot, temporarily, to move things along.

Pillow variation

Instead of spreading out the *ripieno* in a solid layer, use your fingers or a spoon to drop a checkerboard of horizontal and vertical rows (about 1–1½ inches apart) of ½-teaspoon-sized dollops (or whatever size you like) on one half of the dough. Fold the other half on top. Now go over each dollop and press around it with the pads of your fingertips to seal each one shut. Use the *rotella* to cut the ravioli into squares. Each raviolo looks like a pillow surrounded by a larger border of flat dough.

Rolling and filling: The pasta machine method

1. Cut your dough into three pieces. Cover two in plastic. Use your hands to press the other one into an oval-shaped disk. Sprinkle it liberally with flour.

2. Set your pasta machine on the first setting (with the largest space between the rollers). Feed the disk through and retrieve it. Fold it in thirds, like a letter, and feed it through again, short end first. Repeat this step one more time. If the dough starts to tear or get skid marks, sprinkle it well with more flour. If you have a complete failure, reshape the dough into an oval, put it in a plastic bag to rest 20 to 30 minutes, and then try again.

3. Now, *without refolding*, put the pasta through increasingly higher settings, so that each time it becomes a longer, thinner, and more translucent sheet. Your goal is pasta that is very thin, no more than $\frac{1}{16}$ inch. You may have to go to the highest setting on your machine or perhaps the second-to-highest setting on your machine will be best. It will depend on the quality of your flour and dough. (I am not above using a ruler to measure the thickness.)

Lou feeds pasta through his beloved machine.

4. Now you have your *sfoglia* for ravioli. It should be about 4 to 5 inches wide and somewhere between 2 and 3 feet long. Sprinkle your work surface with flour. Lay this pasta sheet down. Don't worry if some hangs off. Fold it gently—from one tip to the other—for the purpose of creasing the dough at the halfway mark. Open it up again.

Be ready. It gets very long.

5. Put some spoonfuls of *ripieno* on one half of the dough, spreading it evenly with a butter knife or some other trowel-like tool—about ⅛ inch thick. It must all be level. Leave a ½-inch empty border at the edges. When you are done, take the clean half of the dough and fold it on top. If it is not meeting all the edges exactly as you would like, gently stretch it just a little. (If at any point you tear the dough, repair it with moistened fingers.)

6. Sprinkle the dough generously with flour and then take your check-ered rolling pin and firmly roll across it, imprinting a pattern of squares and sealing the ravioli shut. Or use a ravioli press (if you're one of the esoteric few who have one).

7. Using your *rotella,* press firmly along the grooves and cut the ravioli. Lift them with your dough scraper and transfer to a tablecloth or sheet to dry. Or if you plan to freeze them, transfer to a cookie sheet dusted with cornmeal, semolina, or wheat flour. Do not let the ravioli touch one another.

8. Repeat the process with the other two pieces of dough.

9. Let the ravioli dry at least a half hour before cooking. If they seem very wet, turn them over to dry both sides. For more information on freezing ravioli, see page 276, step 12.

Pillow variation

Just as with pin-rolled pasta, you can make the hand-dropped pillow ravioli shape mentioned above using your machine-rolled strips as well. After you roll out your pasta, use your fingers or a spoon to drop small dollops of *ripieno*—about the size of a nickel, spaced about ¾ inch apart— in a long row about 1½ inches from the edge of the pasta. Fold the pasta strip lengthwise, bringing edge to edge. Use the pads of your fingertips to press down around each little dollop, easing out air and sealing the individual ravioli shut, taking care not to use your fingernails. Cut a long line with your *rotella* to trim the edge. Then cut the squares for pretty pillowlike ravioli.

Rolling and filling: Using a pasta machine and metal ravioli form

1. Sprinkle fine semolina, cornmeal, or flour all over the form, especially the edges.

2. Machine roll one-fourth of your pasta (¼ pound), taking care to make it as wide as possible, the full 5-inch width of the rollers.

3. Lay your pasta strip over the form, stretching it a little if necessary to meet all the edges. Fill each cavity with *ripieno*, using a spoon. Repeat step 2 and place this second layer of pasta on top of the first. Roll over this with a small rolling pin, or better yet, press down with a cutting board on top of the form. Flip the ravioli form so that the ravioli come tumbling out. Gently separate them at the grooves. If they do not come apart easily, cut them with the *rotella* as necessary.

4. Repeat with remaining dough and filling. Dry or freeze according to the directions on page 276, step 12.

QUESTIONS I FREQUENTLY ASKED MYSELF, AND YOU MAY ASK TOO

Which rolling and filling method is best?
They all have advantages and are subject to personal preference. You will need to decide which you like best. The checkered rolling pin makes for speedy production of relatively small-shaped ravioli, about 1 inch square. The pillow method is more time-consuming but perhaps the prettiest. You get a little more filling, and a lovely puff in the center surrounded by a large border of delicate fluttery dough (assuming you roll it thin). You can also make the ravioli much larger if you prefer. The

form method is a little trickier to use, but it is versatile. You can purchase forms in a variety of shapes—from tiny soup ravioli to large triangles or circles. There are other methods too, like the big round
stamp-type cutters for making pierogi in half-moon shapes. But that is
too much for this book.

What setting on my pasta machine will give me the right thinness of dough?
There are no hard-and-fast rules. It depends on your dough and your
preference. A very soft dough will get thin more quickly; a drier dough
made of hard flour may need to go to the highest setting. Also, if you want
something toothsome, you may not like pasta that is too thin. Or you may
love the delicacy of very thin pasta. Use your judgment, or even boil up
one or two after you've done a batch to see how you wish to proceed.

How many ravioli will I get from a pound of pasta dough?
It depends on how thick you roll out your dough and on how big you
make your ravioli. My checkered rolling pin and thin dough yield seventy to eighty ravioli per pound, depending on heaviness of the filling
and other mysteries I can't explain. By contrast, some factory-produced
ravioli come in packages of sixteen to the pound.

How many ravioli should I plan per serving?
Because it depends greatly on the size of the ravioli and the appetites of
those eating, perhaps it is better to think in terms of weight. My two sons
and husband together can easily eat close to a pound of ravioli as a main
course by themselves. But perhaps you and your friends are modest
eaters, and four of you would be happy with one pound along with a nice
salad. Obviously, for ravioli as a first course, you need much less.

How much water should I add to my dough?
This question continues to engage me, as it is a delicate matter, depending on what kind of flour you're using and the humidity of the day. Start
with a small quantity and add it until your dough is moist but not sticky.
The relationship of liquid to flour is very important. The more you
make ravioli, the more you'll get a feel for it.

I've heard that the best pasta uses only eggs and no water. Why do you use so little egg in these recipes? Why so much water?

The number of eggs in pasta depended, historically, on how wealthy one was, and also on the region from which one came. Originally, pasta had no eggs in it at all. In some parts of Italy, modern pasta is made exclusively with eggs as the liquid. If you'd like a rich eggy pasta, then by all means go ahead and use as much as one egg per cup or per ¾ cup of flour and use little or no water. You'll get a very supple yellow dough, which is common in modern times. But in old Liguria, there was a tradition toward fewer eggs, so I have followed this style. Some say it is because the people were poor and cheap. Perhaps. But there is virtue in a lighter pasta that allows the flavor of the *ripieno* to come through.

What is durum wheat? It's an ingredient in all my boxed noodles. Shouldn't it be used in homemade pasta?

Durum wheat is a different kind of high-protein wheat that is ideal for dried pasta. It is typical of the hotter climates in southern Italy, and especially Naples. But we are not there now. With these recipes, we are in northern Italy.

THE RECIPES

Ravioli

Ricotta Cheese Ravioli
for Beginners and Others

To get started on making ravioli, here is a very manageable and basic recipe that uses a cheese *ripieno*. It makes enough for three or four people for dinner, with a big salad. Use the pasta machine and whichever filling technique you like.

Yield: 3 to 4 dinner servings

FOR THE PASTA
Prepare 1 pound pasta dough according to the basic dough recipe
  on page 269.

FOR THE FILLING
1 ½ cups whole-milk ricotta cheese, preferably small production
  from a specialty shop rather than industrial production
¼ cup plus 2 tablespoons *Parmigiano-Reggiano*
salt and pepper, to taste
a sprinkle of freshly grated nutmeg, if you like
1 egg, lightly scrambled

1. Using a wooden spoon, mix all the cheeses, salt and pepper, and nutmeg (if you are using). Taste to check if more salt is needed. Add the egg and stir to a smooth paste. Add the spinach if you are using it (see the variation below).

2. Using a machine, roll your pasta to ¹/₁₆ inch or thinner. Choose a filling technique—whether the pillow method, ravioli form, or checkered rolling pin. Fill and press your ravioli, then cut into squares. Dry at least a half hour on a cloth (tablecloth or sheet) or on a cookie sheet sprinkled with flour or cornmeal. To freeze for later use, place cookie sheet in freezer. When ravioli are frozen, scrape them off into an airtight freezer bag.

3. Put ravioli into a large pot of abundantly salted boiling water and cook about 3 minutes if fresh, about 5 minutes if frozen. Take one out and taste, to see that they are done, before draining. Serve with any sauce you like.

SPINACH-CHEESE VARIATION: Add 1 loosely packed cup fresh spinach, washed, stems removed, and minced very fine. Recommended.

LOU'S GOAT CHEESE VARIATION: Omit *Parmigiano-Regianno* and replace with 6 tablespoons softened goat cheese. This adds a delicious tang.

Ratto's Ravioli

Before we begin making Genoese ravioli, let's take a moment and pay homage to the earliest published version, presented in 1863 by Gio Batta Ratto in his book La cuciniera genovese. *This is for those who enjoy reading historic recipes. I have adjusted the punctuation slightly, and correctly I hope, so as to clarify for modern readers.*

This is the queen of all the first courses invented by a Genovese cook, and is now known throughout the world because of its excellence.

Take eight escaroles and two bunches of borage. Remove from them all the damaged and tough leaves and let them boil for five minutes. Then squeeze them until all the water is released.

Take then a half kilo of lean veal, 200 grams of lean pork, 300 grams of veal udders, a sweetbread, chopped. Brown in butter. Before removing them from the flame, add brain and 50 grams bone marrow, which you will have first soaked in warm water and removed the hair from. Having chopped everything, that is, the lean meats, udders, greens, etc., very finely on a cutting board with a mezzaluna, then crush it a little at a time in a mortar until it is reduced to a paste. Add to it 150 grams of sausage, place all in a vessel, where you will add eight well-beaten eggs, a small amount of bread crumb soaked in the broth or in the veal gravy, a handful of good parmigiano cheese, a very small amount of finely chopped marjoram, and sufficient salt. Remix well with a spoon and you will have the filling, principal part of the ravioli.

Take then a kilo and a half of wheat flour, dissolve it in warm water to which you will add three fresh eggs. Reduce it to a dough. Work it at length with force until it becomes soft. Then break off enough to form one sheet. Cover the rest with a bowl so that it is not exposed to air and will not dry out. Stretch it out as wide and thin as possible using a rolling pin. Lay it out on the kneading board, and taking the prepared filling with a small spoon, make small equal-sized balls out of it, which one by one you will let fall onto half of the sheet of dough arranged into many horizontal rows and separated one from the other by a small space. Begin covering the first row with strips of dough, then with your fingertips form many small pillows. You will cut this first row with a cutting roller and then with the same cutting roller you will cut the ravioli one by one repeating the same process until the last strip.[1]

Having finished the first sheet of dough, you will move on to form the second, then the third, then the fourth, etc. . . . until you finish the dough and filling, being careful to always keep the dough covered until the end, otherwise it will dry up and become unusable.

Unfold a tablecloth over the table placing on top of it the ravioli separated so that they cannot stick to one another and cover them. When they are dry enough, throw them a few at a time into a large pot of boiling water being careful that it is not too salty and that the flame is very high so that it does not stop boiling. When they rise to the top, press them lightly down to the bottom with a ladle. When they are cooked, remove them with a slotted spoon and let them drain well. Place them in a wide serving dish arranged in various layers and season each layer with the roast gravy and excellent parmigiano cheese.[2]

---

[1] Now, instead of forming many little balls, to expedite the process you can place the filling on half of the sheet of dough, leveling it and connecting it with the blade of a knife, then you cover it with the other half of the sheet of dough and you apply on top of it a square form made especially (a ravioli form), or you can pass over it a rolling pin with grooves that give shape to the ravioli, which are then cut one by one with a cutting roller.

[2] The same ravioli are excellent cooked in a very good broth.

Adalgiza and Tessie's Ravioli

This is the basic recipe that came from Adalgiza and Tessie and their granddaughters. For now, my official conclusion is that the raw meat has no explanation, other than that it is just the way they did it in our family. That's all.

*Yield: 250–300 small ravioli, enough for 10 to 15 people as
a first course for a holiday dinner*

FOR THE PASTA

5 cups flour

3 teaspoons salt

2 eggs (some of my relatives use more)

1 ½ cups water (very approximate; start slow and use judgment)

FOR THE FILLING

2 packages cream cheese, 4-ounce size, room temperature

1 or 2 boxes frozen chopped spinach, thawed, cooked, and all water
    squeezed out

1 pound veal, ground twice so it is very fine (ask the butcher
    to do this)

1 pound pork, ground twice so it is very fine

salt and pepper

dash freshly grated nutmeg, to taste

2 teaspoons fresh marjoram, finely minced, or 1 teaspoon dry
    (optional; this is my addition)

1 cup *Parmigiano-Reggiano*

3 eggs

1. Make your dough and let it rest. (For a review of techniques, see pages 270–72, but remember to use the quantities given here.)

2. In a large bowl, cream the cheese with a handheld electric blender until it is soft.

3. Add the spinach, then the meats and seasonings. Mix well with a wooden spoon to combine. Some members of our family use a KitchenAid mixer. Add the *Parmigiano-Reggiano* and eggs.

4. Roll out the dough very thin, using a rolling pin to create a large circle.

5. Fill half the dough with the *ripieno*, spreading it evenly, not too thick. Fold the other half of the dough over on top of the *ripieno*. Press with the ravioli press (or roll with a checkered pin). Cut with a *rotella*.

6. To eat the same day, dry at least a half hour on a tablecloth or sheet. Or freeze the ravioli on cookie sheets, then transfer them to plastic freezer bags for later use.

7. Cook in abundantly salted water for approximately 7 minutes (longer than other ravioli because the *ripieno* is raw). If the ravioli are frozen, you will need to boil them for closer to 10 minutes. Keep a careful eye. Cooking times take judgment. Taste one before draining.

ALTERNATIVE: As described previously, I once made this filling by cooking the meat first. I began by mincing a small onion, a clove of garlic, a stalk of celery, and a carrot. I sautéed these in olive oil until soft, then added the meat and cooked it until brown, splashing in white wine—I can't tell you how much. After this, I added the remaining ingredients. It was quite good. And you don't need a meat grinder to do this.

Niccolò Paganini's Ravioli

Amidst his great musical works of art, papers, and other documents, the great composer and violinist Niccolò Paganini (1782–1840) left behind a beloved recipe for Genoese ravioli. He describes in careful detail the making of tomato meat sauce (tucco). Next comes the filling, as follows.

In the same pan with the meat you used to make a sauce, cook half a libra [about 1 pound] of lean veal. Then remove, and pound it well. Take a calf's brain, cook it in water, then remove the skin covering the brain. Chop and pound separately. Add a little borage that's called Nizza Borag, and boil it well and pound it, and they are crushed as above. Take three eggs which are enough for 1½ libra of flour. Beat them and, having mixed and newly crushed together all the ingredients mentioned above, add a little parmigiano cheese to them. The filling is done.

You can serve capon instead of veal, some sweetbreads instead of brain, to obtain a more delicate filling. If the filling should end up hard, add some gravy/sauce.

For the ravioli leave the dough a little soft. Leave it for an hour covered under a dish to obtain thin sheets.

Maria Carla Roncollo Guigoni's Christmas Ravioli and Tucco

This is an extravagant recipe. If you begin work early, it can certainly be done in a single day. But I prefer to make this over two days, cooking the meats and making the *ripieno* on day one, then making the pasta and filling it on day two. Note that Maria Carla's dough is richer than my basic dough, and also makes a larger quantity.

I had to make some changes to this recipe to accommodate American cuts of meat. For example, though Maria Carla uses some leaner meats, I have used fattier cuts that braise well. Otherwise, this is her recipe more or less exactly. It is glorious.

Yield: about 300–350 small ravioli

FOR THE PASTA

3 cups 00 flour

1 cup all-purpose flour, preferably with a high gluten content, such as King Arthur's

4 eggs, plus 1 yolk

enough water to make the dough elastic

FOR THE FILLING

1 bunch borage (about 2/3 pound), or substitute spinach and/or escarole

1/4 cup olive oil

2/3 pound veal shoulder or veal stew meat

1 pound beef, the type you would use for pot roast, such as chuck, trimmed of extra fat, or bottom round or top round roasts, which are leaner but still braise well

salt and pepper

2 cloves garlic

1 stem fresh rosemary or 1 teaspoon dried

2 bay leaves

1 cup dry white table wine

1 carrot, minced extremely fine

1 rib celery, minced extremely fine

1 onion, sliced thinly

3 or 4 pieces dried porcini, reconstituted in warm water for 30 minutes

6 cups marinara sauce, already made

1 tablespoon butter

2 teaspoons pignoli

1/2 pound pork, shoulder cut, trimmed of extra fat

1 large piece stale white bread (about 3 inches from an Italian loaf),
  soaked in warm milk
1 cup grated *Parmigiano-Reggiano*
nutmeg, to taste
1 teaspoon marjoram, minced
2 eggs, plus 2 yolks

1. Make the dough with the ingredients specified above. (For a review of techniques, see pages 270–72.)

2. Boil the borage (or whichever greens you are using) 5 minutes in salted water. Let cool.

3. Heat the olive oil in a terra-cotta casserole or large heavy stainless-steel pot. Season the veal and beef with salt and pepper and put them in the pot along with 1 clove garlic, the rosemary, and 1 bay leaf. Brown the meat.

4. Add ½ cup of the white wine. When the wine has evaporated, add the carrot, celery, onion, and porcini. Cook uncovered until the vegetables are softened. Add a little hot water as necessary, to keep the vegetables from scorching.

5. Cover the pot and lower the flame to a very slow heat. Check the veal in 20 to 30 minutes. When tender, remove the veal and put it aside. The time will depend greatly on the size and cut of your meat.

6. Add the 6 cups marinara sauce to the pot with the vegetables and beef in it. Continue to cook the beef on a slow heat until it is falling apart and tender—essentially, a pot roast. This can easily take another 2½ hours, depending on the size and quality of your meat. When it is done, remove the meat. Save this sauce, which is one method for making *tucco*, Genoese for *sugo*, or gravy. You will use it to dress your ravioli.

7. Melt the butter in a separate smaller pot. Add the pignoli, 1 bay leaf, and 1 clove garlic. Add the pork and cook over a medium heat for 20 minutes, uncovered.

8. Add 2 or 3 tablespoons white wine. When the wine has evaporated, add a few tablespoons more and cover the pot. Cook until tender. This may take an hour or more, depending on the cut of meat. Turn off the heat and let it rest.

9. When all the meat is cool, cut it into pieces that will fit into your meat grinder. Set up your meat grinder and fit it with a fine mandrill. Place a big bowl underneath.

10. Put all the meats through the grinder. Add the pignoli and a little of the flavorful fat and wine from the bottom of the pork pot.

11. Squeeze the water completely out of your greens and put them through the meat grinder, followed by the soaked bread.

12. Put the *Parmigiano-Reggiano*, nutmeg, and marjoram directly into the bowl and stir with a wooden spoon so that all is well mixed.

13. Taste. Correct seasoning. Do you need more salt, pepper, cheese?

14. Add the eggs and egg yolks. Mix everything. Your filling is now ready.

15. If you are using a machine, roll out your dough to $\frac{1}{16}$ inch thickness, probably the second-to-last setting. Maria Carla uses the pillow variation (described on pages 276 and 280) to form and cut her ravioli. Choose whichever rolling and filling method you like best.

16. Let the ravioli dry at least a half hour on a tablecloth or sheet. Or place on cookie sheets dusted with flour or cornmeal and put directly in the freezer.

17. When you are ready to cook, put the ravioli in fiercely boiling salted water. Maria Carla adds a teaspoon of oil to prevent sticking. Cook about 3 minutes if your ravioli are fresh, 5 or 6 minutes if they are frozen. Taste to be sure.

18. Gently scoop out the ravioli with a large slotted ravioli lifter—or pour them carefully into a colander so they don't break. Serve in a large bowl with the *tucco*—the red sauce you made in step 6. Cover abundantly with grated *Parmigiano-Reggiano*.

Mushroom Ravioli

Take a breath after that enormous recipe. This one—perfected by Lou—is much simpler and very special. The earthy flavor will win you the devotion of mushroom lovers. Serve it with a light marinara sauce or *tucco*.

Yield: a first course for 6 to 8, a main course for 5

FOR THE PASTA
3 cups flour
1 teaspoon salt
1½ teaspoons olive oil
2 eggs
water as needed, beginning with ⅓ cup

FOR THE FILLING
2 tablespoons olive oil
2 cloves garlic, minced very finely
8 cups mixed mushrooms, washed, sliced, tough stems removed (see
    notes below)
¼ to ½ cup dry white wine, such as Pinot Grigio
½ teaspoon salt; begin with this quantity and add more depending
    on your taste
pepper to taste
3 tablespoons minced flat-leaf parsley, stems removed
¼ cup *Parmigiano-Reggiano*
2 to 3 tablespoons fine bread crumbs
1 egg, lightly scrambled

1. Make the dough with the ingredients specified above. (For a review of techniques, see pages 270–72.) Cover it in plastic and let it rest.

2. Heat the olive oil in a large stainless-steel skillet. Add the garlic and stir a minute or so on medium heat, until fragrant and golden. Add the mushrooms, and stir to coat with oil. Immediately add the wine. You will have a lot of liquid in the pan. Don't worry. Let this mixture cook down on medium heat, and enjoy the intoxicating smell until all the wine has evaporated. Remove from heat and let cool.

3. Set up your grinding machine with a small mandrill and a generous bowl beneath. Run the mushrooms through the grinder. Add all remaining ingredients to the bowl. Mix until you have a nice smooth paste. Your filling is now done. You should have about 2 cups.

4. Follow the procedure for making ravioli using the pillow technique or another of your choice (see pages 272–82).

5. Cook the ravioli in abundantly salted water about 2 to 3 minutes, longer if you freeze. Drain and serve with whatever sauce you like.

Note: Use a nice combination of mushrooms. Lou and I like oyster, crimini, shitake, and porcini. What weight, you wonder? I resist giving this as some mushrooms are light, and some are heavy. So stick with volume, and know the measurement of your own hand when you are in the market. For example, 2 of my handfuls equal 1 cup. So I scoop up 16 handfuls to get 8 cups.

Another note: Mushroom authorities say to wipe each of your mushrooms with a damp towel so as not to waterlog them. Good advice for many dishes, but not this one because the liquid will evaporate anyway. Just the same, wash your mushrooms immediately before using, as they are sponges and will absorb water and deteriorate quickly afterward.

Excellent Everyday Herb Ravioli

This recipe from the fourteenth or fifteenth century is still popular all these centuries later. It is essentially a ravioli magri—that is, lean ravioli.

If you want to make ravioli with herbs or any other filling, take herbs and trim them and wash them; then boil them briefly and take them out and squeeze out the water and chop finely with a knife and put them in a mortar with fresh cheese and dried cheese, eggs, mild and strong spices and grind all together to a paste. Then make soft pasta as you would lasagne and cut out circles with a beaker and make ravioli. When all are made put them to cook and when properly cooked sprinkle with spices and good cheese and they are good like this.

—Libro per cuoco
By an anonymous fourteenth- or fifteenth-century Venetian

Pansotti

Liguria's famous *pansotti* are descended from a long lineage of *ravioli magri*, such as the one above. Note that the dough is made with a bit of wine.

Yield: serves 6 to 8 as a first course, 5 as a main course

FOR THE PASTA
3 cups flour
2 eggs
salt
½ cup dry white wine
water as needed

FOR THE FILLING

2 pounds mixed greens such as Swiss chard, borage, escarole, green
    cabbage, parsley, beet greens, pimpernel, watercress, and
    spinach, washed and stems removed

1½ cups ricotta, *prescinsêua* (page 307), or *prescinsêua* substitute
    (page 308)

¼ cup grated *Parmigiano-Reggiano*

2 tablespoons fresh herbs, such as basil and marjoram, minced finely

grated nutmeg, to taste

salt and pepper, to taste

2 eggs

1. Make the dough with the ingredients specified above (for a review of techniques, see pages 270–72). Cover it with plastic and let it rest.

2. Boil the greens in salted water until just tender, about 5 minutes but it depends on the greens. Drain and cool them.

3. Squeeze the greens absolutely dry by wringing them in a clean dishtowel. Mince them very finely and place them in a large bowl.

4. Add the cheeses, herbs, nutmeg, and salt and pepper. Taste for flavor and adjust if necessary. Add the eggs and mix very well so that everything is a smooth paste.

5. Roll a piece of pasta on the machine at the last or second-to-last setting. Cut this strip into triangles, each about 3 inches long.

6. Place a generous spoonful of filling in the middle of each triangle. Fold this triangle in half, making another triangle. Seal the two open edges. Some people like to join the opposite corners together and seal them shut, something like large tortellini.

7. Cook the *pansotti* in salted boiling water about 3 minutes, more or less, until done. Scoop out and serve with *salsa di noci* (page 304).

Other nice pastas to make

Since you have come this far and already know how to make pasta, it would be silly not to learn some other shapes that are far easier than ravioli. With a little practice, for example, you can easily make a pound of tagilatelle in under an hour.

Tagliatelle

Tagliatelle / Taggiaen

In Italian or Genoese, this name is derived from the verb *tagliare*, which means "to cut"—which is exactly how you make these noodles.

Yield: 1 pound pasta

1. Make a basic pasta dough (page 269) and let it rest. Roll it out by your method of choice—pin or machine—so that it is as even and thin as possible.

2. Gently roll up your sheet of dough, something like a cigar, except loosely, about 3 or 4 inches in diameter, being sure to sprinkle flour constantly and abundantly as you roll it up, to prevent sticking. Take care not to press downward or all the pasta will meld together in a sticky lump. Using a sharp knife, leading with the point, cut ¼-inch slices across. Unfold these ribbons and gather them together to cut them to correct length—you don't want to serve 18-inch-long tagliatelle.

3. Splay your ribbons out to dry in even batches, at least a half hour on a floured cookie sheet, occasionally turning them so that all parts can air dry. If you are making a lot, set out a clean tablecloth or sheet on a table and dry the pasta there.

4. Cook the tagliatelle in abundantly salted water 2 to 3 minutes, depending on how thick you've made your dough. Serve with any sauce in the universe, but especially meat sauce.

VARIATION: Because I love chestnut, I sometimes make this dough with half chestnut flour and half OO flour, served with *salsa di noci* (page 304). Another variation is to cut the pasta very thin—about ⅛ inch, creating "macaroni in the Genovese style actually called *tagliarini*," so described in the fifteenth century by cookbook author Maestro Martino.

Gnocchi/Troffie

Gnocchi belong to the larger archetypal family of dumplings that have existed all over Europe for centuries, if not millennia. In Genoa, gnocchi are often called by their Genoese name, *troffie.* Today, they come in several varieties and shapes. This one, I learned in Ne from Roberto at La Brinca trattoria. It is famous with pesto. Note that it contains no egg.

Yield: 4 servings

1½ pounds potatoes, or about 3 cups, not too creamy a variety
1 teaspoon salt, more or less
4 to 5 tablespoons Ligurian olive oil, or as needed
1½ cups chestnut flour
1½ cup 00 flour

1. Boil, bake, or microwave the potatoes in their jackets. Remove them from the water, and when they are cool enough to handle scoop out the pulp. Rice the potatoes and spread them out to dry on a cookie sheet. This will help the water evaporate and make lighter gnocchi. What, you do not have a ricer? Go get one at the hardware store for a few dollars. Or instead, mash the potatoes extremely fine, removing all lumps, and spread them out thinly to dry. When they are dry, about an hour later, put them in a medium-sized bowl.

2. Add the salt to the potatoes. Add the oil to the potatoes so that they are very moist. Mix well into a paste. You may need more oil, depending on how absorbent your potatoes are.

3. Blend your chestnut and oo flours on your work surface. Make a low hill with an ample hole in the center for your potatoes. Place the potatoes there and gradually work in the flours to form a dough. You may feel like it will never come together as a dough, but it will, just be patient. Sprinkle in a little more olive oil if you must.

4. Knead thoroughly, sprinkling all-purpose flour on your work surface as needed to prevent sticking. Let rest a half hour.

5. Pull off a piece of dough and turn it into a 1- or 2-foot-long rope, about as thick as a small finger, by rolling it on your work surface with your palms. When this rope is uniform, get another piece of pasta and make another rope, the same size. Line up the two ropes side by side.

6. Now, with a sharp, nonserrated knife or the edge of the dough scraper, cut the pasta ropes into ¾-inch squares.

7. Take a thumb or forefinger and imprint each one; this little crevice creates a space to catch the sauce. Sprinkle with flour as needed. Repeat this process until all your dough has been turned into gnocchi.

8. Cook your gnocchi in boiling water. When they rise to the surface, taste to determine if they are done. When they are cooked to your liking, drain and serve with pesto. At La Brinca, they add a little *prescinsêua* to the pesto, creating a slight tang to offset the sweetness of the chestnut.

Silk Handkerchiefs

Fazzoletti de seta/Mandilli di saea

Most Americans think of lasagne as a layered casserole baked in the oven. But historically, the term refers to the pasta itself—a square or sheet—and is used in many diverse preparations. In Genoa, if you order a plate of lasagne you're likely to receive squares of pasta loosely tossed with pesto. A variation of this dish is called "silk handkerchiefs," whereby extremely thin, square sheets of dough are draped in the bowl (like fallen handkerchiefs) and layered with pesto.

Yield: serves 3 to 4 as a main course

1. Make dough according to the basic pasta recipe on page 269. Let it rest, then roll it as thin as possible. Cut it into 4-inch squares and let them dry.

2. Prepare pesto (page 303) and put a dollop in the bottom of three or four serving bowls.

3. Place the lasagne in abundantly salted boiling water and cook 1 to 2 minutes.

4. Carefully scoop out the pasta with a slotted spoon. Layer each bowl with lasagne and a dollop of pesto followed by lasagne, then pesto, then lasagne, etc. Loosely drape the sheets to make them look like fallen handkerchiefs.

Sauces

Enrichetta's Pesto

Pesto/Pestu

It was difficult to find a large mortar (6 to 8 inches wide) for making hand-pounded pesto in the United States. Then, I finally found one, and it was not so easy to pound as I'd expected. For now, I'm sticking with Enrichetta's blender method. Note, there are dozens of variations on pesto throughout Liguria.

Yield: enough for 4

1 handful (about ¼ cup) pignoli
pinch salt (⅓ teaspoon or less)
2 small cloves garlic, each about ¾ inch long and ½ inch deep,
    green germ removed
1 tablespoon extra-virgin Ligurian olive oil or other mild oil
1½ handfuls (about 2 cups) Genoese basil, small- to medium-sized
    leaf, harvested while tender, washed and dried very gently
a little bit of water, perhaps a tablespoon
2 handfuls *Parmigiano-Reggiano,* and then another, and maybe yet
    another if you're Enrichetta

1. Put the pignoli, salt, garlic, and oil in the blender. Process well. Scrape down with a spatula.

2. Add the basil. Process well, pausing as necessary to turn off the machine and scrape down the inside of the blender. Add a little water. Repeat. Process very well.

3. Add the *Parmigiano-Reggiano* and process very well. Add more cheese as necessary.

4. Serve your pesto over pasta. You may wish to thin it out using some hot water from your pasta pot.

Note: The Genoese add a peeled and roughly cut potato to the water when making pasta that will be dressed with pesto.

Walnut Sauce

Salsa di noci / Sarsa de noxe

Walnut sauce is a dream. It goes beautifully over herb-and-cheese-filled ravioli, such as *pansotti,* or other fresh pastas made with chestnut flour. When these special items aren't an option, you can make walnut sauce to dress ordinary dried pasta too, for a quick and lovely dish.

Yield: enough for 6 to 8 servings of pasta

2 cups nice walnuts (about 7 ounces)
boiling water for soaking
pinch salt
1 medium clove garlic, about ½ teaspoon, green germ removed

5 leaves marjoram or basil, or ½ teaspoon dried marjoram if you must

1 cup grated *Parmigiano-Reggiano*, plus extra for garnish

1 cup, more or less, warm milk, or hot pasta water, to thin out the paste

1. Place the walnuts in a bowl and cover them with boiling water. Leave them to soak a half hour or so to leach out the bitterness.

2. Transfer the drained walnuts to a food processor along with the salt, garlic, and marjoram or basil. Pulverize to as smooth a paste as you possibly can, pausing at times to scrape nuts down from the side with a spatula. Add the cheese and process. The mixture will remind you of pesto.

3. When you are ready to serve, you must thin out this paste by adding the warmed milk or some hot starchy water from the pasta pot. Ladle in a little at a time and process. The goal is a sauce that is not too thick, but not too watery either. Aim for luxuriously creamy and smooth.

4. Serve the sauce over pasta. For even more luxury, sprinkle with *Parmigiano-Reggiano*.

Meat Sauce

Sugo di carne /Tucco

This classic Genoese meat sauce used to dress meat ravioli can also be made with veal. It is a practical dish with numerous uses. When this meat is complete and soft, you can remove a pound of it and use it in your ravioli filling. Then you use the sauce to dress the ravioli. Then you serve the meat, sliced on a plate, as the second course.

Yield: 6 servings

3 pounds cut of beef that will make a good pot roast, such as bone-
    less beef chuck shoulder, beef top round, or beef bottom round
salt and pepper, to season meat
3 tablespoons olive oil
1 onion, thinly sliced
2 cloves garlic, minced
1 carrot, minced small
1 stalk celery, minced small
1 small handful dried porcini, or quantity to taste, reconstituted in
    hot water, liquid strained and reserved
½ cup dry white table wine, plus more if needed
one 35-ounce can good-quality plum tomatoes (preferably seeded)
    and juices, mashed with a potato masher or your fingers, tough
    parts removed

1. Wash the meat and dry it well. Trim away excess fat. Salt and pepper the meat. Pour the olive oil into a large, heavy-bottomed pot. When it is hot enough to make the tip of a wooden spoon sizzle, add the meat and brown on each side. Remove the meat to a plate.

2. If your oil is still nice with flavorful brown bits of meat, proceed to add the onion, garlic, carrot, and celery. If the oil if black and burned, wipe the pot clean and start again with fresh oil, bringing it up to heat. Add the onion, garlic, carrot, and celery. Cook over medium heat until golden and soft, being careful not to brown the garlic.

3. Return the meat to the pot. Add the porcini and wine. When the wine has evaporated, add the tomatoes. Cover the pot and turn it to low heat. Cook for at least 2 ½ hours, perhaps more, until the meat is tender to the fork. An alternative method is to put the pot in the oven at 300 degrees.

4. Check your pot from time to time. If the sauce is getting too thick, add a little more wine or some of the water reserved from the mush-rooms. When the meat is cooked, remove the pot from the heat. Serve ravioli as a first course, covered with this sauce. Serve this roast as a second course, sliced thinly and fanned out on a serving plate.

Genoese specialties

Prescinsêua

Quagliata

This kind of fresh cheese was made in families, usually with unpasteurized milk that had gone sour (but was still pleasant, unlike pasteurized milk which turns putrid when old). The addition of yogurt gives back some of the natural bacteria that are lost in the pasteurization process. The rennet forms the curd. This is the recipe I received from Claudio Bassi at the Casseificio Val d'Aveto. I have made some minor adjustments to accommodate American products. See "Resources" (page 320) to find rennet. This is an easy and fun recipe to make.

Yield: about 2 cups cheese

4 cups whole milk (absolutely cannot be ultrapasteurized)
4 tablespoons plain yogurt with active cultures
4 drops rennet

1. Heat the milk to 90 degrees in an absolutely clean pot. Add the yogurt and rennet. Let this sit undisturbed for 24 hours.

2. When you return, you should see a mass of curd, surrounded by liquid whey. Pour off the whey (or use it to cook with or drink, as it is very healthful). Pour the curd into a strainer lined with cheesecloth. Gather up the cheesecloth to bring the cheese close together. Tie it tight and suspend it over a bowl or the sink so that it can drain for 4 hours. Now your cheese is done. It will last in the refrigerator not more than 1 week.

Prescinsêua Substitute

This is an inferior substitute for the real thing, but use it if you must.

To ¾ cup fresh ricotta cheese, add ¼ cup good-quality plain yogurt (with active cultures). Stir together. That's it. What can I say?

Minestrone

Minestrone alla Genovese/Minestrùn

Ravioli—full of meat for celebration times—may have been the queen of Genoese cuisine. But food historian Paolo Lingua says that minestrone is the king. The food of everyday life, this version takes no meat or broth of any kind. Instead, you cook a heap of vegetables and fresh beans in a lot of water for hours, until everything is softened to a dense consistency. The crowning glory is a swirl of pesto at the end.

Your ingredients will vary according to season and to what you've got on hand. After trying many versions calling for enormous amounts of cabbage, squash, celery, eggplant, peas, zucchini, potato, and string beans, I've settled on something simpler. I discovered it in a charming little fifty-page cookbook—*I Battolli e altre vecchie ricette di Uscio e ditorni*—picked up by chance in the town of Uscio, a little bit north of Recco. I've made only a few changes.

Yield: 4 generous servings

8 cups water

8 ounces fresh cranberry beans, removed from pods

6 ounces green beans, trimmed and cut into ½-inch pieces

12 to 16 ounces potatoes, sliced small and thin

8 ounces zucchini, sliced small and thin

1 handful fresh spinach or some other greens you may have

1 to 2 ounces fresh mushrooms (crimini, shitake, porcini, etc.), sliced;
    or 3 to 4 dried porcini, reconstituted

rind from a wedge of *Parmigiano-Reggiano* (see note below)

1 tablespoon salt, more or less to your taste, probably more

pepper, to taste

2 to 4 ounces small pasta of your choice (I especially like vermicelli)

¼ to ½ cup good pesto (page 303)

Parmigiano-Reggiano, for sprinkling

1. Put the water and cranberry beans in a large heavy-bottomed pot on the stove on high heat. Bring to a boil, then turn the heat to medium. Cook the beans in this way for 45 minutes. Add the rest of the vegetables, the mushrooms, and the cheese rind. Cook another 2 to 3 hours (depending on how small you've cut your vegetables), until the potatoes are melty and everything else is very soft and your soup is dense. Taste this now. Add salt and pepper as needed.

2. Add pasta and cook until done.

3. Remove your pot from the heat. Swirl in a generous dollop of pesto. Serve with a sprinkling of grated cheese.

Note: If you normally buy your cheese already grated, ask your cheese seller to sell—or give—you leftover rind of authentic *Parmigiano-Reggiano.*

The vegetable pies known as *torte*—which in my mind share some ancestry with the ravioli family—come in infinite varieties. In Liguria, two major forms emerge, those with crust and those without. I give one of each here. Most that I've seen in Liguria have a crust, like Enrichetta's Chard *Torta*. But the other varieties are important too, and our family had this crustless kind. The food historians Alberto Capatti and Massimo Montanari have observed the genius of the *torta*, which was enormously flexible and therefore enjoyed by all classes—the rich would fill it with luxuries, while the poor would use some simple gathered herbs. But all versions would be *torta*. In this vein, I love our *torta* just as it is and amuse myself by considering how it has descended from the great aristocratic kitchens of the Middle Ages down to my generation, reconfigured with American technologies of flash-frozen spinach and cream cheese in silver foil. My mother still makes it all the time.

Spinach Torta via Hoboken

Yield: serves 10 to 12 as an appetizer or side dish

4 packages frozen chopped spinach
8 ounces cream cheese, at room temperature
8 eggs, beaten
1 cup grated *Parmigiano-Reggiano*
salt and pepper, to taste
parsley, to taste

I. Preheat oven to 350 degrees.

2. Brush about 2 tablespoons of olive oil on the bottom and halfway up the sides of a 9-×-11-inch pan or Pyrex-type dish.

3. Begin with three mixing bowls: large, medium, and small. In the largest bowl, defrost and drain the spinach very well. Expedite this with heat or the microwave if you wish. Place the cream cheese (or other fresh cheese) in the medium bowl. Beat the eggs in the small bowl.

4. Cream the cream cheese, using a handheld electric mixer. Add the beaten eggs to it, then the *Parmigiano-Reggiano*, salt and pepper, and parsley. Mix well, then pour half this mixture into the spinach. Evenly spread the spinach mixture into the oiled pan. Cover the spinach with the remaining half of the liquid egg mixture.

5. Bake about 45 to 50 minutes, or until the top is golden.

Enrichetta's Chard Torta

Torta di Bietole/Turta de gè

This is the recipe Enrichetta Trucco showed me in her kitchen in Montoggio.

Yield: 10 servings

FOR THE CRUST

3 cups flour, such as all-purpose King Arthur

1 cup 00 flour

a little less than ⅔ cup olive oil, plus much more for drizzling as needed

a little less than 1 cup (200 milliliters) water with 1 teaspoon salt mixed in

FOR THE FILLING

about 1 pound thin-stemmed Italian *bietole* or American chard

1 handful 00 flour

about 3 handfuls *Parmigiano-Reggiano*

1 teaspoon of a spice mixure you make yourself to your preference, containing coriander, cinnamon, clove, nutmeg, and ginger

about 1 pound *prescinsêua* (page 307) or *prescinsêua* substitute (page 308)

1½ tablespoons 00 flour

about 2 tablespoons milk

I. Wash your greens for the filling. If you are using thick-stemmed chard, remove the stems. Cut the greens into 1-inch pieces, wrap them tightly in a towel, and set them aside to dry.

2. Now you will make the crust. Mix the flours on your work surface, then form into a mound with a volcano in the middle. Add the olive oil to the center. Then add the salted water. Use your fingers to pull flour from the inside edges of the volcano and form a dough.

3. Knead this very well until it is elastic and soft, about 8 minutes. Add all-purpose flour as needed, but expect an extremely sticky dough. Do as Enrichetta does and knead in every possible direction, turning your dough into various shapes to make sure you're reaching every bit.

4. Cut the dough into five even pieces and shape each one like a round disk. Let them rest on a plate, covered by a damp towel. Set aside.

5. Now prepare the filling. Take the greens out of the dishtowel and put them on your work surface. Sprinkle handful of OO flour over the greens, then 3 handfuls of *Parmigiano-Reggiano,* then your spice mixture. Use your hands to combine this well.

6. In small bowl, mix together the *prescinsêua,* the 1½ tablespoons OO flour, and the milk.

7. Prepare your pan—a large pie pan about 13 inches in diameter. Brush the entire inside, including the rim, with olive oil. Set it atop a small inverted bowl so it is steady and standing about 3 inches above your work surface.

8. Roll one disk of your dough in a circle. Hold it in the air on two fists, and working it systematically around the edge, stretch the dough until it is transparent and very thin. (This is a little like what you may have seen a pizza maker do.)

9. Lay this first layer in your pan. Repeat with another disk of dough and lay that in the pan too. Some dough will be hanging over the edges. That's fine.

10. Now you will fill the pie. Lay in your mound of greens and spread them in an even layer. Drizzle olive oil over the greens. Layer in your *prescinsêua* mixture by putting generous tablespoons around the perimeter. What's left can go in the middle (during cooking it will all even out). Moisten your fingertips with water and run them around the edges of the pie.

11. Roll and stretch a third disk of dough so it is thin and transparent. Lay it on top of your pie, pulling it a little tight so it is not sinking into the center. Drizzle a bit of oil over it. Repeat this two more times, so that in the end you have three layers of dough on top. Naturally, you will drizzle some oil on top one last time.

12. With scissors, cut the overhanging dough away, but leave 1 inch around the edge. With your fingers, form a braid border with the edges of the dough, rolling and tucking in a rhythm all around. As you do this, your top layers of dough will grow tighter, forming a bubble effect.

13. Make a decision for practicality or beauty. If you leave the bubble on top, you'll have to watch it carefully in the oven and cover it to prevent burning. The other option is to take a skewer and prick it in a few places so it deflates.

14. Bake in a preheated 360-degree oven for 40 minutes. Watch the top to make sure your *torta* isn't getting too brown. If it is, cover it with foil or parchment paper.

Genoese Focaccia

Focaccia al olio/Fugassa a l'eujo

Genoa is famous for this bread, and though it is nearly impossible to make it exactly the same here, you can still make an absolutely wonderful and *very* close version. After trying recipes in Italian and English, I've settled on this fabulous version by Carol Field, from her beautiful book *Focaccia*. With baking, chemistry is all. So please follow all of her suggestions to the letter, and rely on weight rather than cups. One exception: I sometimes need to add more flour to my work surface than she recommends.

Yield: one 10 1/2-×-15 1/2-inch focaccia; serves 10 to 12

FOR THE SPONGE
2½ teaspoons (1 package) active dry yeast
⅔ cup warm water, 105° to 115°F
1 cup (140 grams) unbleached all-purpose flour

FOR THE DOUGH
½ cup water, room temperature
⅓ cup dry white wine
⅓ cup light extra-virgin olive oil, preferably Ligurian
sponge (above)
2½ cups plus 2 teaspoons (360 grams) unbleached all-purpose flour,
    plus 1 to 2 tablespoons as needed
2 teaspoons sea salt

FOR THE TOPPING
about 2 tablespoons extra-virgin olive oil, preferably Ligurian
¾ to 1 teaspoon sea salt
onion, if you like (see variation below)

I. To make the sponge: Sprinkle the yeast over the warm water in a large mixing bowl, whisk it in, and let stand until creamy, about 10 minutes. Stir in the flour and beat until smooth. Cover tightly with plastic wrap and let rise until puffy and bubbling, about 30 minutes.

2. To make the dough: Add the water, wine, and olive oil to the sponge. If you are making the dough by hand, whisk in 1 cup of flour and the salt, then beat in the rest of the flour until you have a dough that is very soft and very sticky. Knead on a lightly floured board with the help of a dough scraper and 1 to 2 additional tablespoons of flour for 6 to 8 minutes, or until the dough comes together nicely and is silky and shiny; it should remain soft but not wet.

3. If you are using a heavy-duty mixer, set the paddle attachment in place and add the water, wine, and olive oil to the sponge. Add the flour and salt and mix until the dough comes together while remaining very soft. Change to the dough hook and knead for 3 minutes at medium speed, stopping once or twice to press the dough into a ball to aid in the kneading. Use the 1 or 2 tablespoons additional flour if you finish by kneading the dough briefly on a lightly floured work surface.

4. First rise. Place the dough in a lightly oiled container, cover it tightly with plastic wrap, and let rise until doubled, about 1 hour.

5. Shaping and second rise. The dough should be soft, full of air bubbles, and stretch easily. Press it into a lightly oiled 10½-x-15½-inch pan, dimple it well with your fingertips or knuckles, cover with a towel, and let rise until puffy and doubled, about 45 minutes.

6. Baking. At least 30 minutes before you plan to bake, preheat the oven to 425°F with a baking stone inside, if you have one. Once again dimple the top of the dough with your fingertips or knuckles, drizzle olive oil so it pools in the little indentations, and sprinkle with the sea salt. Place the focaccia pan directly on the stone and immediately reduce the temperature to 400°F, spraying the oven walls and floor with cold water from a spritzer bottle 3 times in the first 10 minutes. Bake the focaccia for 25 to 30 minutes, until golden. Immediately remove from the pan and let cool on a rack. Serve warm or at room temperature.

VARIATION: There are endless variations around Genoa. I like focaccia with onions strewn on top. I believe Adalgiza made this one, which her grandchildren remember as onion pizza. To prevent the onion from burning on top, chop or slice red or white onion thinly. Soak in cold water the night before. Sauté in olive oil. Put on top of your focaccia just before you put it in the oven.

Pandolce

Pandolce/ Pandöçe

Pandolce is the most famous dessert of Genoa. I'm told Adalgiza made this bread in Hoboken at Christmastime with her grandchildren standing around her, helping to sprinkle in the fruits and nuts, which she baked into a light and high, sweet bread.

This recipe was given to me by Maria Carla Roncollo Guigoni. It produces two delicious, shortbread-like cakes, and the first time I made it I sent one to my eighty-four-year-old cousin Catherine. She called to thank me profusely, saying how delicious it was and how she and her husband competed for the last slice.

"But do you want the truth?" she asked.

"Yes of course," I replied.

"This is not *pandöçe*."

And she's right. Maria Carla readily admits that this is not an antique version. With the advent of modern life, bakeries, and a general increase in wealth in Italy since World War II, the cake has changed, relying far more on butter, eggs, more sugar, and baking powders rather than yeast. Today *pandolce*, as it is called in standard Italian, appears in every bakery, in tall and short forms, and most of those are average. This homemade one is excellent.

As to the true old yeast version, like Adalgiza's—well, I still hope to learn. When I met a seventh-generation baker named Adriano Alvigini in Genoa, he told me that he uses a "mother yeast" kept alive in his family of bakers for a hundred years. I asked if he could show me how to make the bread, and he laughed at my naïveté. It was the middle of summer. It would take three days just to wake the yeast from its rest, let alone to even begin the process.

Until I get a lesson, I'm using this delicious recipe that I once had at Maria Carla's house.

Caveat: The candied lemon rind and citron that you find in Italy are very different from the flavorless plastic things you find in American grocery stores. Order some good citron in advance from The Baker's Catalogue (see "Resources," page 320). Or substitute some good-quality dried pineapple or other honest dried sweet fruit. I have left these measurements in Maria Carla's metrics as baking is a formula, and these are more precise. I greatly prefer to use orange blossom water. You can find it in Middle Eastern or Caribbean markets or online; see "Resources" (page 320).

Yield: one 14-inch cake serving 16, or 2 small cakes

4 ⅔ cups (500 grams) 00 flour or cake flour (*not* the self-rising kind)

1½ teaspoons baking powder

2 sticks plus 2 tablespoons (250 grams) sweet unsalted butter, softened at room temperature

1¼ cups (250 grams) sugar

2 large eggs (approximately ½ cup beaten eggs)

1 tablespoon orange blossom water (or Marsala wine, or rum)

1½ cups (250 grams) raisins, softened for 15 minutes in warm water and drained

¾ cup (100 grams) candied fruits, a mixture of orange rind and citron

¾ cup (100 grams) pignoli, preferably from Pisa as they are more aromatic, but more likely you will find the ones from China

1 tablespoon (5 grams) fennel seeds soaked in warm water for half an hour

I. Mix the flour and baking powder. Set aside.

2. In a large bowl, cream the butter with the sugar. Add the eggs and orange blossom water. Then add the flour mixture and mix in.

3. Turn the dough onto your pastry board and work in first the raisins, then the candied fruits, then the pignoli, then the fennel seeds.

4. Form one large loaf or two small ones, about 1 inch thick, slightly domed at the center. Place on greased double cookie sheets (to prevent burning the bottom). Make an X (or a cross if you prefer) in each loaf and open slightly like a flower. Let your loaves rest for a half hour, covered lightly with plastic, ideally in the refrigerator if you have room.

5. Bake at 325 degrees in a preheated over for 1 hour or until a testing stick comes out clean. Turn cookie sheet halfway through baking. Let rest a half hour and very carefully lift to rack. When completely cool, wrap your head tightly in plastic and store it in a cool, dry place. This sweet bread can last many months. Its flavors improve over time.

Note: For a pretty sheen, you can brush the loaves with egg yoke before baking. Also, you can make this cake using a heavy-duty stand-up mixer (such as a KitchenAid), fitted with a paddle attachment, for steps 2 and 3.

RESOURCES

GENERAL COOKWARE

For all kitchen equipment such as rolling pins, dough scrapers, good-quality chef knives, ravioli rolling pins, pasta boards, and pots and pans, I always go online to Fante's first.

Fante's Kitchen Wares Shop
1006 S. Ninth Street
Philadelphia, PA 19147-4798
800-44-FANTE or 215-922-5557
www.fantes.com; mail@fantes.com

For corzetti stamps, to make corzetti pasta
A.G. Ferrari Foods
13 stores in northern California
877-878-2783
www.agferrari.com

INGREDIENTS

For chestnut flour, 00 flour, Ligurian olive oil, good-quality porcini, pignoli, and other Ligurian foodstuffs, I strongly recommend the following importers. Please note that they do not list chestnut flour on their web sites, so you must call to order.

BuonItalia
Chelsea Market
75 Ninth Avenue
New York, NY 10011
212-633-9090
www.buonitalia.com; info@buonitalia.com

Corti Brothers
5810 Folsom Boulevard
Sacramento, CA 95819
800-509-3663
www.cortibros.biz; cortibros@sbcglobal.net

Todaro Bros.
555 Second Avenue
New York, NY 10016
877-472-2767
www.todarobros.com; Eat@TodaroBros.com

For rennet to make prescinsêua
New England Cheesemaking Supply
P.O. Box 85
Ashfield, MA 01330
413-628-3808
www.cheesemaking.com; info@cheesemaking.com

For citron/candied fruit and orange blossom water
The Baker's Catalogue
800-827-6836
www.kingarthurflour.com; customercare@kingarthurflour.com
(You can also try an Arab market for these items.)

For seeds to grow your own Genoese basil, bietole, or borragine
Seeds from Italy
P.O. Box 149
Winchester, MA 01890
781-721-5904
www.growitalian.com; seeds@growitalian.com

For imported jars of pesto made with Genoese basil from Prà
Gustiamo.com
1715 West Farms Road
Bronx, NY 10460
877-907-2525
www.gustiamo.com

COOKBOOKS

In English, the most comprehensive Ligurian cookbook is the wonderful Recipes from Paradise: Life and Food on the Italian Riviera *by Fred Plotkin. In Italian, there are many choices listed in the Bibliography.*

FOOD AND TRAVEL IN LIGURIA

This list is limited primarily to restaurants, food producers, and people I met while research-ing and featured in the book. Of course there are many, many additional excellent resources not listed here.

Note: *When calling Italy from the United States, dial 011-39 before the in-country numbers given below.*

Agriturismo
 Rue de Zerli
 51 Strada per Gòsita
 16040 Ne (GE), Italy
 In-country tel.: 0185-339245
 www.ruedezerli.com; francadamico@tin.it
 Franca Damico and her family offer a bed-and-breakfast at their farm in Ne, a few miles from Chiavari and Lavagne. You can find Franca's products in specialty shops all around the Riviera di Levante. She also has a small shop at her farm.

Culinary tours
 Micol Negrin
 Rustico Cooking
 917-602-1519
 www.rusticocooking.com; micol@rusticocooking.com
 Classes and tours to Liguria (and other regions), led by an Italian native, expert cook, teacher, and award-winning cookbook author.

For information on local cheeses, and to visit the shop in Val d'Aveto
Caseificio Val d'Aveto
In-country tel.: 0185-870390
www.caseificiovaldaveto.com; info@caseificiovaldaveto.com

Cooking classes
Sergio Rossi and his mother, Enrichetta Trucco, give
occasional classes on Genoese cooking and traditions.
They are held in Montoggio and conducted in Italian.
For more information, telephone (in country) 327-4404811;
or email sergirossi@tiscalinet.it.

Gerri Sarnataro teaches pasta making at her school Cucina della
Terra in Umbria (and also at the Institute of Culinary Education in
New York City). For more information, telephone (in New York)
646-761-8037 or email gsarnataro@rcn.com.

Genoa's Pesto World Championship
www.pestochampionship.net
This is a new event, scheduled every two years.

Trattorias serving traditional Genoese foods
La Brinca
Campo di Ne 58
16040 Ne (GE), Italy
In-country tel.: 0185-337480
www.labrinca.it (English version available); labrinca@libero.it

Da ö Vittoriö
Via Roma 160
Recco (GE), Italy
In-country tel.: 0185-74029
www.daovittorio.it; info@daovittorio.it

La Manuelina
Via Roma 278
16036 Recco (GE), Italy
In-country tel.: 0185-74128 or 0185-720779
www.manuelina.it; manuelina@manuelina.it

Antica Trattoria della Rosin
Frazioni di Tre Fontane
16026 Montoggio (GE), Italy
In-country tel.: 010-938955

Trattoria Sa Pesta
Via Giustiniani 16R
Genoa (GE), Italy
In-country tel.: 010-2468336

Antica Sciamadda
Via San Giorgio #14
Genoa (GE), Italy

Guido Porrati and family's wine and specialty foods shop
Parlacomemangi
Via Mazzini 44
Rapallo
www.parlacomemangi.com; scrivi@parlacomemangi.com

Recommended for pandolce
Pasticceria Tagliafico
Via Galata 31R
16212 Genoa (GE), Italy
www.chococlub.com/pasticceria/tagliafico;
pasticc.tagliafico@libero.it
In-country tel.: 010-565714

For more information on Ligurian foods
  Conservatorio delle Cucine Mediterranee
  Director: Sergio Rossi
  President: Giovanni Rebora
  www.conservatoriocucine.it (English version available)

SELECT BIBLIOGRAPHY

Andrews, Colman. *Flavors of the Riviera: Discovering Real Mediterranean Cooking*. New York: Bantam, 1996.

Aroldi, Mario. *I Battolli e altre vecchie ricette di Uscio e ditorni*. Uscio, Italy: Pro Loco di Uscio, 2001.

Artusi, Pellegrino. *Science in the Kitchen and the Art of Eating Well*. Translated by Murtha Baca and Stephen Sartarelli. Toronto: University of Toronto Press, 2003.

Balma, Mauro. "Liguria: A Multipart Song from the Alps to the Sea," in *European Voices: Multipart Singing in the Balkans and the Mediterranean*. Edited by Ardian Ahmedaja and Gerline Haid. Schriften zur Volkmusik. Band 22. Vienna. Boehlau Verlag, in press.

Ben Amara, Radhouan, and Alessandra Guigoni. *Saperi e sapori del Mediterraneo*. Cagliari, Italy: AM&D Edizioni, 2006.

Braudel, Fernand. *Memory and the Mediterranean*. Translated by Siân Reynolds. New York: Alfred A. Knopf, 2001.

Bugialli, Giuliano. *Bugialli on Pasta*. New York: Simon & Schuster, 1988.

Calvino, Italo. *Italian Folktales*. Translated by George Martin. New York: Pantheon Books, 1980.

Capatti, Alberto, and Massimo Montanari. *Italian Cuisine: A Cultural History*. Translated by Aine O'Healy. New York: Columbia University Press, 2003.

Cogliati Arano, Luisa. *The Medieval Health Handbook, "Tacuinum Sanitatis."* Translated and adapted by Oscar Ratti and Adele Westbrook from the original Italian edition. New York: George Braziller, 1976.

Davidson, Alan. *The Penguin Companion to Food*. New York: Penguin, 2002.

Delle Piane, Padre Gaspare, dei frati Minimi di San Francesco. *Cucina di strettissimo magro*. [1880.] Reprint of 1931 edition, Genova, Italy: Feguagiskia' Studios Edizioni, 2004.

DeSalvo, Louise. *Crazy in the Kitchen: Foods, Feuds, and Forgiveness in an Italian-American Family*. Bloomsbury, 2004.

Downie, David. *Enchanted Liguria: A Celebration of the Culture, Lifestyle and Food of the Italian Riviera*. Photographs by Alison Harris. New York: Rizzoli, 1997.

Faccioli, Emilio, ed. *L'Arte della cucina in Italia: Libri di ricette e trattati sulla civiltà della tavola dal XVI al XIX secolo*. Torino, Italy: G. Einaudi, 1987.

Field, Carol. *Focaccia: Simple Breads from the Italian Oven*. San Francisco: Chronicle Books, 1994.

Frisoni, Gaetano. *Dizionairo genovese-italiano e italiano-genovese*. [1910.] Genova, Italy: De Ferrari of Devega, 2005.

Hazan, Marcella. *Essentials of Classic Italian Cooking*. New York: Alfred A. Knopf, 1992.

Helstosky, Carol. *Garlic and Oil: Politics and Food in Italy*. New York: Berg, 2004.

Laurino, Maria. *Were You Always an Italian? Ancestors and Other Icons of Italian America*. New York: W. W. Norton, 2000.

Lingua, Paolo. *La cucina dei genovesi*. Rome: Franco Muzzio Editore, 1989.

Marchiori, Mario. *E riçette de mæ moé*. Genova, Italy: Nuova Editrice Genovese, 2003.

Martino, Maestro, of Como. *The Art of Cooking: The First Modern Cookery Book*. Edited by Luigi Ballerini. Translated and annotated by Jeremy Parzen. Berkeley: University of California Press, 2005.

Minuto, Luigi; Angela Bisio; Francesca Perucchio; and Virgilio Pronzati, eds. *Preboggion e prescinsêua*. Genova, Italy: Feguagiskia' Studios Edizioni, 1997.

Pellegrini, Sandro. *Recco Ieri*. Rapallo, Italy: Officine Grafiche Canessa, 1971.

Perry, Charles. "Notes on Persian Pasta." In *Medieval Arab Cookery: Essays and Translations*, by Maxime Rodinson, A. J. Arberry, and Charles Perry. Devon, England: Prospect Books, 2001.

Platina. *Plantina, On Right Pleasure and Good Health: A Critical Edition and Translation of De Honesta Voluptate et Valetudine*, by Mary Ella Milham. Asheville, N.C.: Pegasus Press, 1999.

Plotkin, Fred. *Recipes from Paradise: Life and Food on the Italian Riviera*. Boston: Little, Brown, 1997.

Pradelli, Alessandro Molinari. *La cucina genovese*. Rome: Newton Compton Editori, 2002

Profumo, Emanuela. *La cucina di Enrichetta Trucco*. Genova, Italy: Feguagiskia' Studios Edizioni, 2003.

Ratto, G.B.e. Giovanni. *La cuciniera genovese* [1863.] Genova, Italy: Fratelli Frilli Editori, 18th ed., 2003.

Rebora, Giovanni. *Culture of the Fork: A Brief History of Food in Europe*. Translated by Albert Sonnenfeld. New York: Columbia University Press, 2001.

Rodinson, Maxime; A. J. Arberry; and Charles Perry. *Medieval Arab Cookery: Essays and Translations*. Devon, England: Prospect Books, 2001.

Rossi, Emanuele, comp. *La vera cuciniera genovese*. [1867.] Bologna, Italy: Arnaldo Forni Editore, 1992.

Rossi, Sergio. *Cucina di guerra*. Busalla, Italy: Edizioni La Lontra, 2005.

Santich, Barbara. *The Original Mediterranean Cuisine: Medieval Recipes for Today*. Chicago: Chicago Review Press, 1995.

Scappi, Bartolomeo. *Opera di Bartolomeo Scappi M.: dell' arte del cucinare*. Venice, Italy: Presso Alessandro Vecchi, 1610.

Serventi, Silvano, and Françoise Sabban. *Pasta: The Story of a Universal Food*. Translated by Antony Shugaar. New York: Columbia University Press, 2002.

CREDITS

Photos:

pp. iv, 1, 129, 137, 142, 201, 259, from *Obiettivo Su Recco: Una Storia in 1000 foto*, 2nd edition, 1986, Sandro Pellegrini and Emilio Razeto, published by Microarts, Recco. Used with permission.

p. 74, Picture Collection, The Branch Libraries, The New York Public Library, Astor, Lenox and Tilden Foundations.

p. 55, Carbone and the Parco del Basilico in Prà, Italy.

p. 207, Massimo Angelini, Associazione Consorzio della Quarantina.

pp. v, 80, Courtesy of the Hoboken Public Library.

All food photography by Dan Epstein.

Recipes:

Focaccia, p. 314, from *Focaccia; Simple Breads from the Italian Oven,* by Carol Field, 1994. Reprinted with permission of Chronicle Books, LLC, San Francisco. Visit Chronicle Books.com.

ACKNOWLEDGMENTS

MANY THANKS to the National Italian American Foundation, which generously funded some research and translations for this book. I am also indebted to The New York Public Library for refuge, once again, in the wonderful Allen Room.

Tremendous gratitude to the cousins who were so kind: Linda McDonald for sending the very first recipe card, documents, and many photos over the years, some of which appear in this book; Catherine Flanagan who gave me stories I needed, the details about family history, and was always (of course) absolutely right; her daughter Valerie Walker who lent me Adalgiza's rolling pins and let me use them such a long long time; Rosemary Schenone Pagano who sent the *rotella*, photos, film footage, and voices; Donna Annillo for her amazing photo of Salvatore and Adalgiza on their wedding day; Chris Bacigalupi for the stories of Tessie; and of course Millie McCarthy and Susan Kazala, ravioli heroes extraordinaire.

In Italy—*mille grazie* to Alessandra Guigoni who opened the first door in Genoa, and to her generous and kind parents Maria Carla and Guido for whom my esteem is obvious. Thanks also to Ebe for the bible, and to Giovanni Rebora for making time to talk and Harriet Metcalf who translated. I thank Mauro Balma for leading me to the vocal traditions of Liguria, making recordings for me, and sharing his expertise. I am forever indebted to Marialuisa Schenone for finding me and bringing me to her wonderful family in Lumarzo, and to her mother Giuseppina Giuffra who not only demonstrated ravioli but let me hold her pin.

Many thanks to the Ligurians who took time from their busy food businesses to talk to me: Franca Damico and her beautiful Rue de Zerli, Guido Porrati of Parlacomemangi, Gianni Bissou of Da ö Vittoriö, *troffie* makers Giulia and Meri Senarega, as well as Claudio Bassi, Violeta Bachvarova, and the staff at Caseificio Val D'Aveto. Special thanks to Roberto and Sergio Circelli of La Brinca who let me in their kitchen and made the best ravioli I have ever tasted.

In the U.S., my sincere appreciation to Fred Plotkin for sharing expertise and deep knowledge of Liguria. I also thank Rachel Lauden, whom I am fortunate to know. She has expanded my thinking regarding pasta and food history in general. Gratitude to food historian and journalist Charles Perry who was generous with Arab pasta history and even translated a recipe from Persian (which to my regret didn't make the final cut). And my thanks also to Micol Negrin of Rustico Cooking, who shared contacts and sent me in the right direction at the beginning.

More thanks: to Eve Spencer, Christina Baker Kline, Jackie Coleman-Fried, and Kayhan Ekinci for skillful reading and comments on manuscript; my dear in-laws Colleen Schaffner and Filippo Aureli for the science insights; Marie Leone Meyer for the Italian tales; and the Association for the Study of Food and Society and its Listserv members whose insights guided me.

Grazie mille to my translator and fabulous teacher Phyllis Ignozza of The Language Institute in Caldwell, New Jersey, and to Diane Rosenblatt who brought good cheer and assisted in recipe testing and organization when I needed it most. Many thanks to the wonderful Regina Flanagan for photo research, and the friends who tested recipes: Chef Susan Calhoun, Lina Panza, Nancy Star, Larry Goldfield, and Danielle Svetcov, and a special thanks to John Ritz for ravioli testing.

In the publishing world, I am blessed to have as my editor the fabulous Amy Cherry who is a dream to work with and so many things I'm not, amongst them: organized, calm, and steady. Her editorial skill and insights helped shape and improve this book. I thank my agent and friend Arielle Eckstut, a wonderful advocate, advisor, and force of goodness. My appreciation to Andrew Marasia and the staff at W. W. Norton for their beautiful work (and tolerating my delays), and I also thank the sharp-eyed Elizabeth Pierson for her extremely hard work in copyediting.

In addition, there are several people without whom I never could have written this book. In my closest circle, I thank Lou Palma—mentor and dear friend—and his wife, Susan, both of whom have welcomed me on countless times in their kitchen, providing inspiration not just in cooking, but life. I cannot possibly express my thanks to Nancy Ring, friend and coach, who called daily and pushed me to finish, read manuscript, helped me sort through the demands, and reminded me of art.

I am profoundly grateful for Sergio Rossi who took me places I never would have gone, told me things I never could have known, made introductions, and answered countless questions for more than a year. His expert knowledge and passion for the food history of Genoa and its mountains are deep and true. He enriched the journey beyond measure. I also thank his mother Enrichetta Trucco for welcoming me into her kitchen and teaching me, the outsider.

Without my father, I could not have written this book or this story. I thank him for our shared history and the roots he gave me, his encouragement, his ravioli memories, his story, and for raising me in a home where there was song. I thank my sisters, Andrea and Lisa, for their love and understanding, and my mother, Marcia Schenone, for her help in countless ways, for telling me the stories while she cooked, and especially for telling me not to wait.

Above all, I thank my husband, Herb Schaffner, love of my life, who has unfailingly encouraged that I write, seek, and travel, though it would have been a million times easier for him if I didn't. He is a keeper of promises, loyal, and true, at my side, a constant champion who tells me to never give up and helps me find the way.

Finally, I thank my beloved sons, to whom this book is dedicated, for being who they are, wonderful guys, fun travelers, insightful and fabulous pasta eaters, my inspiration and joy.